SAINTS AND SKELETONS

Praise for Ana Manwaring's
JadeAnne Stone Mexico Adventures

Coyote   Recipient of the Literary Titan Silver Award for Fiction 2023

US Review of Books
In this fourth book of her JadeAnne Stone Mexico Adventure series, Manwaring picks up the story after JadeAnne and Lily escape from a life of sexual servitude and torture. The novel's action is fast-paced as JadeAnne must evade vicious cartel members. Nowhere is safe, and the author does a wonderful job of describing the tension and terror that pervades JadeAnne's life. The protagonist, a headstrong woman who sometimes balks at being kept hidden inside, is at times at odds with her father, Quint, adding to the underlying tension. JadeAnne's beloved dog, Pepper, and Lily's dog, Maya, with her five one-month-old pups, also offer moments of suspense and stress with their dangerous but necessary trips outside. This novel, with its backdrop of human trafficking, is a riveting read that puts one into the center of Mexican culture with its descriptive narrative of landmarks and cuisine.

Nothing Comes After Z   Recipient of the Literary Titan Silver Award for Fiction 2022

Literary Titan Review

Nothing Comes After Z is a riveting crime thriller with a strong female protagonist. I appreciated the grounded nature of the crime and how it relates to some headlines we see in the news today. Before she can safely leave Mexico and return to her life, she has to uncover some hard truths and catch the perpetrators. I enjoyed how well the emotion is weaved into this action novel because it ensure we're invested in the protagonist and we're biting our nails when the action intensifies. Author Ana Manwaring knows how to create a storyline that easily sets up the hard-hitting action.

M.M. Chouinard, USA Today bestseller of the Jo Fournier Mystery series
"A well-written, engaging story with a bad-ass protagonist I loved spending time with. Bring on more JadeAnne!"

The Hydra Effect

Lisa Towles, Bestselling and multi-award-winning author of Hot House, Ninety-Five, The Unseen and Choke
"*The Hydra Effect* sizzles with action, tension, and peril. Great writing combined with regional flare and international intrigue make this sequel a delightful ride!"

Jan M Flynn, award winning author

"JadeAnne heads to Mexico City for a break from her partner and now ex-boyfriend. But her sharp intelligence, curiosity and inability to stay in her own lane land her in a snarl of trouble. In short order she's evading cartel thugs, uncovering a human trafficking network and confronting high-level Mexican politicos with questionable connections, all in a lushly realized setting one can just about smell. And taste—JadeAnne might be in the middle of a gunfight, but she's never immune to the temptation of a good plate of tacos al pastor. She and her loyal dog Pepper are a team you can't but cheer for."

Set Up

Heather Haven, multi-award-winning author of the Alvarez Family Murder Mysteries
"This is a blowout of a story. It starts on the backroads of Mexico in the middle of the night—just a woman, a dog, and Mexican Banditos—and escalates from there. If you are looking for a fast-paced, action-filled thriller about the adventures of a young PI and her lethal but well-trained dog, this will be your cup of tea. Or should I say Margarita? Jack Reacher step aside. You have met your match in JadeAnne Stone.

Judy Penz Sheluk, Amazon international bestselling author
In her debut mystery novel, Author Ana Manwaring offers up more twists and turns than a Mexican rattlesnake. Fast paced, with well-crafted characters and a strong female lead, there's plenty to like about this world of power, politics, and Mexican money laundering. I especially enjoyed the strong sense of place, which Manwaring uses to great effect. Well worth adding to you TBR pile.

Kirkus Reviews
"With a likeable duo and a vivid, appealing setting, this adventure series is off to a promising start"

Copyright © 2023 by Ana Manwaring

Published May 2023
by Indies United Publishing House, LLC

All rights reserved.

No part of this publication may be reproduced, distributed, or transmitted in any form or by any means, including photocopying, recording, or other electronic or mechanical methods, without the prior written permission of the publisher and/or author, except as permitted by U.S. copyright law.

For privacy reasons, some names, locations, and dates may have been changed.

Edited by Cindy Davis
Book Cover by Vila Design

FIRST EDITION

ISBN: 978-164456-616-9 [Paperback]
ISBN: 978-1-64456-617-6 [Mobi]
ISBN: 978-1-64456-618-3 [ePub]

Library of Congress Control Number:2023937509

INDIES UNITED PUBLISHING HOUSE, LLC
P.O. BOX 3071
QUINCY, IL 62305-3071
INDIESUNITED.NET

Other Books by Ana Manwaring

Set Up (2018)

The Hydra Effect (2019)

Nothing Comes After Z (2022)

Coyote (2022)

Coming 2023
Backlash A JadeAnne Stone Mexico Adventure #5

For
Fernando

I loved you; I hated you; I forgave you.

and

Parsley

You were a true companion. I miss you.

Acknowledgments

This memoir has been in the making for almost thirty years and many people deserve my gratitude. First, Fernando. *Muchas gracias,* there wouldn't have been anything to write about without you. Then to the host of angels who appeared when I needed help: my cousin Marty and friend Pattie top the list. Both kept track of me and my possessions, giving me lodging, storage, respite, and paying attention when I was out of touch too long. Then to the many people I've met along the way like Hal Miller, who drove me across the border and paid his own airfare back to L.A., Frank, Nora, Enrique, my language teachers and hosts, Dr. Appendini, and all who helped with a loan, a meal, a place to camp. Thanks also to the nameless man who instructed Fernando and me how to stay safe in a bad neighborhood. You all contributed to my adventure of a lifetime, and helped ensure I'd make it home.

Over the years I've written this book, many teachers and writers have guided me. My gratitude especially goes to teacher Susan Bono and her critique group who gave me the foundation for writing memoir. As always, I couldn't have done it without JAM—JC Miller and Mark Pavlichek and my Beta team, Jan M. Flynn, Lisa Towles, Bruce Johnson, Aletheia Morden, Susan Savage, and Mac Daly. You kept me honest and kept me going. Thank you.

I'm grateful to my publisher Lisa Orban, who is letting me publish in a new genre, and to my editor Cindy Davis, and Tatiana Vila, my brilliant cover designer, who turn my rough drafts and half-baked art ideas into award winning books.

And as always, to my darling David— my greatest supporter. I love you.

SAINTS and SKELETONS

A Memoir of Living in Mexico

Magic, Mole, and the Mexican Who Would Break My Heart

ANA MANWARING

INDIES UNITED PUBLISHING HOUSE, LLC

Prologue

Mole

In a dusty roadside restaurant somewhere in the north of Mexico in 1973, I first tasted *mole*. I remember the land was flat and heat radiated in waves off the pavement of the narrow highway as we drove toward the border. The sparse vegetation choked under dust. My college boyfriend and I were thirsty too. Ahead, rising out of a distant mirage, loomed a faded turquoise cinder block structure with a weathered sign in front: *Lonchería Carta Blanca*. The Cart Blanche Lunch House, a place where anything goes. We rattled the pickup to a stop in front. It looked like "anything" was already gone.

Inside the cool interior were empty metal tables and folding chairs painted in Coca Cola advertisements. Other than a couple of fat red hens roosting near the kitchen door, we were the only patrons.

A small wiry man dressed in the color of dust brought us a menu and a toothless smile. "The chicken *mole* is delicious today," he said.

Influenced by the chairs, I ordered a Coke; my companion ordered a Superior. The drinks refreshed us after our hot drive up the coast from Guaymas and we were ready to order. Having heard so much about the mystical, ancient dish made with meat and chocolate, I ordered the *mole*.

My plate arrived. On it, a chicken leg drowned in what looked like a dollop of slightly runny chocolate pudding. The chicken's skin curled up as though gasping for breath; the meat drifted in strings. It tasted thick, sweet, viscous.

"How can anybody eat this stuff?" I pushed the plate away. "It's disgusting. Too much chocolate." This from a confirmed chocoholic. Instead, we enjoyed Kirby's huge plate of *enchiladas verdes, frijoles refritos, arroz mexicano*, and plenty of hot homemade tortillas while that poor chicken leg vanished back into the kitchen's maw to the disapproving clucks of the hens.

For over two decades I continued to visit Mexico. I told my chicken mole story that first day at an intensive Spanish course in Oaxaca. As part of the curriculum we had the choice of weaving classes, pottery making, or cooking lessons—all in Spanish. Every day I cooked wonderful dishes like *chili rellenos, gorditas, tamales* and *enchiladas*.

On the first day, Doña Carmen, our instructor, marched us to the central market. It was a *mole* experience. There were vats of *mole*, tubs of *mole*, mountains of *mole*. *Mole verde, mole rojo*, the famed Oaxacan *mole negro* and *mole* of every color in between. Each stall crowded into the huge market building brimmed with *mole*. *Mole*, spicy and chocolaty, pervaded the air with its fragrance. It blended with the meat smells of the butchers' corridor, mingled with the sweet ripe smells of fruit and the pungent herbaceous odors of vegetables in the greengrocers' section. The scent of hot bread and tortillas baking melded with the *mole*, becoming an almost palatable smell. Our every breath was wrapped in *mole*. It settled over the household goods and wafted through the clothing aisles, spilling out the many doorways, down the narrow sidewalks, and into the dusty exhaust-choked streets of the city. *¡Que rico!* was the only way to describe it. I thought back to *Lonchería Carta Blanca* and the indignant hens clucking over my untouched lunch.

"Perhaps," I commented to the group, "I could be persuaded to try *mole* again."

In class I pestered Doña Carmen for a promise to demonstrate *mole*.

"Oh, *mole*. It takes too long to make," she replied as she spread out the ingredients for *picante salsas*, sweet *atole* but no *mole*.

On our last day of class, Doña Carmen greeted us in the kitchen at four o'clock as we straggled in from our sumptuous lunches on the plaza. By this time the class had dwindled to the hardcore. The long wooden table was laden with tomatoes, plantains, sesame seeds, raisins, four kinds of dried chilies, almonds and oil. On the counter stacked thin patties of crumbly soft Oaxacan chocolate wrapped in pink paper. Doña Carmen announced we were going to make *mole negro* —the quick way.

She allowed us to select only the finest of the fruits and vegetables. Classmate Tom and I had to hand-pick the plumpest of the half kilo of sesame seeds. Only the reddest tomatoes were good enough; the plantains could not be bruised; the raisins needed to be juicy. Jacquie ground the almonds to a paste in the *molcajete*. Linda roasted the *chipotle* chilies on the *comal*.

Two hours later the ingredients were ground to paste and simmered in broth to a velvety smooth sauce. When the sauce was thick but not too thick, we added just enough of the chocolate to deepen the flavor to a rich complexity. The little kitchen smelled divine. In moments the sauce adorned the tender braised chicken resting in a brown-painted clay serving dish with the fluffed rice. I set the table and we began the feast.

Someone passed the *mescal*, and toasting ourselves, and our crown of creation, we dug in. We ate, and ate; and we ate some more. We invited the weavers, the potters, and the guitar students. We invited the director and the teachers, and we all ate. When the feast was gone, and I was cleaning up, I found myself licking the *mole* pot. So this was *mole*—truly food for the Gods.

Chapter 1

Robbed

September 30, 1991

Five days after my forty-first birthday, and sixty-eight days in-country, I screeched into the receiver of a pay phone near the police station in downtown Oaxaca long distance to Marin County. "Sam, they stole *all* my clothes. Five suitcases! I've got my pajamas and the jeans I had on last night." My dog Parsley whined and leaned into my thigh as though to comfort me.

"I'm sorry, Ann, but I hope your birthday was happy," my ex-boyfriend said.

Yeah, happy birthday. At least the *ladrones*, thieves, hadn't found the secret compartment Sam had built in-between the front seats, which held the computer, my Nikon camera and lenses, and a pullout Clarion tape deck. *That* was a consolation.

"Have you reported it to the authorities?" Sam's calm voice grated on me.

"Yes. They aren't going to do anything. Six bathing

suits Sam! And the sandals I had made in Denver." I felt violated, like a heavy weight pressing on me. Or was it guilt for calling my ex? I started to cry.

"You still have the valuable stuff—money, your computer. What do you want me to do?"

I sniffed and wiped the back of my hand across my eyes. He was right. I still could plug in and write, the reason I gave for my trip to Mexico—launching a new career. Not the barely recognized truth: I was escaping my mediocre life. And Sam was part of that life, but what was I going to do? Was I so weak I couldn't go buy myself some new clothes and get on with it?

"I have a trunk of clothes in my storage. Get me the red sleeveless t-shirt, the peach flounced dress, my deck shoes…" I ticked off the list of clothes I wanted and started to cry again. Why would anyone break in to my bus and steal my clothes? All the stuff sold together wouldn't be as valuable as the 350 HP Honda generator, but the *pendejos* left that.

His voice softened. "I'll fill a suitcase for you, Ann, just pick me up next Saturday at the airport. Four o'clock."

The guilt settled into my neck and shoulders. I was only going to hurt him again. "I've lost weight, Sam. I'm size eight now, I guess. Tell Mom to get me some clothes. See you in Mexico City."

I hung up and slumped into the stone side of a building, stiff with tension, tears streaming off my chin. Pedestrians gave me a wide berth and funny looks, but none as funny as I gave myself. But left with only the jeans and t-shirt I was wearing at the time, I didn't know who else to call.

SAINTS AND SKELETONS

From his tone, I knew Sam had construed my call as an invitation. There was no justification for my selfishness. I didn't want him in Mexico with me. I claimed I wanted to stand on my own. To stop relying on Mr. Wrong to fill me up.

What had I done?

Sam cleared customs at the Mexico City airport on October 5th, lugging the promised suitcase along with his own bulging duffle. In those few days, I had fallen into the easy groove of Spanish classes, cooking lessons, lively cultural exchanges at *Instituto Cutural Oaxaca,* a Spanish language school, and I'd settled comfortably at my hosts', the Maldonaldos, home with Parsley, my twelve-year-old German Shepherd mix. The Maldonaldos loved Parsley and she settled right in.

The drive from Mexico City back to Oaxaca took about twelve hours in the old VW bus, and we planned to drive all night; I didn't want to miss any lessons. Sam, Parsley, and I had traveled by car plenty over our eight years together: through the Pacific Northwest, several trips down the Baja Peninsula, once pulling a twenty-three foot sailboat on a trailer, up the Australian eastern seaboard, Brisbane to Cairns, and a month in Mexico and Belize. We had it down: the rhythm of the road. Drive and ride, drive and sleep, pit-stop, walk the dog, eat, change drivers.

"I'll drive first—you sleep," I offered. "I can get us out of the city and onto Highway 190 through Cuautla by dark. Then you drive." It was six p.m. I'd left Oaxaca at five that morning. I yawned.

West of Cuautla the sun disappeared behind the distant dead volcanoes, their dark peaks worn to two-dimensional flatness against the yellowy haze of sky fading to ash with the twilight. Earlier in the day, I'd crossed this prehistoric valley with its moonscape of cones jutting from a vast expanse of empty grassland and experienced the strangest sense of déjà vu.

I planted corn kernels in this rocky, fertile soil. My brown stick-like legs jutted from the thread-bare hem of my rough jute-colored tunic, my dusty feet bound to leather soles by strips of tanned hide. My pointed stick plunged into the ground; I saw my calloused hand dip into the cloth bag, drop the seed into the hole. I saw the others, dark-skinned against their light tunics, ragged black hair flowing forward across bent shoulders—dig, reach, drop, dig, reach, drop—against the backdrop of smoking cones.

This was why I'd come to Mexico—to decode my night-time dreams. I wanted to dig my ancient roots, uncover an obscure heritage within my blood. And I was going to write about it. I'd been in Mexico for over two months and, so far, this valley held the strongest pull, the sharpest vision. I thrilled to my discovery.

"Ann, I can't live without you." Sam's voice crashed between our Caddy seats, urgent, jarring.

I flinched, startled back from my past-life musings. "What?"

SAINTS AND SKELETONS

"I need you— give me the excuse to finalize the divorce," he mumbled, his hang-dog body language barking "loser."

"Get over it, Sam. Don't bring me into it—if you don't love your wife and don't want to be married to her—get a divorce."

I'd dumped Sam two years before when he ran off to Belize to chase drug smugglers on what I thought was a DEA contract. I didn't want him following me around Mexico, spoiling my big adventure. But I was the one who called for help, and there we were, driving toward Oaxaca and the *Instituto*.

Why did I think I needed him? I had agreed that I would show him around —*as a friend*—if he brought me some new clothes and a printer for my portable Toshiba computer. Now he was rooming with me. This was more than I'd bargained for. I'd moved on. Why hadn't he?

After our session at the *Instituto* ended in late October, Sam and I headed out of Oaxaca City onto the narrow country road winding toward the Pacific. We cruised my 1969 VW pop-top camper as though chugging an old Chris Craft along the sloughs of some sleepy delta. The ride felt thick and smooth—I had installed air shocks in place of the regular stiff factory stock.

Villages with tongue-twisting names peeked from under profusions of blooming vines. Churches, soccer fields, and markets overflowing with fresh vegetables and fruits, plots of marigolds pungent-ripe with golden flowers, and dark skinned families carrying pottery and crafts along the road, drifted by our open windows. The countryside smelled of fresh tortillas, burning chilies, chickens, goats, and the ubiquitous corn. As we ascended the foothills, the terraces of maize stretched into the clouds that hung around the high peaks above us like wooly ruffs.

Sam drove. I popped some old Moody Blues into the tape deck and cranked it up, making it impossible to talk, and leaving me plenty of time to savor the shifting view of Mexico as I settled into the divots of my wide, red-leather seat, which some previous owner had pulled out of a Cadillac and installed into the cab. The seat matched that owner's rear, but over time, it reformed to fit me.

I felt Sam rankle. I didn't care. I was still pissed-off that he'd followed me from California to Oaxaca—even though he had done me a huge favor. It was bad enough that he'd signed up for the same session at my language school, and then he finagled lodging with my hosts. We argued about it. Worse, we'd shared a room for three weeks and I'd settled right into the old relationship. I hated that it was so familiar, so easy, but mostly I was disgusted with myself for stringing Sam along to soothe my own apprehensions about travelling alone. I'd managed to take care of myself from Mazatlán to Oaxaca over the last two months. What was the matter with me now?

Sam claimed from the start I was nuts—out of my mind—to make this trip. Crazy? Probably. Who else but a lunatic would close a viable business, pack up a geriatric dog, and drive to Mexico in a VW camper at age forty? To write a novel—or that's what I told myself I was doing—but I'd had plenty of time to consider the truth on my long drives. Call it a mid-life crisis, or just plain running away from everything I thought was wrong with my life: my lousy choices in men, my dysfunctional family, my lack of distinction. I'd been stuck in a dead relationship and bored with keeping books and preparing taxes. My family dynamics weren't going to change, so why not get out while the getting was good? My therapist advocated I take a break and have a good look at my life and my choices—as far from my normal life as possible. She was right. I needed to figure it out, and let go of my anger with my family, with Sam, and with myself.

I returned my attention to the cab and the ribbon of tar, at times barely a car width, which wound higher into the Oaxacan mountains. Astringent scents of mountain pine and wood smoke swirled through our open windows, the afternoon air crisp and fresh. In places, the mist hung heavy in the trees as adobe huts gave way to wooden cottages scattered farther and farther from their neighbors. The spectacular scenery unfolded around each bend. Freshwater streams spilled over tumbled stones and fell down steep cliffs, disappearing into fern-lined canyons. In sunny pockets, brilliant red, yellow, and orange flowers crowded against the dark forest. The people we saw wore woolen clothes and hats, stout boots, and thick woven shawls to protect against the chilling dampness of the shadows. We shivered in shorts and sandals from the biting breeze flooding into the cabin of the bus, and the awesome beauty of the cloud forest as we reached the summit of the range.

A compact wood-hewn restaurant with white smoke billowing from the chimneystack sat atop the pass.

"I'm cold," I said. "Let's stop for some lunch and change into something warmer. Parsley needs a walk, too. Are you hungry?"

"I could use some coffee. This road beats hell—what have you gotten me into?" Sam said.

Inside the snug restaurant a bright fire burned in a large fireplace along one wall with local crafts and paintings hanging above it. Hand-loomed yellow cloths brightened the cluster of square wooden tables filling the room. Opposite the fire a little bar and the door into the kitchen took much of the wall-space. Most amazing was the north-facing picture window overlooking rugged peaks ranging farther than my eye could see.

The restaurant wasn't listed in any of my guidebooks, but, like the miraculous vision of a saint—it materialized when we most needed it. We'd changed into sweats, socks, and shoes inside the camper then hunkered down in front of the restaurant's fireplace to sip our steaming mugs of sweet *café de olla* while we waited in silence for the *dueña* to serve her sweet and spicy *mole de guajillo*.

Back on the road, a black blanket of clouds extended below us to the horizon covering the lower range and foothills as we began our westerly descent from the peaks. We slipped under the clouds into a torrential downpour that turned the twisting mountain road into a churning mud-laced rapid. The cloud-forest had thinned and lush tropical jungle crowded over the narrow road.

Storm-tossed leaves and branches rained down like confetti over a wild parade. We crawled along in first gear.

"God, do you think this road is safe?" I asked Sam. "What if it washes out while we're on it? What if one of these trees falls on us?" The road was dark and slippery. Thunder rocked the bus. Brown churning rivers cascaded down the hillsides briefly illuminated by the white glare of lightning. I smelled the ozone and wrinkled my nose.

"We should pull over and wait it out," I said.

Sam shifted into second gear, dismissing my suggestion. "Let's just get down this damn mountain. I can't see a damn thing. Wipe off the window."

I bristled but pinched my lips tight against the angry tempest close to bursting from me. Not the time to argue.

Soon the torrent slackened and trickled to mist then cleared around us, the air perfumed with exotic flowers and damp loam. The road, still curvy, wasn't so steep, and it was no longer a muddy flash flood. The deep black sky lightened. I saw people walking with their burros and baskets from banana groves at the end of the day's work. Girls clutched stacks of tortillas in embroidered cloths, grandmothers bent under tumplines of firewood, and mothers carried steaming blue enamel pots on their heads while herding their children to dinner. We had arrived in Pochutla. It was the first town since Miahuatlán back on the east slope, and it flanked the intersection of *Ruta* 200 and *Ruta* 175 from Oaxaca.

"Turn right at the intersection," I directed.

"To where for God's sake? Let's stop and have a

beer," Sam said as he maneuvered the bus into a parking space.

Once we'd made ourselves comfortable at a small wooden table in the window of a restaurant on the main street, Sam demanded the map, asking "Where the heck are we?"

"Here." I stabbed Pochutla with my index finger. "We go north on the Pacific Coast Highway," I continued, tracing our route. "Look. To Puerto Escondido; there's a trailer park."

My pals from the Instituto planned to visit this "anything goes" haven for young gringo surfers—a snarky crowd and certainly not Sam's type, but I wanted to hook-up with my friends, especially cute, dancing William after Sam's jealous outburst the day before.

"Puerto Escondido? The surfer-dude hang-out?" Sam banged his beer bottle onto the scarred tabletop. "We're going to Huatulco—to Club Med."

"Sorry, Sam, everyone else is going to Puerto Escondido." *Everyone* meant a couple of the other students from our language school. "Anyway, you agreed to meet William tomorrow night for the World Series. There's a bar with satellite TV."

"That must have been the tequila talking. God, I hate baseball. You want to see your new boyfriend from the *Instituto*," Sam baited me. "You and William looked pretty chummy dancing at the party last night."

My stomach clenched in irritation. What part of "just friends" was so hard for him? William and I danced a few times at the end-of-session party. So what? But I resented myself for being so transparent. It was true. William, a classmate, was handsome, witty—new. And old Sam was here. End of story.

I bit back a rejoinder. What purpose would it serve? Instead, I pulled a 1000 peso coin out of my pocket.

"I'll tell you what—I'll flip you: Quetzalcoatl says we go north, and the eagle with the snake points to Huatulco. You flip it."

I shot the coin across the table. Moisture from the storm hung heavy in the hot coastal air and I was anxious to get going; anxious to let the rush through my open window cool me and drown out Sam's tiresome accusations. I'd heard enough of his entreaties and his wallowing jealousy. What had I been thinking when I agreed to spend the next ten days traveling with him? Stupid, stupid, stupid.

He flipped the peso into the air. It bounced back to the table clanking dully.

Quetzalcoatl—I won—we'd go north to Puerto Escondido. Sam fumed.

I pushed a salsa tropical mix into the cassette deck as I considered the coin toss. Maybe Sam was right that this wasn't such a good idea. But he had already nosed the camper out of Pochutla's *centro commercial* and turned north onto the highway.

Puerto Escondido for only a peso, but costly in the end.

Chapter 2

*Mariposas bailan en mi pecho—
butterflies dance in my heart~Maná*

October 26-27, 1991

The late afternoon sun angled toward the Pacific, painting our first view of Puerto Escondido a rosy gold that blushed across the buildings, fanning up the hillside from a strip of sand. Puffs of cumulus clouds congregated above the ocean, and reached toward the lighthouse that presided over a point rising sharply behind the old fishing village, marking the north corner of the mouth of the bay. The cobbled waterfront thoroughfare, shaded by tall coconut palms on the beach side was closed to all but foot traffic. We parked and walked. Trees, bushes, and vines, blooming in a Crayola rainbow of colors, cascaded down the slope from every wall, gate and rooftop on the opposite side of the street. Stone steps twisted up between the tourist and surf shops, restaurants, bars, and *tiendas* brimming with ripe mangoes, succulent papayas, trays of astringent smelling limes and oranges, and sweet, bee-attracting pineapples. I craned around corners and doors, snapping pictures, hoping to discover the mystery of each enticing passage as it disappeared around the high, glass-topped stone walls. Parsley strained against her leash, sniffing the smells with gusto. For an old girl she maintained her curiosity, and in Mexico, everything smelled interesting to a dog.

Sam stopped in front of a bar, sniffing the air. "Aren't surfers a bunch of stoners?" he asked, wrinkling his nose.

"Keep your DEA badge in your pocket."

"What are you getting at? It's a Marin County sheriff's badge." Sam's look would have frozen hell. "Let's get going. Quit taking pictures. I'm tired and hungry," he complained.

I focused my lens on Sam's familiar frown. Click. Click.

"Put that damn camera away."

A trio of pedestrians turned toward us, inquisitive.

"Quit nagging me. You're such a stick-in-the-mud." I raised my eyebrows at the tourists, as if to say it was out of my hands.

"You're selfish and irresponsible. I'm going to find somewhere to sleep tonight." He spun on his heel and stalked off in the direction of the parked camper. A sensation of giddy lightness came over me. I grinned at the passers-by.

"Are you coming?" he demanded from several feet away.

A slight gust of wind rattled the palms. "I thought

you were leaving," I said, slowing my pace.

"Don't sound so happy."

In 1991, Puerto Escondido boasted two trailer parks right on the beach. Las Palmas Trailer Park hunkered in a coconut grove at the north end of the bay. The camping spaces, defined by the trees, had brick barbecues with metal grates. Although the park was sparsely populated, I felt safe enough because of the tall chain link fence separating me from the beach, but Sam complained that it was too empty.

"Where are all the surfers staying?" He squinted his eyes in a frown as if the surfers had purposely gone into hiding.

I ignored him and checked the bathrooms. They worked. They had real toilet paper rather than rolls of brown crepe paper that might be left over from some celebration a decade past like the t.p. at Pepe's Trailer Park in Zihuatanejo. The shower water even felt warmish—a plus.

"The bathrooms are okay. We'll stay."

Business was brisk at the nearby restaurants, and people were heading out to the clubs. Music spilled down the rough paved streets, echoing off the stone walls lining the hillside above us.

"Too noisy. Let's go," Sam said.

"Then let's take a look at the place down the street."

Although not fenced, the other park was private and pretty, set about with flowering hibiscus and blooming hedges. It was also uninhabited and dark, making me nervous. Sam, ever cautious, turned us back to Las

Palmas. For once we agreed.

We staked our claim halfway between the beach and the bathroom. I sat in the wide side door of the bus and gazed toward the mouth of the bay across a fleet of low, open boats drawn up on the beach like colorful beached whales, but I didn't unpack. Instead I thrust a folding chair toward Sam and handed him one of the Pacifico beers I picked up at the *tienda*. I figured he couldn't talk if he had a beer bottle to his lips.

Parsley gave me that "feed me" look, so I fixed her bowl. "That place smells good," I said of a tiny taco joint visible at the edge of the trailer park. "Let's get dinner."

"Are you nuts? Looks worse than the roach-coach back home."

"Then what do you want?"

"Aren't there any coffee shops here?"

"Sam, we're in Mexico, not Marin."

"Whatever. Let's go."

Once Parsley finished eating, we strolled onto the esplanade.

"What about that one?" I pointed to a place tucked under a thatched roof with blaring salsa music.

He looked at a menu posted by the entrance. "I want a hamburger," he grumped and walked on.

"You won't find a Lyons."

We strolled to the end of the esplanade, reading menus and quibbling over which to choose. Each was too dirty, cost too much, or served the wrong food, according to Sam. All I wanted was some dinner—a quesadilla, tacos, whatever.

"Isn't that where you're supposed to meet William

and Kathleen?" He nodded to a dumpy looking cinderblock building with faded paint and peeling trim, squatting at the edge of the street. An old sign said "Sports Bar". The familiar flicker of television lit the interior. Sam trudged up the several steps to the door. "They have hamburgers."

"You've got to be kidding," I said when we stepped inside. A sports bar, indeed. Two huge TV's showed games with the patrons crowding the small, smoky room shouted and cheered in English. Sam marched toward a table, but stopped and threw himself into reverse like a cartoon character when he realized the smoke was coming from numerous joints passing through the crowd.

"Let's get out of here," he said.

I looked forward to coming back for the World Series and sampling some of that Acapulco Gold—Sam was sure to stay away!

We settled on a fish restaurant on the other side of the esplanade from Las Palmas and up a few steps. The palm thatched roof covered half walls open to the elements. Diners perched on stools at tall tables, surrounding a central kitchen open to view. Our obliging waiter brought a dish of scraps along with the bowl of water we ordered for Parsley. My *huachinango mojo de ajo*, Pacific red snapper drenched in garlic, was fresh and grilled perfectly. Palm fronds clacked in the gentle sea breeze and the balmy night smelled fresh and salty. The fish was so delicious, I forgot to notice if *mole* was on the menu.

After dinner with our bellies full, and our attitudes toward one another kindlier, Sam and I cruised arm-in-arm with the flow of tourists, lovers, drunk surfers and locals, noting places to explore in the coming days. We located the bank, the post office, and the only grocery store that was open, where we bought purified water and a few provisions before going back to the *bus* to set-up camp. I pulled out the sling-back chairs and unfolded the bench to make the bed, while Sam retrieved the table from the luggage rack then set it up under the glow and hiss of my Coleman lantern. We both felt optimistic when he said good night.

Sam snored inside the no-see-um-netted bus when an orange VW camper pulled into our trailer park close to midnight. I paid little attention, lost in Gabriel Garcia Marques' *Love in the Time of Cholera*. Parsley, on-duty at the edge of my tiny circle of light, kept watch on the two men who emerged from the VW, set-up camp, and disappeared back into it, pulling the door closed behind them with a thwunk.

The laughter of fishermen awakened me the next morning. The clock read 7:00 a.m. and the camper was already a slow-cooking oven in the heat. A sheen of sweat made my skin slick. I stretched and pulled myself out of the sheets to look through the gauze of the no-see-um netting velcroed into the door opening. The edge of the bay lay about seventy-five feet away from my front door. Tiny waves foamed onto the shore. The fishermen, a jolly lot, clustered together, mending nets, preparing to launch the green, yellow, and red *pangas*. Some cleaned early catches. Catcalling and laughter between boats drifted my way, but gulls, squabbling over bits of discarded fish guts, drowned out the fishermen's conversations.

Presently, four or five stout women in shiny dresses appeared, hefting gigantic blue enamel pots and baskets laden with steaming tortillas wrapped in bright napkins. They dished up breakfast for their men into clay bowls that materialized from the baskets. The rich smell of tortillas and roasted chilies got my stomach to rumbling. Sam, already up, sat in the shade in one of the folding oak "archaeologist" chairs and watched the scene.

"It's about time you woke up." My shoulders tensed at the sound of his voice.

"It's barely seven."

"I'm ready for breakfast. C'mon. Hurry up."

"Did you make coffee?" I hauled myself out of the camper and into the cooler, dappled shade of Las Palmas. Sam hadn't bothered to set-up the stove and drip a pot.

I grabbed my towel and my cosmetic bag from the locker then ambled off to Las Palmas' shower house. Luxuriating in the warm stream, I complimented myself on my ability to pick a park and thought about the trailer park I'd stayed at in Puerto Vallarta on my way down the coast.

My bus had limped into town after losing a shock absorber in the process of my first harrowing trek down a drenched and treacherous mountain road. I didn't take the time to check out the facilities before paying the tariff, triple what I paid elsewhere. It turned out the park was located just south of a pig farm and the breeze off the ocean blew right through the sty into my windows. To make matters worse, there was not another soul camping there. If I hadn't been so tired from the arduous drive from Mazatlán, I might have noticed the lack of company and the barnyard smell, but as it was, I paid the twelve dollars and dropped into bed.

In the morning, when I went to the bathhouse for a shower, I found, as the night attendant had claimed, the water was hot and would last as long as I would, but he neglected to mention the reptiles, insects, and mad dogs who would be bathing with me. That bathroom was filthy. It was the first hot shower I had encountered since Tucson, and I couldn't touch anything—including the water. Learning my lesson, I moved to a hotel—check the bathrooms first.

"The showers are great, Sam. This park was a good choice."

"I'd be more comfortable in a hotel in Huatulco. Can't you hurry up?" How did he manage to survive without a Hilton in the jungles of the Petén while he chased drug runners for the DEA—or whatever he was doing? His secret missions were a big part of our break-up.

I pulled the green embroidered drop-waist *ropa típica* sundress, bought in Oaxaca City after my suitcases were stolen, over my head, and we left Las Palmas to rustle up some breakfast. The orange camper glowed through the palm trees in a shaft of sunlight.

Sam chose the most gringo-style restaurant on the walking mall. His limited taste in food ranked high in my canon of reasons to break up—but not as high as becoming a narc when his private investigation firm tanked.

Runny eggs seasoned with Sam's snipes for breakfast, I envied the fishermen their happy banter and delectable smelling tidbits served from the giant blue pots. It didn't matter what triviality we argued over, for me it was always about the same thing. And I was still angry about it: Sam claimed to have taken a contract job with the DEA, chasing cocaine dealers through the jungles of Belize two years before, and our relationship strained to breaking. I threw him out one night in the midst of a lamp smashing, shouting match on our houseboat in Sausalito. We had been split-up until I arrived in Oaxaca to study Spanish.

Although Sam had followed me down to my language school with a suitcase of clothes, I was enjoying my single status and not rushing to make up. He hoped I might change my mind, but I resented his presence. Why couldn't he understand that I didn't want him there? This was my big adventure—he'd had his. But I couldn't send him packing.

I still don't know what I was thinking! I was fine, Parsley was fine, and they were only clothes after all, but Sam and I had always enjoyed traveling together—Australia, Belize, Mexico—camping or sailing or touring, it was an adventure. Somehow during the shock and sense of violation after the robbery, I forgot another of our canon: I am the adventurous one. Left up to Sam, we'd have stayed in a seedy hotel bar drinking Miller and eating grilled cheese sandwiches on Wonder bread, and that's exactly what he wanted.

SAINTS AND SKELETONS

Breakfast over, and our provisioning accomplished at the under-stocked, over-priced tourist grocery store, we returned to camp to put on bathing suits and get ready for the beach. Three months in Mexico and I had lost an entire dress size.

"Must be the salsa!" I told Parsley as I slid out of my dress and into a new bikini and sarong for my day at the shore.

"Your turn," I said, stepping out of the bus, smoothing the netting back into place.

"Why don't you trot over there and meet the guys from California. I bet they want to go to the beach with you." Sam spoke in his most snide tone and gestured his shining, hairless pate toward the orange camper. *Now what was he mad about?*

I glanced over to the lifeless bus whose license plate read: Mexico DF—*Distrito Federal*.

"It's from Mexico City."

"Whatever. Take them to the beach," he said.

"Aren't you coming with me?"

I hoped Sam didn't hear the glee in my voice as I walked off toward the gate, Parsley at my side.

Parsley and I hit the beach at about 9:30, trudging through the sand with towels, lotion, water, book, hat, and all the accoutrement needed for a heavy day of leisure by the sea. I found a likely spot under a thatched umbrella shading an unoccupied weather-beaten wooden chair stationed in front of a funky beachside restaurant playing some good old rock-and-roll.

The surf was higher on this side of the bay and the deep sandy beach sloped to the water's edge. On

Sunday morning, both tourists and locals were staking claims to the beachfront real estate. Kids ran in and out of the water splashing and laughing; girls basted themselves with coconut oil, stretching out to roast in the sun; surfers, stalking the perfect wave, passed by carrying their boards; young men milled around the restaurants eyeing the girls while dealing in low voices, and greeting arriving friends in loud voices, "*Que onda, guey?*" Lots of palm slapping. Mothers, aunts, and grandmothers sat in the shade of the *palapas* and fussed over picnics, children, and each other. A skinny, dark-skinned ten-year-old came up and asked what I would like to order. He soon returned with my first Negra Modelo of the day.

Sam never showed up. I passed a relaxed beach day drinking beer, meeting people, eating fresh fried fish, swimming when I felt hot, and learning all the local gossip. In the afternoon, a band set-up and played reggae. A handsome kid, Anibal, asked me to dance. He was probably no more than twenty, but he was charming and claimed to have some "killer *mota*." It wasn't hard to convince me to hook up with him later that evening at a popular salsa club on the hill. Anibal promised that I would get "*muy prendida,*" stoned, and he could teach me more Spanish. All right! William joined me during the afternoon and agreed to check-out the club with me—after the World Series game ended. I bet myself that Sam would refuse to go. Where was he, anyway? I half hoped he'd stay there.

Shadows stretched behind me. I gathered my things, paid my bar tab, then Parsley and I trudged back to Las Palmas through the sand. Sam, it turned out, lay in bed, miserable with a debilitating case of *turista* and told me to go out and leave him alone. I took another shower and tossed on the melon-colored flounced sundress he brought from home, added a bit of green eye pencil, some lipstick. Voila! I was ready to knock 'em dead at the salsa club.

"*Hola*. Hallo! Do you want a drink?"

A pale, soft-looking man with cropped black hair hailed me in heavily accented English from his barbeque pit at the trailer park. One of the orange camper neighbors.

I waved Hi, and walked over to introduce myself. "*Yo soy Ana*," I said as I extended my hand.

"My name is Gerardo from the north of Mexico City," he replied, pumping my hand a bit longer than necessary and breathing what I took to be the exhaust of a tequila distillery.

Did everyone in Puerto Escondido speak English? Gerardo appeared to be thirty-five, or slightly older. It was hard to tell because, up close, he had that worn look of an alcoholic. After a minute or two of polite small talk in a combination of my broken Spanish and his slurred English, I declined his offer of a cocktail and made an excuse to leave. As I turned to go, on that evening of October 27, 1991, the door of the orange camper slid open and, like in the movies, time slowed.

A slender man of medium-build with light brown hair curling into ringlets onto his forehead and neck stepped out. He looked young, twenties maybe, in his ancient pair of flowered Hawaiian baggies with dress tassel loafers. Nothing else. My feet rooted into the sand. I melted into jelly knees and rubber elbows with a wildly beating heart. Dazzled, I couldn't take my eyes off his golden aura as he strode across the sandy path from the orange camper. He looked young, sleepy-eyed and innocent, but something in his manner said he was older. He sauntered over to me and took my hand. Butterflies danced in my heart.

"*Fernando Leon, a sus ordenes*," he introduced himself, his smile lighting up his sea blue eyes. Warmth flowed through him.

Fernando. Fernando Leon. Fernando from the orange VW camper, from the north of Mexico City. His name played like a mantra. I was still holding his hand, gazing into the vast Pacific of his eyes when I heard myself inviting him out for the evening, drawing him toward the esplanade.

"*Voy a encontrar unos amigos en el club de salsa anoche. No quieres venir? Te gusto bailar?*"

"Oh! Wait!" I remembered Sam, sick in my bus. "I have to go say goodbye to my traveling companion. I'll be right there—¡*espérame, espérame!*" I ran to my VW bus and leaned in to tell Sam I was off to the video bar to meet with William and Katherine.

"Sam, you're welcome to join us if you feel better," I fibbed, crossing my fingers and surreptitiously slipping a condom into my tiny black suede shoulder bag along with a fistful of pesos and my lipstick. With a final, goodbye, I skipped off across Las Palmas, my excitement a cloud of sparkling particulate whirling around me.

Closer up, Fernando looked to be in his thirties. Not

a huge age difference, I thought as he, Parsley, and I set off to the video bar with Gerardo lurching behind us. Fernando whistled to Parsley and took my elbow, urging me to walk faster. I thought he was embarrassed by his drunken friend —a childhood companion. He practically yanked me into the video bar when we reached it.

Inside, the last game of the World Series blared from four screens placed around the small bar. The Minnesota Twins were crushing the Atlanta Braves at the Metrodome in their second World Series win in five years. William, glued to the screen, clutched a sweating Corona. Four empties littered the bar in front of him. Katherine hadn't arrived yet. I wondered if she'd made it to Puerto Escondido at all.

"So, William..." I sidled up and seated myself next to him. "Are you hungry?" Fernando took the stool next to me and ordered coffee.

"Not yet. It's only the fifth inning. I'll grab a bite here." His eyes never left the game.

"How's the food?" I looked around to see who was there and what the food looked like. The patrons were mostly American surfer types with long sun-bleached hair and fabulous tans. There were a couple of seedy-looking men sitting alone, sipping beers. Soldiers of fortune in between wars? Dealers waiting to score? Spies? The few women mostly hung with the surfer crowd: bleached blonds in miniskirts or short-shorts and bra tops with maximum tans and fresh faces. Even the bartender was a middle-aged gringo, graying at the temples, but fit and healthy-looking in a light blue *guayabera*-style shirt and white jeans. An escaped nine-to-fiver down for a surfing holiday who never went home?

Surfer regalia decorated the bar: a couple of boards floated under the thatch, plastic Hawaiian leis draped surfing photos, a few colorful croton plants stood in the windows, and a ceramic sculpture of a woody with boards on top sat on the juke box, which played every surfing hit from the 1960's. The Beachboys, competing with the televisions, invited us on a surfin' safari.

People munched piles of fries with ketchup, meat sandwiches that resembled hamburgers, and one guy even had a Ballpark frank. The plates were served with frijoles and rice instead of potato salad and pickles, but this *was* Mexico.

English cheers and boos erupted around us. Fernando looked uncomfortable. Gerardo managed to find us and sucked up his third tequila slammer. He was having trouble sitting on his bar stool. I didn't think he'd make it to dinner.

"What do you want to eat?" I asked Fernando.

"Tacos," he responded, immediately.

"I love tacos," I gushed. "Where shall we go?"

I was one of the lucky tourists—I could eat just about anything I wanted without getting diarrhea, but I'd never eaten a street taco. Fernando glanced at Gerardo, his head sagging almost to the bar top. He grabbed my arm, spun me toward the door, and ran me out into the fading sunlight. Parsley, determined that she loved this new guy, bounded happily at his thigh. Bars bored her, but she liked restaurants. Fernando escorted me up one side of the mall and down the other in search of tacos, talking the entire time in a slow, simple manner that I could almost understand.

We found a spotlessly clean *taquería* he approved of. It was a platform of concrete raised up perhaps three feet above the pedestrian mall, with thatched umbrellas shading a collection of very tall, very tiny round tables, a popular look in Puerto Escondido.

Fernando showed me how to eat the miniscule folds of tortillas stuffed with *sesos*, *cabeza*, and *al pastor* (brains, cow cheeks, and marinated pork) slathered in *picante salsa* and introduced me to Mexico's popular icy, sweetened tamarind drinks. He regaled me with the story of his three years in Germany with a German girlfriend he met in Cancun while he was working at a resort. She spoke a smattering of Spanish, but he knew no German.

"I completely understand your frustration," I said. I felt the same way—here I was with a young god, and all I could do was gaze at him and hope he didn't think I was too stupid. Gazing wasn't that bad, actually.

I ate my *tacos al pastor*, thin-sliced pork layered over a giant skewer, which revolved in a heating element, cooking continuously until the skewer emptied. Reddish in color, the meat tasted vaguely like honey-baked ham. The best *al pastor*, I came to find, was cooked on busy city streets and dusted with exhaust carbon and automotive lead by every passing bus and car, but Taqueria La Concha in Puerto Escondido turned out a pretty good al pastor, too. We drank our *tamarindos* and gazed in each other's eyes. I ordered a Tres Equis. As I sipped it, he said he didn't drink, wooing me with his clean living.

Meanwhile, Gerardo, an accountant and school

chum of Fernando's, lumbered past us, drunker than before, slurring epithets under his breath, swearing at the people he ran into. On his third pass, he happened to look up and see Fernando. He staggered on the steps, poured himself into the empty chair at our table and began an obnoxious diatribe against Americans in Spanglish. We paid our bill then hurried out into the evening, leaving Gerardo behind, muttering indignantly.

It was too early to go to the club, but we searched out the stairs that led to it and the village beyond. From the stairs, we saw that Puerto Escondido wrapped around a shimmering, open-ended bay stretching south from the point where the lighthouse stood, around to a natural outcropping of rock jutting up through the sand into the water. Most of the town was built on the mountain, but the tourist section had been drawn along the littoral, right in the sand, the main street a walking mall with a few hotels, restaurants, and many shops.

Fernando and I stood side-by-side on a bougainvillea-covered wall and watched the sunset as lights twinkled up the hillside.

Lightning arced between us.

Chapter 3

Caravan to Zipolite

October 28, 1991

Tequila-laced sweat pricked at my skin and plastered my hair to my scalp. I lifted my head to look out the no-see-um netting, but the hammering inside my skull sent it burrowing back to my twisted pillow and soaked sheets. My clothes, wedged against the bus's wall, smelled like a skid row bar.

The sun was already inching up the sky, and the trailer park cooked. It was going to be a hot one, for sure. The fishermen were gone.

"It's ten. Get up," Sam growled from somewhere outside in the shade.

I groaned and sat up, legs dangling in the doorway, then rooted around in the cargo net strung from the curtain bar behind the seats for the bottle of aspirin. I would have to get up and close the pullout bed if I wanted cold water from the cooler to wash down the aspirin tablets. I groped in the closet for something to wear and dragged my green shift over my head. It was almost clean. I didn't have much of a choice since my suitcases had been ripped-off. Even in Mexico, replacing a wardrobe was costly.

"How're you feeling?" I asked Sam when I eventually stepped out of the bus.

"Better than you look. You and your new boyfriend have fun last night?" His tone was angry, mocking. Parsley wagged her tail but stayed put under the table, a worried expression in her eyes. She knew that tone; so did I.

I bent down to pet her, conveniently keeping Sam from seeing my face. I replied in a neutral voice, "Yeah. It was a gas. Too bad you didn't come. You'd have liked the band. I think the style of music is called salsa tropical."

"Who told you that—William?"

"I didn't even see William. I met up with people from the beach."

"What happened to your buddies from the VW?"

I looked across the trailer park to the closed-up orange camper. A bolt of excitement ran through me. Was Fernando still sleeping? We got in from our tryst on the beach barely before the sun came up. *La madrugada*, he called it. I needed to look that up in my dictionary, which lay on the table by Sam's elbow—later.

Sam's expression frightened me. I should have adjusted my face. Uh-oh, I realized I was smiling. After ten years, he could read me, but he didn't know what he was reading. However, he knew I never smiled before coffee. I'd better be careful.

"You were smoking marijuana. The smell nauseates me."

"They don't speak English. Smoking doesn't require language."

"Are you asking to visit a Mexican jail?"

"Don't start your narc shit, Sam."

"Stay away from marijuana."

"You're so uptight."

"Just don't get caught. I don't have any influence in Mexico."

"What about your get-out-of-jail-free card? Don't you have your badge?

Maybe your DEA ID?" Now I was doing the baiting. I wanted to deflect him from questioning me about the residents of the orange camper. I knew from long experience that an argument would do the trick. "Maybe you'd like to bust all the people smoking pot at the club."

"Christ. You're never going to forgive me, are you?"

I busied myself collecting my towel and toiletries for the shower, wondering how I was going to ditch Sam. He felt like a heavy anchor dragging me down, drowning me in negativity.

The aspirin, a cool shower, the plate of eggs I scrambled with chorizo, and a pot of coffee soothed my hangover. The orange camper showed no signs of life. How could they sleep in that tin can in this heat? Fernando couldn't have slipped out without Sam or me noticing, could he? I itched to see him. I kept my back toward our neighbors, but my ears were tuned in. I felt like a teenager sitting by the telephone waiting for some boy to call.

Sam made it clear that he detested Puerto Escondido. "I've seen everything here."

"Pot-smoking surfers turn me off." "I don't give a damn about your classmates from the Instituto." "There's nowhere I can eat."

Paying attention to Sam's inane and querulous conversation was torture.

"I want to go to Club Med, do some sightseeing, rent a sailboat," he finally said in a petulant voice.

That wasn't a bad idea; I loved to sail. Sam had sent me to sailing school on Richardson Bay in Sausalito before we bought a boat in the mid-eighties. Later I crewed for a friend until she deemed me expert enough to sail our boat by myself. I only sailed solo once. The problem with sailing alone was there wasn't anyone to take the tiller when it was time to moon the elegant diners at the Spinnaker. The problem with sailing with Sam at Club Med was—Sam.

"I had something else in mind." I didn't say I wanted to see what was going to happen with Fernando. I thought he'd said something about caravanning to a place called Zipolite, notorious as being one of Mexico's two nude beaches.

"There was some talk of getting up a caravan to a cool beach farther south. Ever heard of Zipolite?"

"Oh, you and the pot-smoking Mexican from the VW bus are planning to go?"

Was he reading my mind? "All of us, Sam. Maybe some others from the club too." I talked too fast, mentally crossing my fingers against the lie.

"When did you plan on mentioning it?"

"Right now. I don't know if it's going to happen."

"So what is it between you and that, what's his name?"

"Fernando and Gerardo. We're travel friends," I said.

Sam and I had traveled and he knew how, after a night of shots and laughs in some backwater bar in Baja, or Belize, or the Outback itself, the folks Sam and I met would become instant friends. "They might be gay," I dissembled. What I was up to wasn't his business. Even if I did feel guilty.

The sun shone directly overhead, filtering through the palms clacking faintly in a freshening afternoon breeze. I lounged in my folding sling chair finishing a novel, *The Sum of All Fears* by Tom Clancy. It was on the bestseller list that October and Sanborns, where I shopped in Mexico City, carried all the bestsellers—but I couldn't concentrate. The orange camper remained parked at its campsite. I had that sinking feeling. Fernando was gone and I would be stuck with Sam forever.

Sam, in the meantime, paced, fidgeted and complained.

"Take Parsley for a walk, why don't you?" I directed Sam.

"Aren't you going to the beach?"

"No, too much effort. I'm reading. Find somewhere for dinner."

Sam shambled off in the direction of the sports bar, towing Parsley behind him like a reluctant dinghy. She glanced back at me with a mournful look on her face. I felt guilty for disrupting her peaceful slumber in the shade, but no one on this bus got a free ride, and her job today was to entertain Sam. I took a deep breath and let it out slowly. Maybe I'd drop Sam in Oaxaca for the next session, then go on to Mexico City. Maybe I should go home. Really, what was I doing in Mexico?

Like the grating of stone pestle on mortar, the unmistakable sound of a VW bus side-door opening vibrated through my bones. I felt liquefied, all except for my now-racing heart. I maintained my cool, nose in book, dying to turn around and see who it was. With my luck, it would be Gerardo, hung over and mean. I read the same sentence six times.

"*Buenas tardes, Anita.*" He greeted me from his camp.

It was him! Fernando. "*Hola.* Sleep well?" I called back.

"*Sí, gracias. ¿Tú?*" he said, his tassel loafers crunching the packed sand.

"Come over. I have coffee."

Fernando and I drank a carafe of fresh coffee and I made him some eggs. The charge passing between us felt stronger than the night before. He talked about all kinds of things in his rapid fire Spanish, most of which I couldn't understand, but he slowed down when the topic came around to Zipolite.

"Where's your friend?" he asked.

"Sam's taking a walk with the dog. Gerardo?"

"Still passed out. Let's go when he wakes up."

"Go to Zipolite?" I had to repeat things to make sure I understood what Fernando said.

"*Bueno*, let's do it. I'll get my things."

He was going to jump Gerardo's ship and ride with us? I wondered how you say, "hold your horses" in Spanish. But the problem was solved when the camper door ground open again and Gerardo clambered out. He trudged over to join us. The energy surrounding him was like a swarm of angry black bees. I handed him a cup of coffee and he sat down. Fernando outlined the caravanning plan to him. Gerardo didn't appear pleased; they argued briefly but calmed down when he learned that Sam was going too. This was going to be interesting. Now there were two guys to ditch.

Sam stalked back to our campsite with Parsley still in tow. He glared at the Mexicans lounging in our chairs, his arms tightly crossed over his chest. I introduced the men and busied myself with collecting up the cups, maps, books, and miscellany that littered the table to begin packing the bus for the drive south. Fernando shook Sam's hand, making some polite remarks then left. Gerardo was determined to cause trouble, but Sam didn't have a clue what he blathered on about between his poor English and the fact that he'd guzzled three Tecates from my six-pack on an empty stomach. Neither did Gerardo, I had begun to think, but it was obvious by his scowling, tight-lipped face he wasn't a happy camper. He and Sam should have ridden together; they made quite a pair.

"You actually spent time with that drunk?" Sam scoffed as we finished tying down the cargo restored to the bus's roof.

"Drunk? You should have seen him last night. We ditched him. Fernando doesn't drink."

"Just smokes pot."

"Haven't we had this conversation? It's called *mota* here, anyway."

"So you want to drive off to some beach and smoke with this guy?"

"Actually, Sam, I've heard of Zipolite and Puerto Angel. They're off the tourist circuit and beautiful. The beach at Zipolite is clean and empty. My adventure in Mexico is about going to as many of the out-of-the-way places I can to take pictures and lie on the beaches. If you don't want to go, you can stay here. I don't care. You're not going to spoil it for me—as hard as you're trying."

Sam shut up, but fumed as he paced around our campsite.

Chapter 4

Not What we Expected

October 28-29, 1991

Our Zipolite caravan commenced just after two o'clock, Gerardo's orange camper in the lead. I followed with a visceral giddiness, windows down and tropical sea-air streaming in. Reggae, Sam's least favorite music, blasted from the Clarion tape deck. I cranked it up louder for *Lively Up Yourself* and received several thumbs-up from surfers carrying their boards across the highway and hearing the refrain. Sam was not amused.

We doubled back to Pochutla but turned left when we came to the junction with Ruta 175. The flat coastal lowlands gave way to green forested hills and there was no evidence we were only about five miles from the Pacific. We twisted our way down a sandy, hard-packed road to a bluff above the rock and jungle ringed bay of San Angel. This was truly the postcard-perfect sleepy fishing village. The rusting trawlers, bright colored paint fading, bobbed at their buoys and the familiar *pangas* littered the narrow beach. Sam gasped. I turned down Jimmy Cliff's *The Harder They Come* for the breathtaking sight.

Busses rumbled over a bridge where the mouth of the creek fed into the bay and chugged back into the jungle for another three or four miles north. If Zipolite was anything like San Angel, I was on my way to paradise. It was late afternoon. I looked forward to a margarita and dinner at whatever beach restaurant presented itself. As wild and ridiculous as it seemed, I envisioned fresh *dorado mojo de ajo* melting on my tongue. I salivated.

The orange camper pulled over and Fernando hopped out of the passenger door wearing his ridiculous tassel loafers. I pulled up behind them, idling.

"We're here," Fernando said.

"This is Zipolite?" I looked around. A stretch of blinding white beach dropped to the surf. A few scrubby palms dotted the top of the beach and a series of hovels and animal enclosures, mostly overgrown with trumpet flower and bougainvillea vines strung out on either side of the road. The dense jungle crowded up against the sand. I didn't see any restaurants.

"Look for somewhere to park," Fernando said.

"What do you mean?"

"We have to negotiate a place with one of the families."

"We what?" This was not what I expected.

"Follow me," he said, clopping back to his ride.

Sam scowled as I hopped back into the driver's seat. "So there's nowhere to stay?" He demanded. "Your new boyfriend doesn't know what he's doing."

"It's an adventure, Sam. Relax." I replied, hoping he wasn't right.

The orange camper cruised slowly, turning into one beachside compound after the next, Fernando asking what the rate for car camping and meals would be. The locals eyed two buses with city slickers and gringos. They weren't having anything to do with us. We scouted until the mid-point of the broad cove. A señora agreed to put us up for a modest price—something in the region of five dollars a day for all of us. We'd get the use of the outhouse, a water ration, and *comida* in the afternoon. Fernando signaled me to pay her.

"Why doesn't he pay the woman? Do you know what you're in for?" Sam smirked at me.

What a tedious man.

I opened my bus's side door to get my purse and let Parsley out. Chickens and mongrels scattered in a cacophony of yips and squawks. Parsley ignored the dogs, but chased after the nearest hen. I sprinted after her, zig-zagging across the sandy yard until I grabbed her tail and she stopped. The yard cackled and crowed until the dust settled.

"This is not going to work out," I said, panting, when I had my dog secure on her leash.

Fernando thanked the woman. We revved up our buses and slowly moved on down the sandy road. Finally, at the end of the cove, a family took us in. The *dueña* was a skinny short woman with dark scraggly hair and a shiny navy blue dress topped by the ubiquitous plaid pinafore. She looked shifty to me, but she only wanted a couple of dollars a day for each vehicle, and she would give us food.

The compound was a hovel. The fences had collapsed and grown over with beach-tolerant shrubs and vines. The one-story house perched atop a concrete slab with two windowless sides and supported a large over-hanging corrugated tin roof, which gave the whole thing the look of a carport. The front and back walls were stacked about a meter high in cinderblock cemented over structural steel bar. Everywhere metal rusted and flaked, including the exposed steel bar, an unidentifiable piece of machinery, and the old pickup in the yard. Chickens lived in a small pen enclosed by rusted wire; a goat strolled through the compound nibbling weeds, rags, tin cans, and geraniums. I watched him wander into the house to be chased out by a couple of grubby kids.

I paid for the night, thinking the Club Med in Huatulco may have been a better choice after all. Then I unloaded the table and chairs, the stove, and my dishes for dinner. We weren't getting electricity in the deal.

While Fernando and Gerardo busied themselves in the cabin of the orange camper, Parsley sniffed out her new territory, keeping out of the way of the goat. Sam pouted in the shade once I'd gotten the canopy up. I handed him a beer.

The sound of the beer caps popping off brought out our hostess's father, a cheerful, wizened coot who looked a bit like Emiliano Zapata in a straw cowboy hat. A sullen teenager also appeared, the oldest son, I guessed, and slouched just out of conversation range like a wannabe orbiting the fringes of the hipster high school group. He watched our every movement.

SAINTS AND SKELETONS

"I have a bad feeling about this," Sam said.

The Mexican's side door scraped open and my heart made a little somersault as Fernando stepped out and ambled over, Gerardo on his heels. I motioned my head for Fer to come to the door, whispering, "Sam doesn't think we're safe here."

"I don't either. Let's invite the old man and the kid for a beer," he said and I nodded.

He raised one of the bottles toward the old man and another to the boy with an inviting look. *"Oye, viejo, joven. ¿Cerveza?"*

He handed Sam and Gerardo theirs then offered the unoccupied camp chair to the grandfather. The old man shuffled over, accepted a beer, but squatted in the sand, calling for the boy. I turned up the tape deck—Linda Ronstadt's *Canciones de Mis Padres*. Fernando took a quick turn to the salsa beat and grinned at me before squatting down with the old man; Gerardo helped himself to my chair. I stayed in the doorway of my bus. Soon the four Mexicans were having a lively talk, laughing and slapping their thighs. I couldn't understand any of it, but I trusted that Fernando was winning our hosts over with his charm and wit. The señora scowled from the shadows of her covered patio kitchen, her arms folded tightly across her scrawny bosom.

"Fernando agrees with you, Sam," I said in English. "It's too late to leave now, but we'll get out of here tomorrow."

"If we aren't murdered in our sleep. Have you taken a good look at the woman?"

"I sure have. She's totally pissed off that the old

man and her kid are sitting with us."

Sam craned around to see what she was up to. She had lit a small fire of twigs and placed a large round *comal* over it, propped on cinderblocks. She dumped the cheap vegetable oil I'd seen street vendors using across the surface, tossed on several whole fish, added the sweet green onions I loved and left the food to cook. Then she scooped a handful of *masa* out of a blue napkin-covered bucket and patted out fresh tortillas, cooking them around the edges of the *comal* then stacking them in a tortilla towel to stay warm. When the fish was cooked, she piled it and the onions on a platter, added a bowl of red salsa. Next, she brought the meal out to us.

I dished up the fish and onions, and the men helped themselves to tortillas and salsa. The grandfather chatted on, but declined to join us in the food. The kid slinked off when no one offered him a third beer. I fell into fresh fish heaven as the sun, a huge orange ball, sank into the Pacific.

I lit the Coleman lantern as Emiliano Zapata tottered off to his hammock. Dinner had tasted fresh and savory, but we all knew we had a serious problem. The vibes coming from the mother and son shouted out: robbery! We decided that someone had to stay with the buses at all times; everything had to be locked up tight while we slept. I wasn't looking forward to that. I was used to sleeping with the windows and side door wide open, the fans running, and all the no-see-um netting velcroed into place to keep out the bugs. I sure didn't want to be locked into my bus with Sam and Parsley. We'd roast—even with the offshore breeze that blew the mosquitoes away.

But the food had tasted rich and fresh; it was the fish I'd imagined, even if it did come from a sullen woman's dirty kitchen. Fernando dropped his fork onto his plate and trotted over to thank the Doña. I saw him helping her tidy up as I did with our dinner dishes— I used our bottled water to wash rather than the Zipolite family's stored rainwater. Sam popped another beer as Gerardo staggered to his VW, parked several feet behind mine, and poured another *copa,* cocktail. The afternoon shadows reached into dusk while Linda Ronstadt crooned '*tu solo tu, eres causa de todo'*—you, only you, you're the cause of everything....

"Where's the lantern fuel?" Sam asked, as the Coleman sputtered, almost out of gas.

"In the cabinet. Can you stick in Dr. Loco while you're inside?" After eating, I was feeling frisky— maybe a little *baila* to "*Mueveté*" would be in order. Dr. Loco's Rockin' Jalepeño Band was made up of a bunch of university professors and students, some from Stanford, and often played in the Bay Area. I'd bought a cassette at a concert at College of Marin, one of my two tapes in Spanish. This would impress Fernando, I thought.

"Let's listen to Simon and Garfunkel."

"Sure, after."

"Trying to impress your new boyfriend?"

Oh good lord, Sam had to go! Where was Fernando? It was completely dark and the roar of the waves breaking on the shore sounded closer and louder than before. The heat radiated out of the sandy ground in the cooling evening air; millions of stars pierced the navy blue sky. It would have been perfect, if only…

"Here's to you Mrs. …" played.

I glared at Sam, but it was hard to be angry with Simon and Garfunkel singing. He screwed a new canister of propane onto the lantern, set the Coleman onto the table, lit it with a soft pop, sat down, and tossed the empty to me.

"So we'll get out of here in the morning and go to Huatulco. Club Med. Without the Mexicans," he said. "Hand me my book, would ya. It's on top of the cabinet."

"Sure." I distractedly tossed the spent canister into the garbage bag and handed him a dog-eared paperback. Fernando had just stepped over the low wall surrounding the "house" and my stomach did that little *baila*—butterflies dancing—as the Maná song went.

"Hey. What's up with the old lady?" I asked him, gesturing toward the wing chair.

"Religious. She doesn't approve of men and women traveling together. I said you and Sam are married and she relaxed." He drummed his fingers in time to the "59th Street Bridge Song (Feelin Groovy)" and smiled. *"Me gusta mucho Simon y Garfunkel."*

"Hey, good musical choice, Sam. Fernando likes them too," I said in English, and then in Spanish, "So you think we're safe?"

"Ask him if these bandits are going to rob us in the night," Sam demanded.

"We'll be okay," Fernando said.

"Okay? He said okay?" Sam leaned around the hissing lantern to see me on the other side of the table.

"Sam, you've studied more Spanish than I have.

You can understand him. We're okay. Tomorrow, after checking this place out, we'll leave."

"What do you mean? We're leaving first thing. As soon as it's light."

I rolled my eyes at Fernando, who could see me clearly. He jerked his head. "Come on, let's go explore the beach," he said.

"What did he say?"

"Fernando wants to know if we'd like to walk down to the beach." Parsley perked up her ears at the word walk.

"And just leave our stuff alone? You go with your boyfriend, I'll stay and watch camp," he said, his words trailing off into the implied *it's what you want. Poor me.*

"Come, Sam. We'll lock up. Everything will be fine." I crossed my fingers behind my back to mitigate my lie then stood up. Parsley woofed and bounded from under the table, snuffling and wagging into Fernando's open hands. They'd already fallen in love, and I saw the shadow of recognition cross Sam's eyes. He knew what was coming. If my dog loved him, I would too.

Sam got up and pushed past me into the bus. "I'm going to bed. Take your key." he almost spat the words at me.

Fernando had followed the exchange closely. "*¿Todo está bien?*"

"*Sí, vamos a la playa,* yes, let's go to the beach." I grabbed my chair.

He grinned and collected his.

"Night, Sam. We'll be back soon," I said as he slammed the door shut.

Fernando and I skirted around the silent hovel guided by my flashlight. I flicked it off when we cleared the house, hitting the deep sand that shined under the brilliant sky. The waves breaking onto the shore rumbled peacefully, a lion purring in its slumber. The rich odor of un-groomed seashore tantalized my nose—it smelled like home, or the home in Sausalito's Waldo Point Harbor I'd given up to come on this crazy adventure. I felt a little prick of hot tears at the corners of my eyes. For just a moment I missed my houseboat and my funky Schoonmaker Building office, my eclectic bunch of bookkeeping and tax clients, my family, and yes, even the almost ten years I'd shared with Sam—but that had ended when he signed up and left to chase drug shipments through Belize and the jungles of Guatemala. He left me behind and I'd learned to live just fine without him, thank you very much. Now I was on my own quest. But what was I looking for?

Whatever I was after, the ghostly white beach, the rich balmy air, the gentle roar of the surf, the luminescent foam cresting off the waves, and a hot guy slipping his hand into mine as we trudged to the tide line, lit me on fire. I trudged into my future, giddy with anticipation. The past wasn't holding me back, no matter how nostalgic.

I was on my way.

Chapter 5

Two Roads Diverged

October 29, 1991

The moon, a shrouded waning crescent, slid silently into the Pacific during breakfast. Fernando and I had dragged ourselves off the beach just before daybreak, but the heat in my camper forced me up to join Sam and Gerardo at the coffeepot.

"What time did you come in?" Sam asked, his eyes squeezed to narrow slits—the trademark skeptical look I knew all-too-well.

"I dunno. Late. One?" I took a gulp of Sam's weak coffee. Tepid. "Why didn't you drip this into the thermos?" I asked.

"Yeah? My clock said it was five."

I flicked the coffee into the dirt. "I'll make another pot. Move." I pushed past Sam's seat blocking access to the storage cabinet and rummaged around for the coffee making supplies. We spent the night on the beach? I hadn't realized—time had shifted from normal hours and minutes to something non-dimensional—a perpetual now marked only by the rising sliver of moon who projected her pale beam across the placid sea in steadfast transit to the eastern horizon.

"Did you set your watch back? No daylight savings here. I'm not even sure what time zone we're in, are you?" I tipped purified water from the *garrafón* into the kettle and set it onto a burner.

"*Buenas días,*" Fernando greeted us, as he came around the bus from the direction of the latrine. He yawned and rubbed at the scruffy looking stubble on his chin. I noticed dark circles around his eyes and wondered about my own face. Fernando and I'd stayed up most of two nights running—and not relaxing, restful nights spent meditating. I prayed that Sam wouldn't pitch a fit. I didn't have the energy to fight with him.

"Good morning, Fernando. Coffee?" I asked.

"*Sí*. The old guy went fishing. Give me a couple of pesos and I'll get a fish for breakfast."

"Sam, do you have a couple of pesos? Fernando will buy a fish," I translated.

"Why should I buy your boyfriend's breakfast?"

"I'll make eggs and snapper with salsa." I hoped my tone was enticing. In Spanish I asked, "Fer, can you get fresh tortillas, too?" I heard the slap-slap-slap-slap—of hands patting balls of masa to flat corn pancakes. I fished into the cargo net hanging over the seats for my purse and a five thousand peso note, about forty-two cents. I handed it over to Fernando. He could go charm the fishwife and close that "bad eye" that cast a withering stare in our direction. I thought we'd resolved her issues the evening before.

I found *los campesinos*, country folk, inscrutable. The people I'd encountered during my three months in-country had always been wonderfully kind to me, but I'd sometimes felt an undercurrent of—what? Resentment? Mistrust? Jealousy? Well, Fernando could deal with it and I wasn't going to worry about some woman who didn't approve of me and my entourage. What was the worst she could do? Kick us out?

That day on the beach in Zioplite is etched into my memory, in part by the photographs in my scrapbook and the notes I kept in my datebook. After breakfast I donned my bright flower-patterned maillot and favorite earrings, the moon-and-sun earrings, a solid silver ball suspended inside a silver hoop. Gone is the shark's tooth-shaped black coral pendant set with an opal I wore on a twisted silver chain. I think I gave it to Fernando—a love token? Studying the photo, I can't determine if he shaved, but he looks sexy in a skimpy aqua and black zebra stripped bikini trunk. Sam, though, looks dowdy in my canvas "outback" hat from our trip to Australia, a white undershirt and black leather tennis shoes. His legs jutting from stone-colored shorts are bleached white like a cadaver.

In the photo of me, I'm grinning. In the other, the men smile at each other: Fernando like a cat about to spit, and Sam in disgust. The caption:

"D Day" October 29, 1991 On the beach at Zipolite
Fernando Leon Torrens vs. Sam H. Miller.

A sense of timelessness overcame me as we bathed in the sun near the spot where Fernando and I had stopped time the night before. The sand was thick near the cliffs at the end of the beach. We conversed in a desultory Spanish. Fernando knew almost no English, and how tired we were made it hard to do much beyond give each other goo-goo eyes. Gerardo had stayed back at his vehicle to drink.

Parsley, panting, got up from the driftwood she'd been gnawing, and stretched.

"You want to go for a walk girl?" Sam asked her.

"She probably wants water." I poured a cup from my bottle. She lapped it greedily. My dog wasn't much of a sun worshipper. "Let's go down the beach and see what we can find. Doesn't that look like a beach restaurant?" I pointed into the distance.

"Yeah. Maybe they have beer," Sam said.

We picked up our towels, suntan lotion, and books. Fernando and I slipped on our flip-flops to start the trek to the south end of the beach. The sandy tide frothed over my feet at the shore. I picked up tiny limpet shells and colored stones. The beach at Zipolite was empty and clean. Few shells, pieces of driftwood or flotsam lined the intertidal zone. This was a wild beach, quiet except for the surf and the crunch of our footfalls. Didn't the people who lived here at the beach go to it? There weren't even any *pangas*. My sixth sense of unreality grew stronger. Nearing the structure we'd seen from the north side of the cove, I realized it sat empty. A former beach restaurant, and definitely closed for beer. I plopped down in the warm sand just beyond a mini escarpment carved by the waves. Fernando joined me.

"Nothing there. I think I'll catch a few rays before lunch." I spread out my towel.

"We're leaving." Sam's voice sounded petulant. He'd lost the battle, and he knew it.

"This is so peaceful, Sam. We'll leave after lunch." I hopped up and ran into the surf, dove beneath a breaking wave and paddled in the cool swells. I was too tired to think, but had I considered my situation, I might have realized I was giving up the old blackened pot for a raging forest fire. What was that I read in some self-help book? If you feel like you're on fire when you meet, you probably are. Caution! Three alarm.

Fernando joined me in the water, but we kept our distance. I wasn't ready to slap Sam upside the head with it. I watched him wander along the beach into the shade with Parsley, then swam to shore. Fernando bobbed beyond the breakers for a few more minutes and returned to his towel. I slathered myself with sunscreen, then stretched out on my stomach.

"Let me have some of that." Fernando tipped his head toward the Coppertone.

"Sure, here." I tossed him the bottle and drifted into a nap.

By the time I woke up the sun had shifted in the sky. My skin burned. Fernando lay next to me sleeping. I raised my head looking for Sam and Parsley, but the palapa was empty. I flipped over and reached out to wake Fernando. Before I realized what I was doing, we embraced each other passionately and began kissing like newlyweds, or maybe teenagers.

"What the hell do you think you're doing?"

I glanced up to find Sam loping across the sand, Parsley happily bounding beside him.

Busted! Fernando and I flew apart and sat up. Where did Sam come from? He was spying on us. Well, not hard to do—we were right out on the beach.

"I'm sorry, Sam! I don't know what happened," I fumbled.

"I've been watching you carrying on under my nose. You think I don't know what you're up to? I'm leaving. Get up and drive me to Oaxaca." He turned and stormed off in the direction of my VW bus.

Sam wouldn't get very far unless he stole my ride, or so I thought, because I wasn't about to drive the eight hours, half after dark, to Oaxaca. I stayed put.

"What did he say?" Fernando asked me.

"*¡Le voy!* He's leaving." I grinned. I suddenly felt elated. A great weight lifted from my shoulders, and I gleefully threw my arms around my new *novio*.

Fernando and I sat on the beach for another hour. Slowly we wended our way to the señora's compound to get cleaned up and see about dinner. My bus was right where I left it next to Gerardo's. Sam and Gerardo were nowhere in sight. I unlocked the door to fix Parsley's dinner. Sam's duffle was gone, but he'd left all his dirty clothes. While I gathered up the dinner things, Fernando wandered the compound looking for Gerardo. Eventually he appeared, coming through the señora's kitchen.

"*Hola*, Gerardo. *¿Que onda?*" Fernando greeted his friend.

"You fucking slimeball," he yelled, rushing Fernando.

"*¡Que pasó?*" Fernando sidestepped the swing Gerardo took at his nose. The momentum rocked Gerardo off his trajectory and he stumbled, almost falling on his face. Fernando steadied him, but Gerardo shrugged him off.

"Her boyfriend left—took a bus back to Oaxaca. I drove him to the station. Now you're leaving me and going with her? I saw her first. ¡*Ladrón*! Thief."

As if Gerardo saw anything beyond his next drink.

The men shouted at each other in Spanish I couldn't understand. I figured that Gerardo had a jealous hissy fit. He should have driven Sam back to Oaxaca.

Fernando and Gerardo joined me to eat a silent, tense meal. After dinner, I settled down with my book and Fernando went to schmooze the señora, who called him over to her kitchen. Peeking around the bus, I saw him gesticulating and heard angry words. It didn't appear to be Fernando's evening. He had trouble everywhere, but soon he was back, attempting to explain that the owner was throwing us out because my husband had left and Gerardo blamed Fernando, or I think that's what he said. It didn't matter. We were out of there first thing in the morning. I was probably driving back to Mexico City, about two days away, and I'd better get some sleep.

I said goodnight and went to bed, locking myself and Parsley in. Fernando returned to the orange camper to keep the peace.

In the morning, I paid the woman for our luxurious stay and packed up my gear. Fernando and Gerardo yelled at each other some more. What a mess!

Chapter 6

Es mi destino

October 29-30, 1991

As the sun rose from behind the mountains shooting rays toward the Pacific, Fernando slipped out of the orange camper before Gerardo emerged from his drunken stupor. I didn't know if Fernando would come with me or not. but as I made my final check that all was properly stowed and battened down, he tossed his bag into the back and slid into the driver's seat.

"Let's go to Huatulco," he said.

We fled the señora's compound, making our way back to Ruta 200 through beautiful Puerto Angel then south down the heavily forested two-lane coastal road as the sun rose from behind the mountains to what I think was called Huatulco Bay. Checking the map, saved these many years, I begin to understand the limits of my memory. I cannot find anywhere called Bahía de Huatulco although I have an orange-headed pin stuck in the map mounted on my wall, indicating I slept at a location next to a nameless curve of coast west of the town of Santa Maria Huatulco. The entire area is called Bahías de Huatulco—the Bays of Huatulco. There are nine of 'em and none called Huatulco. I am confounded. Where were we for those two days in 1991?

Our minds have strange ways of bending memories. I look back, surprised that my trip to Huatulco—and not Club Med, mind you—took place only over the last two days of October. But here it is, marked on my 1991 Audubon Engagement Calendar. I remember long, lazy days playing on a snowy-white beach, which curved around a rugged bay. I can see the brilliant layered sunset washing into the sea at the edge of the world. I smell our campfire and the fish and tortillas cooking. I feel the feather of breeze, tickling my mostly bare skin as the Mexican night closes us into its warm embrace. My memories of the waves and salt and sand of Huatulco, and the total, absolute merging with Fernando in ecstatic infatuation, stretch time into weeks of beach bliss. But the story didn't turn out exactly like that.

It didn't take us long to establish our routine that morning. Fer (be sure to trill your rrrr!) loved to drive the bus, a pleasure I didn't share, wrestling the cumbersome beast around the sharp mountainous curves of coastal Oaxaca. He possessed infinite patience with "UYOLKAN[1]," her license plate name

---

[1] The word on my vanity license plate, today affixed over the door

meaning "heart of sky" in not quite grammatical Yucatecan Maya. He understood her limits and was happy to promenade at a pace I found gruelingly slow when I drove. I had plenty of time to see Mexico once Fernando became my chauffeur.

That morning he took pride in showing me his country, stopping as often as I wanted, allowing me to photograph anything that caught my eye. While he drove, he talked. And talked. And talked. Notes in my dictionary, never far from my reach, tell me I looked up words having to do with Mexico's history, politics, and social order. I may not have known specifically what he said, but I recognized an on-going discussion of President Salinas de Gotari's plan to give legal status to the Church, something he applauded, and abhorred simultaneously.

Although I spoke very little Spanish, I fell under Fernando's *mágico* from the moment we met, and I understood the gist of his dissertations. The problem was, I couldn't respond. When I really needed to say something, I resorted to English, but Fernando only spoke Spanish and German.

Fer had lived three years in Munich with his German girlfriend. He thought he would marry her, but found living in Germany was not for him. He hated the climate and the rigid culture as compared to the land of *mañana*; he struggled with the language. He described feeling isolated and lonely, therefore he did all he could to make my experience more pleasant. I loved him for that. And though at times, frustration got the better of

---

to my 2nd story writing studio loosely translates to "Heart of Sky" in Yucatecan Mayan.

me, we got by in a simple, child-like Spanish when it was necessary to communicate with full understanding, mostly regarding common daily necessities like food, gas, a place to sleep and the daily routine: feed the dog, get a beer, find a bathroom.

While Fernando talked incessantly when we drove, conversation wasn't our big connection in Huatulco. Once we got away from Zipolite, Sam, and Gerardo, we couldn't keep our hands off each other. I quickly learned the true meaning of *caliente*—hot traces left as he ran his soft fingertips over my bare skin.

Fernando, at thirty-one, was cute with thick curly brown hair, gorgeous sea-blue eyes, plump lips, often grinning around straight white teeth, and he had a way of appearing like an innocent puppy—so adorable I just wanted to pet him all the time. I've never met a man who looked better waking up slick with sweat in the back of a VW bus in a PEMEX station, three-day whiskers scruffing his face, and rumpled clothes sticking to him. Sam couldn't compete with the sheer sex appeal of this *mexicano macho*. And Fernando turned out to be the quintessential Latin Lover—in all its connotations., good and bad.

As I sit at my keyboard reminiscing and trying to remember the name of the beach we camped on thirty years ago, I'm overcome with the same giddiness I felt on October 30th in Bahías de Huatulco. My heart is thrumming and I feel the blood effervescing in my veins. I may not recall the place names, the exact conversations, or everything we ate in those early days together, but I have a visceral memory of the feel of Fernando's smooth skin next to mine. The rasp of his beard on my cheek. The faintly sen-sen scent of his breath. The burning trails left by his lips across my thighs. I can feel the weight of his arm as it draped over my shoulder. Our first night in Huatulco counts as one of the top-ten hottest nights of my life.

Fernando and I passed the entrance to Club Med, today Las Brisas Huatulco, on Bahía Tangolunda. I half-smiled at the irony: Sam wanted to go there. Snippets of bay viewed through the dense forest revealed a beautiful location, but I had some concerns about money. Anyway, why would we go to a hotel? We could meander farther down the coast and find the perfect camping spot. After all, we drove our hotel.

I don't know how we did it, but we landed on a large deserted bowl-like bay surrounded by mountains. We cruised right out onto the sand and set up camp, the only folks there on a late Wednesday morning. I think we camped on Bahía San Agustín, which is the closest bay to the town of Santa Maria Huatulco. The wild, empty beach ran down to the foaming surf—not your average tourist shore with gentle waves. I still hear the crash and thunder of waves colliding with shore.

Fernando had not participated in the setting up of my campsite before arriving. He was interested in how I'd built my rolling home, what I'd included, and how it all worked. The bus gave him stars in his eyes. There is something compelling about being able to go as you please, dependent on no one and nothing (except PEMEX—Petroleos Mexicanos—in our case. And the money I'd inherited from my father's father.) Even the illusion of freedom is heady, exhilarating.

He loved the pop-top and the no-see-um netting, the fans and lights, and the canvas canopy that matched the canvas on the folding chairs. He marveled at the two, red five-gallon gas cans, which swung away from the back of the bus on hinged mounts making it possible to open the back window. He immediately got the hang of threading the canopy through the track and staking it in place with telescoping poles and lines tied with trucker's knots then whipping the folding chairs off the roof, hanging the canvas seats in place and *"¡ya, listo!"* Ready to relax.

Fernando claimed the VW bus was his responsibility in Huatulco. I gladly handed it over; I had little mechanical sense for taking care of it. I'd dealt with bus problems since crossing the border and I realized that, even though in those days, any guy on the road could fix a VW engine with some wire and *chicles* —chewing gum—I was ill-equipped to handle problems. Ebbie, my mechanic at home, had showed me how to check the oil, keep the carburetor clean, and set my points, but other than the basics, car maintenance wasn't for me. Looking back, car maintenance informed many of my choices in Mexico.

Lady Luck had graced me two months before I met Fernando, at about ten p.m. on the night of August 29th, when my custom-installed air shock came loose on the empty highway between Tepic and Puerto Vallarta. It could have turned out badly.

I'd left Mazatlán that morning after having a

carburetor noise checked in Mazatlán. About four hours later, near Tepic, I'd gassed up and added oil because the bus was running hot . The station attendant told me Puerto Vallarta was another two hours south.

Well, it took six.

Since the ominous clanking came from the front and the VW's engine was in back, I knew it wasn't an engine problem, but that didn't assuage my terror. The two-lane highway snaked over a little mountain range. The only traffic for hours had been a military convoy I tailgated, using their headlights during a torrential downpour, which followed a spectacular thunder and lightning storm. The truck finally pulled over, forcing me to go ahead and I was on my own in the dark. The rain ceased and the noise started. I knew I should pull over and assess the trouble, but that made me a sitting duck for whatever evil might come my way. And the rain-saturated ground made a perfect duck pond. I slowed down but kept driving.

Finally out of the mountains, the road straightened and I saw, in the steamy distance, an electric light marking a gate, and two men, their heads leaning under the hood of a pickup. *Should I risk stopping?* I debated with myself for several moments, but reckoned that I'd be safer as the initiator in the exchange than a victim broken down by the side of the road.

"I'm sorry, can you help me?" I stumbled through my poor Spanish.

"Sure, we'd be glad to help you. But we don't know anything about mechanics either," an attractive indigenous-looking man told me in Spanglish.

It turned out my savior, named Romeo, and his

cousin, hailed from Oaxaca and sold handmade crafts to tourists on the beach at the Camino Real in Puerto Vallarta—PV. Both wore spotless loose white pants and *guyabera*-style white shirts with huaraches, but they climbed onto the muddy ground under the VW to figure out what might be wrong.

Romeo, now a sullied mess, offered to drive me in my bus the rest of the thirty or so kilometers and install me at the trailer park. He said he'd return the next day and make sure I found a repair shop.

"You speak English!" I exclaimed once we got rolling and clanking again.

"No," Romeo replied, dashing my hopes for an enjoyable conversation—trying to have a meaningful conversation in Spanish was impossible for me at that point in my trip, but Romeo and I did enjoy each other's company. He returned the following day to make good on his offer to help me find a *taller* to repair my *amortiguador.* Once the shock absorber had been re-installed, Romeo took me into town for a hamburger —my cure-all for existential pain and trauma in Mexico.

On Playa San Agustín, Fernando and I set up camp and made lunch. We'd picked up groceries, ice and water in Puerto Angel as we passed through, and a fish in the town of Huatulco for dinner. After we ate, we settled Parsley under the bus, locked the doors, and took off down to the water to swim. At about this time, a pickup trailering two jet skis pulled out of the forest onto the beach near our camp. We sauntered back; soon

SAINTS AND SKELETONS

Fernando had engaged the driver in conversation. It turned out he was an American living in Huatulco in a house-trailer with his Mexican wife and two children. She worked at a school, I recall, and he played at the beach with his jet skis. That day, he and his little boy and a couple of adult friends came out to ride the skis. I can't remember how they got them into the water, or how Fernando convinced them to let us ride one, but I do remember jetting across the bay, my hair streaming behind me in the wind as we bounced from wave to wave. I felt exhilarated and scared and clutched Fernando tightly around his waist. We zigged and zagged, sending up great rooster tails of spray while passing sparks between us.

I still see the bay, ringed by mountains and dark green forest. The mouth yawned wide, but two or three rocks jutted up, forming small islands on the ocean side. The heavy, grey-blue water surged and chopped into whitecaps as the wind came up. We seemed to be far, far from shore. I worried about capsizing, but Fernando raced us into the wind, across the wind, and with the wind until we flew. Neither of us wanted to give the machine back at the end of our ride.

The American, Jerry, invited us to spend the night at his trailer park. He and Fernando had hit it off, probably because they each had foreign "spouses" in common. We had other plans, and wanted our seclusion.

By late afternoon, Fernando and I were alone. I set up the sun shower off the back of the bus. The sun shower was a brilliant piece of low-tech technology, consisting of a heavy plastic bag, clear on one side and black on the other that held a couple of gallons of water. A two-foot hose with a red shower nozzle at the end was attached at the bottom, and a cord for hanging attached at the top. When left black-side up in the sun, the water heated to as hot as I ever wanted it. I bought it with a heavy-duty shower curtain designed to hang around the mast of a sailboat from West Marine in Sausalito. I had devised a way to set up the curtain and sun shower off the back of my camper, but alone on the beach, we skipped the curtain and washed off the salt with a shared "tank" of hot water in glorious nature.

Clean, dry, and back in shorts, we wandered down the beach. I picture it devoid of shells, driftwood, seaweed, and trash—a perfect white crescent in a perfect green and blue bowl. The energy that arced between us had taken on a faint tinge of cerise. I was holding the hand of a perfect man. In our short acquaintance, Fernando had treated me, and my dog, kindly, gentlemanly: he held my door, my towel. He helped me to sit and to stand up. He carried my parcels. He drove my car. And he looked at me with a visage of warm loving acceptance, which I had never before experienced. Fernando gently cared for Parsley. He took her for walks, saved treats for her, and spent plenty of time petting and scratching her. We had fallen under his spell, and I felt certain he had fallen under mine. He'd certainly fallen under my doggie's spell. Perhaps it was happening too fast, but I knew Fernando and I were destined to be together.

We wandered to the water at the base of the cliff jutting from the beach, forming the right boundary of the bay. There, atop the rock face grew a giant cactus of the *nopal* variety with broad flat paddles, and swooping down to that cactus, a snake dangling from its talons, flew an eagle.

Fernando grabbled me in a bear hug and danced me around the sand. "I knew coming home [from Germany] was the right thing to do! That's the symbol of Mexico. See it, see it? That's my symbol. I'm *cien por ciento mexicano* and I'm back in my place. And now I've met my Anita. *Es mi destino*—it's my destiny."

One wouldn't think it possible to ramp up the energy between us any more than it was, but this eagle with the snake, the symbol for Mexico displayed on their flag, supercharged the emotions and sensations running through us. We spent much of the next seven months joined at the hip.

Chapter 7

Jet Skis and Malathion

October 31, 1991

Halloween started on the beach. I've always loved Halloween, and I'd never missed an opportunity to celebrate it. Mexicans celebrate All Saints and All Souls days, November first and second, and not All Saint's eve, but Halloween 1991 turned out to be one of the spookiest I've experienced—and without costumes!

We woke up and prepared a leisurely breakfast with plenty of coffee. Fernando, a great short-order cook, chopped the chile serranos, cilantro, and tomatoes into *salsa fresca.* He taught me how to properly cook a tortilla and how to properly use a tortilla as a fork. According to Fer, the tortilla should not be crispy, but moist and pliable, and stored in a cloth to stay hot. I stuffed the steaming tortillas in my mouth as they came off the griddle, *comal,* until he told me to save some for him. When the eggs and half-kilo stack of tortillas were ready, Fernando's way was to tear off a bite-sized wedge of tortilla and scoop up the eggs, pour a healthy dollop of salsa on top and pop the bite into his mouth. His *huevos mexicanos,* scrambled eggs loaded with the salsa, cooked over our camp stove count as some of the best I've tasted. I cleaned up and we settled in with our books. We had the whole day to think up something to do. Secretly we hoped Jerry would come back with his jet ski.

I wanted to go into town and buy ice and fresh food, but that meant breaking down and stowing our camp and equipment back into the bus. Once we shopped, we'd have to re-set up camp. Maybe it would be better to go in the afternoon when it got hot. Morning on the beach at Bahías de Huatulco seduced us. We lounged in the early sun, sipping coffee, sharing bits of our books, and gazing at each other in that way of new lovers.

I'd flown to my cousin's in Mexico City earlier in the year with a trunk full of the city clothes (Mexico City was relatively formal in those days) and books I thought I'd want while I traveled in-country. Once I arrived in my bus, I used my trunk as my "home base" swapping out wardrobe and books as circumstances dictated. Often I gave the finished paperbacks to English speakers I met; my hardbound books went to my cousin or my friend and host, Pattie. I floated a wake of novels across Mexico as I chugged along.

What I don't see in my mind's eye is the title of the book I was reading that morning. I can squint and peer into the memory, but all I see is Fernando. The truth is, we didn't get much reading done in that first month.

Warming up with the heat of the day, we raced each other down the slope to the surf and Fernando dove in. The waves came in too fast and strong for me; I was afraid to swim. I preferred the gentle rolling surf of Puerto Escondido and suggested we go back there. Anything was possible. I had enough time and money to travel the country, and now with a native speaker who knew something about VW engines, I could do the exploring I'd convinced myself I'd come for. I'd planned to research the novel I'd started, *Stonecarver*, which would require trips to ruins in Mexico, Belize, Guatemala, and Nicaragua. Some of the places I wanted to see I could not go alone, and, I'd already determined, having a man aboard who spoke the language opened doors for me.

I absently watched Fer swim and contemplated our next move. As it turned out, we headed back to the bus to make love until beach visitors disturbed us and we deemed the time right to head into town.

Parsley grinned from her spot under the bus as we packed up. She jumped in, settling onto her seat before we finished. Shade-free beaches were too hot for a German shepherd. Anyway, she took offense at sand falling in her water and food. She'd grown accustomed to living by salt water in Sausalito and enjoyed swimming in it, but only where there were no waves. She liked the bus, however, and until the day she died, she rode like a queen.

We tooled into Santa Maria de Huatulco and found the trailer park and our new friend, thinking we might take him up on his offer of an overnight. Fernando pushed to get us there. I didn't realize why at the time.

SAINTS AND SKELETONS

Once the tops popped off the Coronas, the three of us settled around the oilcloth covered picnic table crowded with ashtrays, baby bottles, dishes, packaged food, books and magazines. In the open space between the trailers, vans, and campers, even a boat on a trailer, which folks called home, the pipe appeared and my compatriot lit the bowl. Fernando reached for it before Jerry finished his toke.

When the pipe came around to me after a bogart on Fernando's part, the pot tasted sticky with resin and hit me quickly—I passed after a couple more hits, remembering how potent the Mexican weed here tasted. Not like the harsh, dried up stuff I'd pretty much given up in the '70s. Marijuana never was my drug of choice. I didn't like the feeling of separation and paranoia I got when I smoked. I wasn't opposed to a little recreational use, but I preferred the sociability of beer and margaritas, and by the '90s, I'd moved out of my youthful "hippie" phase—although some might think living in a VW bus and traveling around foreign countries smacks of the freewheeling gypsy bands of the '60s.

Stoned, I drifted off into my own thoughts while the men blathered on in Spanish about whatever men talk about. Unbidden, Sam's image crept into my mind. My behavior in Zipolite had been inexcusable, so much so that I felt the shame flushing my cheeks as I thought about it. I shoved Sam back into a dark closet of my mind and looked around the park.

It sprawled over a half block of level, tree-studded land between two boulevards. Huatulco, a sleepy backwater tourist destination, didn't have much traffic and it was pretty quiet. Most of the park's denizens were off working or doing whatever they did in the afternoon. Our host's wife had taken their older son to his school for some sort of event. Jerry had charge of the newborn baby—a pickled-looking, week-old girl sleeping in a portable cradle on the table. I remember feeling uncomfortable that this father smoked bowl after of bowl of potent dope when responsible for the tiny life.

Relaxing in the dappled sun, drinking beer, eating mangoes and chatting, I listened to the birds in the trees and watched a couple of hens peck around other tables. Jerry's homestead consisted of an old travel trailer built to house a couple, not a family. I never saw the inside. It was parked near one of the streets and I had a clear view of the comings and goings of the Huatulcans. Over the two hours we visited, I noticed few people on the sidewalk, but one group caught my attention. A mother hurried several children past the park, around the next corner and out of sight. It wouldn't have been noteworthy, perhaps they were late for an appointment, but on their heels came an aroma lacing the salty air, which I found both familiar and alarming. I sniffed.

"Do you smell that?" I turned back to the table and asked the men.

"*Mota*." Fernando gestured an offering with the pipe.

"No, thanks. I mean that chemical smell. What is it?" I looked over my shoulder toward the street again. Now I saw a dense fog-like cloud enveloping the street, billowing toward us. The chemical smell got stronger and my tongue salivated with the greasy aftertaste.

SAINTS AND SKELETONS

What was it? Some sick Halloween joke?

"Malathion!"

Jerry looked at me blankly for a beat, "They spray a fifth of the area every day." At the drone of a plane approaching, we looked up.

"Get in your bus. Close the windows and cover your faces!" shouted our host as he grabbed the baby and bolted to the door of his trailer. "Don't come out for at least forty-five minutes!" That was the last we heard before the door slammed.

The bug bomb moved closer. Fernando, *muy prendido,* appeared confused. He hadn't understood the man's direction delivered in English and didn't understand that we were being fumigated. I grabbed Parsley by the scruff of her neck and pushed her into the bus then pulled Fernando in after me, explaining in my broken Spanish, "*Veneno*, poison!" I grabbed some towels, dampening them with bottled water to wrap our heads. I held Parsley down with a towel over her nose for the requisite time.

The closed bus grew hot and stagnant. We sweated. I feared that Parsley would die. She panted heavily and slobbered all over the towel. Her eyes took on a dull cast. Periodically I peeked past the curtain to see what it looked like outside. About an hour and a half later the air finally cleared and the day returned to its warm placidity. We clambered out of the bus.

The poison left a slick over everything it touched. Dead insects littered the table and ground. I saw a dead bird and I wanted to leave. Fernando wanted another toke, and knocked on Jerry's door, but the American refused to answer. Were they okay?

I yelled, "Thanks for the beers—we're outta here."

What kind of town poisoned its air and citizens? A town that hosted Club Med, that's what kind of town. I'd used Malathion to kill mealy bugs on my houseplants back in the '80s, but soon realized that it was dangerous stuff when citizens of many California agricultural counties protested the aerial spraying to eradicate a Med Fly infestation. A carcinogen, it's also known to cause ADHD in kids. Besides, it stinks.

We got back into our bus and pulled out of the trailer park. The sun arced toward the ocean as shadows lengthened. It was too late to go anywhere and almost time for dinner.

"It's safe to eat here, isn't it?" I said, my mouth full of tender pork cooked in tomatillo sauce. We sat in a little dive a few blocks from the trailer park. I worried that we ate pesticide-tainted food, although the table had obviously been scrubbed and the dishware gleamed spotless.

Fernando looked up and caught the *dueña*'s eye. "It's safe to eat here. She didn't open until after the spray cleared. This is a *comida económica* and doesn't open until late afternoon."

"What?" I slurped a gulp of my tamarind water.

"This kind of restaurant opens late and only serves one choice each day—home-style cooking. Let's go to Veracruz."

"Veracruz? Now? Why don't we go back to the beach? It should be pesticide free."

He knit his brow and thought for a moment, "It's

only a day's drive. On the Gulf—"

"The other side of the country? I have to go back to Oaxaca and give Sam his clothes." And apologize.

The proprietress, a thin, smooth-skinned woman with straight black hair and a green plaid pinafore, brought a new stack of steaming tortillas to the long, typically oilcloth-covered table where we ate. Fernando had selected the restaurant through a mysterious process of elimination as we circled through the center of Huatulco. From the street, I couldn't tell the difference between them. He showed no interest in the places with posted menus. This hole-in-the-wall only had a large stovetop with five blackened *cazuelas*—giant clay pots—steaming over the burners, A top loading refrigerator with chipped Coca Cola logos and an opener screwed to the side, the one long table, and, according to Fer, Vincente Fernandez blaring from a cassette deck. Our dinner for two cost 32,000 pesos—about three dollars.

"Forget him. He left. You'll like it there. We'll stay with my friend Francisco in San Isidro. He has a sugarcane plantation on a river outside Veracruz."

I ripped a small triangle of tortilla. "I can't forget Sam. We were together for ten years." I felt my face coloring as my gut clenched. I'd acted shamefully—I knew it. "Anyway, we need to find somewhere to sleep tonight."

Fernando's face drooped into a pout. Something was up—besides Malathion. Jealous?

The *dueña* stood over Fernando's shoulder stirring one of the bubbling pots. I could only think of Macbeth's witches, 'Double, double, toil and trouble.

Fire burn, and *cazuela* bubble,' and wonder what she had cooking.

"Let's go back to the beach. Tomorrow stop in Oaxaca, do laundry, give Sam his clothes, stock up on food, and go from there."

"To Veracruz," he stated, squinting his eyes into slits. His stern look.

I laid my hand over his. "I'm not going back with him, Fernando." I mustered the sweetest look I could. "But I must try to smooth things over," I added.

Did Fernando think I'd dump him off in Oaxaca? No way. He was the hottest guy I'd ever met, and I wasn't about to let him go. But my guilt over the graceless way I'd dumped Sam festered, and I knew I'd never fully enjoy my affair with Fernando without making some amends. Thinking about facing Sam turned my stomach into knots. Hadn't I made myself clear we were not getting back together? I pushed my plate away. I'd been bad—really, really bad. I couldn't fix this. On another level, I didn't want to, did I?

The answer was no.

Fernando beamed his glowing smile onto me. "You're right. That's why I like you, Anita, you've got integrity."

Yeah. That was a laugh.

I pushed some pesos across the table to him. He settled up our bill, and we rejoined Parsley in the bus.

"Let's leave now—head back to Oaxaca," Fernando cooed. "Come on, Aneeta."

"It's getting dark."

SAINTS AND SKELETONS

"*No te preocupes.*"

"Don't you tell me not to worry about it!"

"I will tell you about San Isidro while we drive."

As he motored east toward the mountains, he began the story of meeting Francisco at University. We rose higher and higher into the range. The evening darkened into night. Finally, we pulled onto a wide, sandy shoulder at the top of a ridge. The cold air stung our bare arms and legs as we walked Parsley. We bundled up into sweats. Parsley grinned. This was a climate she could relate to. Using my sleeping bag and towels as blankets, we hunkered down in our bed to sleep under the brilliant, icy stars.

Chapter 8

Día de los Muertos

November 1, 1991

I dreaded returning to Oaxaca City. Sam had said he was going to attend another session at the Instituto and, his laundry aside, he'd only come to Mexico to help me in the first place. I edged open the curtain to watch the black silhouette of mountains jagging below pinpricks of stars lightening to corona-lit shadows, black to grey to deep green. Dawn on November first covered me anvil-like. Cold and heavy. I snuggled closer to Fernando, who shifted. Parsley crawled from under the bed, stretched and stuck her nose above the mattress, chuffing and wagging. I reached across Fernando and patted her head. She wanted to go out.

Since we'd slept in our sweats and socks, I gingerly crept over Fernando groping around the floor for my tennis shoes. There wasn't much I could do about the rumble and grind of the door opening. I slid it open enough for Parsley to slip through and for me to dangle my legs out while I tied my shoes. It was freezing! I vaguely recall pulling a shawl around my shoulders to stroll along the empty two-lane highway with my dog. Rocks, leaves, and twigs along the edge of the turnout sparkled under rays of early sun illuminating the frost. Wisps of fog lifted from the trees as the air warmed. The westerly peaks ranged downward toward the vast Pacific, a thin haze on the edge of the horizon. We meandered away from the bus and squatted behind a rock. Relieved, Parsley sniffed her new territory while I meditated on the awakening of the day.

Soon the sun lifted off a peak to the east and bathed our campsite in the watery glow of early morning. I fed Parsley then set up the cooking table and stove to get the coffee going. Fernando emerged from the tangle of towels, sleeping bag and comforter, sleepy-eyed and gorgeous to accept a mug of steaming coffee.

"Good morning. Sleep okay?" I asked.

"Like a baby. It's the cool air."

"There was ice on the ground when I got up."

He grinned.

"Breakfast?" I asked. "We have eggs and *longanisa*."

He nodded and went off to "look at the view" carrying his mug. Neither of us was garrulous first thing in the morning, which suited me just fine. Sam had always wanted to talk. I preferred silence until I finished my coffee. I couldn't help make comparisons and it got me thinking about Sam again. I shuddered. I didn't want to see him. I could throw his dirty clothes over the cliff and never go back to Oaxaca—except, I still had some possessions at the Maldonado's house. It would be beyond shitty of me to completely blow Sam off. Fernando thought I had integrity. Maybe I ought to act like it.

I'd do Sam's laundry, deliver it back while he was in classes at the Instituto, and leave a note. An apology. Fernando could fool around in *el centro* while I was visiting the Maldonados.

Fernando had argued I should never see Sam again. I looked up *jealous* in my dictionary: *celoso* or *envidioso*. He had used the word *invidioso* the day before, but I hadn't known what it meant. He denied it. Liar. With my limited language skills, I had to read him through intuition and body language, but Fer was an open book in that conversation.

I said, *"No necesitas sentir invidioso. Sam y yo, estamos terminados."* I wrapped my arms around him and sank into that blissful state of excitement and contentment I felt near him. No—Fernando had nothing to worry about.

We worked out a plan over another pot of coffee. In all the time we dallied, not one vehicle passed by on the mountain road. I found something magical about being the only humans on the top of the world, like we were the first explorers. Together we discovered the secrets of the Sierra Madre Occidental. At least, until that first logging truck chugged by, roaring, farting and squealing as the *camionero* downshifted and tipped into the steep grade toward the sea. We packed up and moseyed on, neither of us in a hurry to confront Oaxaca, or Sam.

A couple of hours later, we descended that same road Sam and I had ascended only five days before. It seemed like a lifetime had passed since the orange camper pulled into the trailer park in Puerto Escondido.

Fernando and I blasted all the tapes I carried and sang along to Bob Marley, Jimmy Cliff, and the Beatles as we rocked back and forth through the mountain curves, only turning down the music when we finally landed in Miahuatlán. Something was going on. Families laden with bundles of marigolds, I identified from the scent washing through our open windows, marched along the highway and streamed into the graveyard. I craned to look past Fernando to see activity around the headstones and monuments.

"What's up—*¿que pasa?*" I asked.

"What day is it?"

"Friday, I think. Why? All those people are in the *panteón.*" I pointed down the slope.

"*Creo que es el día de los muertos. ¿No es el primero de noviembre?*"

I checked my datebook. Yep, November First, the Day of the Dead. "Let's go!"

Fernando grinned and slowed down, nodding to the folks with flowers and cleaning supplies, I realized. Some also carried baskets of food. I wondered what was happening. I heard music in the distance and twisted my hips in a little seated-salsa groove. Fernando laughed and launched into an explanation of day of the dead customs. I was right; the flowers were marigolds, *flor de muertos or cempasuchil* in *Nahuatle*. He said the old customs were kept more in rural areas and small towns than in the cities, but even Mexico City had celebrations. The main activity was to go to the graveyard and clean and decorate it with fresh flowers, foods the deceased enjoyed, and, of course, his or her favorite libation, particularly tequila. Later, in early evening, he said, the families would come back and picnic on the graves.

"Tenemos tiempo," he said, *"Vamonos buscar un lugar descansar. Regresamos mas tarde."* Let's look for somewhere to rest and come back later. We have time.

"Tiempo para qué? ¡Párrate! Stop!" I commanded.

He swung the bus onto the shoulder of the road and stopped. *"Reina, no quiero molestar las familias ahora."* He didn't want to bother the families.

And later would be better? I was already piling out of the bus. We locked up, put Parsley on a leash, and joined the throng parading into the *panteón*. People greeted us politely but we both felt the suspicious glances along with the fear of the dog. I kept Parsley close. We weren't one of them. Fernando moved among the graves working his magic, chatting everyone up, and lending a hand to whoever needed it. I read the headstones and murmured platitudes: *Que bonitos niños. Lo siento. Que amable. Sí, gracias,* shaking hands and smiling a lot. Pretty soon a stout matron suggested we come back later and picnic with the family. Perfect! We said our *"hasta tardes"* and wandered around shooting silly photos until Parsley was too bored and we returned to the vehicle.

We dove on down the highway until we came to a pullout into a huge, weedy field and drove in. We planned on napping until late afternoon, but in time the farmer showed up wanting to know what we were doing on his land. Fernando explained how our new friends had invited us to come to the celebration in the cemetery and we were relaxing until it was time. I imagine some pesos passed hands. I wasn't as generous as Fernando and left those things to him. Whatever happened, the next thing I knew, we were having lunch with the farmer and his wife. I remember a delightful time with a sweet grandmother who asked about me and my travels and patiently listened to me prattle in my sketchy Spanish. The joke was, after everything I said, she turned to Fernando to translate—Spanish into Spanish.

We enjoyed a meal of some sort of meaty stew with hunks of *chayote* and potatoes, *arroz*, and tortillas. The *señora* sent us off to the cemetery with fresh *panes*, breads, to share. These moments turned me from an observer into a participant in the lives of the people I had come to Mexico to know. Even if my Spanish was simple and ungrammatical, I could participate and connect. For a woman with a distinct lack of language learning ability, as demonstrated through six years of failing French, I'm still delighted and proud I've come to be semi-fluent in what I think of as my second language.

As the sun sank behind the western mountains, Fer and I made our way back to the cemetery. Parsley stayed in the camper to protect it. We found our family lounging on a rug spread across the burial plot, and joined in. Bowls of *frijoles*, stacks of *tortillas*, fruit, *pan dulces* and even a slice of *tres leches* cake had been arrayed in front of the family monument. The rest of the cake took pride of place in the center of the group with clay dish after clay plate brimming with delicacies. The adults drank beer and tequila and the many kids darted in and out with their *refrescos,* soft drinks. Everyone told stories and jokes about Tío Juanito, Abuelo, and *las abuelas.* Since we sat with an ancient couple called *abuelo y abuela,* I surmised the dead grandparents were the great-great grandparents. Everyone teared-up when they talked about the babies. The *señora* pointed out three tiny markers belonging to three children she'd lost.

While the stories got funnier and more outrageous, Fernando retold some of them later in my simple language, the drinking and eating escalated as night descended. Lights came on: lanterns, candles, flashlights and torches. All around us, families gathered, ate, drank, laughed and cried. People called from one group to another to relate a story. Some got up to walk, or stagger as the case was, with many, to stop in with friends for a drink or a joke. The atmosphere felt electric and joyous. The deceased truly rose, thickening the air.

A band we'd watched set up began to play. The entire celebration joined in singing old familiar songs. Some danced. More toasted. As the toasting increased, the families with children packed up. I watched mothers and grandmothers dragging off their kids and drunk husbands. Meanwhile the place filled up with a new crowd, the young people, mostly men. The evening wore thin. The vibe changed. I felt the hostile stares—the shift from friendly acceptance to suspicion and resentment. Fernando said it was time to go. I said a little prayer for my grandparents, long gone, and a special prayer for my dad, still alive but suffering from diabetes and related kidney problems.

Once back in the bus, we had to decide what to do. Miahuatlán didn't have a hotel, and pulling into a field on a night roaming with drunk revelers was a scary proposition. We dove down into the valley toward the city of Oaxaca, a couple hours east. The night thickened black and redolent with pungent marigolds. We traveled in our bubble of headlights, unable to see any of the landscape beyond their reach. The moon wouldn't rise for several hours. Fernando drove slowly, worried he'd run over a drunk or hit a cow strayed from her field. Exhausted, we kept our eyes out for a motel and miraculously (everything was miraculous in those days) what I've dubbed "Hotel 6" shined a light at the gate; it had rooms available for a modest price. The clerk welcomed Parsley as well. Heaven! We lugged our overnight needs in from the bus and flopped into bed, the cicadas serenading us to sleep.

I awoke early the next morning to take Parsley out. I hadn't seen much the night before and stepped into an open area of trimmed grass crisscrossed with tiled walkways bordered in red geraniums. Surrounding the garden ran a crumbling roofless colonnade, stained over time from rust, lichen, and the elements. Beyond the colonnade, the tiled hacienda spread out in a U-shape, whitewashed walls with terracotta red trim, and the expected matching tile roof. Arches let into the interior, one of which we had passed through the night before to register. It held bronze statuary on banquets, which we walked between to enter the building. Our wing of guest rooms angled to the right of the entry and sported a red door set with a four-paned window recessed into the whitewashed wall directly centered between the columns. A classic hacienda—in near ruin. I discovered the hacienda was three-hundred years old and up for sale. It would have been a bargain at 600,000 pesos, about $60,000.

Parsley chased her tennis ball, rolling luxuriously on the lawn, enjoying the cool, overcast morning, while I imagined what I could do with the place—if only I had more than the twelve dollars our night's stay cost. Everything was included: pigskin furniture, flowerpots, beds and bedding, Spanish antiques, the statuary, maids and gardener. I might now be a retired *hacendera* writing about my life in California before emigrating, that is, if I managed to avoid being stung to death by the resident hive of African bees. The bees chased Parsley and me into our room, waking Fernando.

Once he was up and ready, we took off for the dreaded encounter with Sam in the city of Oaxaca, but not until he'd talked for ages with the owner. "The bees are part of the sale. I think it's why he wants to sell," he told me in the bus once we were underway. The two-lane highway remained empty for much of the drive. I noted many homes in the area had thick paths of marigolds leading to their doors.

"Fer," I shouted over Pink Floyd, his favorite, "What's up with the marigolds?"

He looked where I pointed. An orange trail wove

along the path to the entry under tiled eaves of a tidy *casita*. "*Todo el día de almas.*" I looked up *almas,* souls, while he explained the country folk believed the souls of the departed needed the marigolds to lead them back to their loved ones on November second.

"*No entiendo*—I don't understand. Wasn't that yesterday?" I asked.

"No *moñeca*. November first is *día de los inocentes,* Day of the Innocents, when the gates of Heaven are opened and all the children are allowed twenty-four hours to visit their families."

"So why is Day of the Dead on November first?"

"Tradition."

I thought about the ether filled with babies and children following paths of marigolds to their families' waiting arms until the outskirts of Oaxaca loomed ahead. I felt my blood pressure rising and dread sinking into my gut.

"We better find a laundromat first," I said.

The day remained overcast, spreading humid gloom over the city. We located a *lavandaría* near my old *Instituto,* where I deposited my, Sam's, and Fernando's dirty clothes with the proprietress to wash, dry, and fold by six p.m.

It was mid-afternoon. Sam would be in his classes, and the Maldonados would be at work. Time was right to check out the city—Fernando hadn't been to Oaxaca before—eat lunch and find a motel. We started in *el centro*. I was learning Fernando's preferences. He preferred market stalls and hole-in-the-wall restaurants to the more elevated "eaterias", especially the tourist places around the central plaza. Fine by me. I didn't want to run into any of the students or instructors from my language school who might have heard about my treatment of Sam. Not that he'd gossip, but I felt more comfortable in the bustling market. As if I could feel comfortable anywhere, with my pending meeting looming as oppressive as the cloud cover.

Fernando and I silently strolled hand-in-hand down the aisles of the huge market. I could tell he felt both empathetic and guilty, because he remained quiet, other than to chide vendors trying to overcharge us while I bought groceries to stock the *combi,* as the camper was now called. I quickly learned an oft repeated phase, *"¡Yo soy cien por ciento mexicano!"* I'm one-hundred-percent Mexican.

Standing over the counter by the brimming blue plastic bowls of red salsas with our plates crammed full of tiny tacos, I asked, "Why did you say you're Mexican?"

In his slow and simple Spanish, he explained, "The vendors think we're gringos and raise the prices over the prices for Mexicans. I'm not letting those old *señoras* get away with it. Everywhere we go, people think I'm a gringo and rich—*rico.* It's tradition to cheat the rich."

I laughed. I would never have realized I was being cheated, the prices were so low. I usually shopped where prices were marked, anyway. *"Manzanas $4.35/kilos"* or *"jitomates $3.17/kilo."* The prices, pesos, were pennies on the dollar—apples at approximately thirteen cents a pound. A kilo is 2.2

pounds and a dollar equaled about twelve (thousand) pesos before the 1993 adjustment when the government lopped off the zeros and reissued the money. The vendors couldn't have been making much, regardless.

After lunch and shopping, we hustled back to the combi to take Parsley for a walk. I'd saved a couple of tacos for her and she scarfed them down in a blink. Under Fernando's tutelage, my dog was becoming a *taquera,* as was I. During our time in Mexico, Parsley came to enjoy many new foods. Dog food was expensive and not always available. Beans, rice, and tacos were. She didn't complain, she loved the new smells and tastes surrounding her and deserved treats for guarding the combi so well. With Parsley in the vehicle, it was safe. But that posed an immediate problem for our overnight stay. I'd already been robbed of most of my clothes in this city. I needed a secure, locked-gate place to park the camper, and us.

We'd meandered back toward the laundry and the Maldonado's home, stopping at an *heladería,* ice cream shop, for a snack. I hadn't seen a motel that looked promising. We'd inquired at several establishment closer to the tourist center, but either the cost was prohibitive (I wouldn't pay more than about $15) or they wouldn't allow dogs, or both. Further out of the center, the places looked too run down; many didn't have secure parking. While we slurped our coconut and *mamey* ice creams, we agreed once the ordeal with Sam was over and I'd collected the rest of my stuff from the Maldonado's, we should see some of the surrounding country. Oaxaca state has a plethora of ancient sites, *artesanía,* and specialties, including mezcal. We would get to bed early and leave with the rising sun.

We returned to the combi to explore the road out of town. Sure enough, we found a little motel for about thirteen dollars per night with hot water *en suite*, a cushy big bed, and no restriction about dogs. The gates would be closed and locked at ten p.m. We got our key, Fernando went in to the heavily red-decorated room for a nap and Parsley and I took off to collect the laundry and see Sam.

Things are always easier than anticipated. Worrying only fans the flames of fear. The Maldonados were happy to see me. The *señora* and I had talked about my relationship with Sam and knew we'd broken up a year before. She sympathized with my plight after the robbery my first night in town and understood Sam's motivations for coming to Oaxaca. While the kids played with Parsley and Mrs. Maldonaldo cooked supper, we chatted about the difficulties of relationships. She and her husband had seen their share of trouble before they finally got married.

I collected my belongings, mostly mementos, and my books from the *Instituto,* exchanging the wrapped package of Sam's laundry for my box of souvenirs in the combi before Sam and the *señor* arrived home from the institute.

Sam was happy to see me, not to mention his clean clothes. We closed his bedroom—formerly my bedroom —door behind us to talk privately. Our conversation is blurred by my anxiety and the many years that have passed since the event. I remember we didn't fight. We cried a little, knowing this was the end, but I was able to leave without turning Sam into an enemy. What I remember is feeling drained and untethered. He'd been a part of my life for ten years. I'd leaned on him for a decade, and I'd now closed the door on the security that brought. We may not have always gotten along or approved of one another, but we'd developed a deep connection over the years and knew we could count on one another.

No longer.

Chapter 9

Boil the Water or Drink Mescal

November 3-4, 1991

Mescal found me on November 3rd. We motored out of Oaxaca City after church (Fernando was a "practicing" Catholic) with the plan of visiting the ruins at Mitla and staying overnight in a hotel. Fernando loved to talk to anyone and everyone. He connected with some locals and learned about a place called Hierve el Agua, Boiling Water, a natural rock formation high in the dry mountains. It sounded pretty cool, so off we went after breakfast to a small town called San Lorenzo Albarradas. The steep road wound up the mountain to the highest point in the Sierra Madre de Oaxaca at 5500 feet. The overloaded, underpowered bus slowly climbed behind a yellow public transportation bus, more overloaded and underpowered than Uyolkan. Even the roof was jammed with passengers clinging on. We made a spectacle pulling into the town and stopping outside a thatched adobe *casita.* Between the passengers disembarking and townsfolk gathering to view the newcomers, we stopped too.

"What's going on there?" I asked, pointing to the structure.

"It's a *tienda,* store," Fernando relied.

"How do you know?"

"I can see the Coca Cola cooler."

"I'm thirsty. Let's get a drink," I said.

We hopped out; I opened the door for Parsley, attracting attention. Neighborhood Watch, I thought. Fernando locked up. People checked us out as we walked over and entered the store, passing a skinny indigenous-looking woman drinking out of a Coke bottle. She followed us in. We paid for our Cokes, which we had to drink in the store so the owner wouldn't lose the bottle deposit money. I looked around and smiled at the several people loitering inside. It was obvious these were friends socializing on Sunday afternoon. One ancient white-haired man in particular smiled at me with a gap-toothed grin. The old woman tipped her bottle and said something I took as an invitation.

I asked Fernando, "What is it?"

"*Mescal.* You don't want that."

I'd tried *mescal*, a less refined alcoholic beverage made from the agave plant tequila was distilled from, at my language school. "Yes, I do," I replied.

Soon we were a jolly group swapping stories and sipping from the Coke bottle. I don't have an entry in my trip accounting for the cost, but if I spent eighty cents, I'd be surprised. I liked the taste and the more sips I took, the more Spanish I understood. The old man told his story about signing up to fight in the Revolution (Nov. 20, 1910-Feb. 5, 1917) early in the war. But, as he told it, he was only eleven when he signed on. He laughed at how he'd lied to get in. Soldiers needed to be fourteen, he claimed, but he was big for his age. The old soldier was tiny, at least two inches shorter than my five four. He described his glory years and how his revolutionary armies defeated the *Porferiato*—President Porferio Diaz's corrupt regime. His understanding of history may have been flawed, but his storytelling amused the increasingly crowded *tienda*.

Word got out around the neighborhood. People turned out to gawp at the *chilango* and the *gringa*. Of particular interest was my bus. People wanted to know how it worked. How we could live in it. By this time the liquor had crept up on me; I was pretty wasted. The *mescal* was running out. The party at the *tienda* was breaking up. I led a tour of women and children through the workings of my bus.

Fernando was mortified. He hustled me into the passenger seat and off we drove, reprimanding me for the next ten minutes."

"Are you *loca*? Those people are poor. They'll try to rob us. We have to find somewhere safe to sleep."

I didn't believe him, but he was driving. What would they steal? He'd talked to some of the men at the store to learn how to get to Hierve el Agua and also the name of a place to eat. We skipped the food then drove into a rock quarry to camp. We had our own food. Besides, the quarry offered us a good hiding place until the early morning when a couple of trucks with work crews arrived. I woke up to thundering of rock hitting metal truck bed as the men heaved rocks in. Or was it the hangover? I swallowed aspirin, covered my ears, and marveled at men actually laboring in this manner. The trucks were filled by hand!

Fernando chatted up a couple of workers, learning where a good mescal still was located. I shot a photo of Fernando shaking hands with one of the men. As I study the image, he looks like a giant next to the compact Oaxacaños. He stood two and a half heads taller.

We pulled up stakes, visited the remarkable geologic formation of Hierve el Agua—a white river of petrified minerals appearing to cascade over cliffs from thermal pools—then found Alicia's kitchen. She invited us to camp in her yard where I spent the day cooking with her. She taught me to husk large ears of *maiz*, remove the kernels, grind them on the *metate* then turn the ground flour into *tortillas,* which we cooked on a giant *comal* over an open wood fire. We made beans, rice, and a stew with turkey meat. This was our meal for the evening.

As it grew dark, five or six men straggled in from their work and sat down to eat. These were Alicia's regulars. For a small weekly sum, she fed them dinner and breakfast. The house and "restaurant" had no electricity or indoor plumbing. The kitchen was a lean-to along the side of the house. Alicia raised turkeys and grew *maiz,* beans, tomatoes, and *chilies.* She dried what she could and collected rainwater into barrels for household use and irrigation. She earned enough to send her kids to school and maintain the basics. I'm sure I paid her ten times the going rate. Especially for the turkey pullet Parsley killed.

Fernando had much to say about the inequities in Mexican economics. He hated the poverty, yet he held *prejuicios,* prejudices, against the *campesinos,* county folk, especially *los indios,* saying they were slow, stubborn, and ignorant. We often debated our beliefs on our long drives. I didn't feel it was the fault of the *indios* they were poor and ignorant. I learned Mexico had a huge divide between the city people and the country people. Education in the country was limited; many couldn't afford the uniforms and books. I blamed the class system, not the class.

On the morning of the 5th we had plenty to debate driving back to Oaxaca with my stash of fresh *mescal,* dripped right out of the still. We filled every bottle and jar we could find. I carried *mescal* on a trip back to California the following June.

Chapter 10

One Long Party with Confession on the Side

November 5-19, 1991

Oaxaca City was a utility stop, nothing more. We did laundry, bought food at the Blanco, a supermarket, and ate in the central market before finding Hotel Fortin. I paid 20,000 pesos for the room, so it must have been a real dive. The thing was, Fernando and I were shiny new and walking on clouds. Everything looked rosy, even crummy hotels.

We passed the days on the same wavelength. Everything was exciting: buying food, exploring, talking, making love. We electrified each other. Our worlds had collided and a week later, it was as if we'd always been together. The days slowed and amplified. We had nothing to do, and all the time and resources to do it with. Fernando and I were on a *luna de miel,* honeymoon. I was sure everything had changed. My life was working out! He was so excited he wanted to take me to Veracruz to meet his brother and best friend. We finished up our shopping and bugged out of Oaxaca east over the mountains to green Veracruz.

There wasn't anywhere to camp in the *combi,* as Fernando called my camper, in Veracruz City. The night of November 7th, we found Hotel San Martín, a place we could take Parsley for just over three dollars a night. The next day, Fernando took me to meet his oldest brother, Victor, Victor's wife Ana, and their little girl Karla. Everyone was polite, but a current of tension ran through our visit. I couldn't follow enough of their Spanish to fully understand what was going on. When I asked Fer about it on the drive to see his college buddy, Francisco, he confessed he'd left school because he'd gotten married and had to get a job. He described his wife as a wannabe socialite, always buying the latest fashions, demanding an expensive apartment and upscale furnishings. She craved the high-life. Fernando went to work as a salesman for a pharmaceutical company and did well, but it wasn't enough. He hated the job and couldn't put up with his wife any longer.

"She wanted more and more and more. I couldn't do it. I couldn't live like that." He left her.

Alarmed, I asked, "Are you still married?"

"No, we're divorced," he said and launched into a discourse on the Church's views on divorce. I gleaned that only the state recognized the divorce. The Church recognized the end of a marriage upon the death of a spouse and through annulment. Fernando was "living in sin" with me. I heard the klaxon sounding, but it was far in the distance. I ignored it.

SAINTS AND SKELETONS

Francisco delighted me. He was a propertied sugarcane farmer with a great sense of humor. After our visit, Francisco led us out along one of his fields and helped us set up camp on the banks of a river. The night was magic, between the gurgle of the water, the symphony of insects, the haloed silver slit of moon overhead, and the melding of our bodies to one. In the morning we knew we had fallen in love.

After a whirlwind of sightseeing and dining we spent another night in Veracruz. We both liked to eat, especially Mexican food.

Early, we retreated back over the mountain to Oaxaca, stopping in Miahuatlán again for mass on the 10th. I might have looked at this as a warning, but I was too head-over-heels to think much about it. We were going back to Puerto Escondido, the sacred ground of our meeting, and booked into Bungalows Acuario for three nights. The bungalows, set amid tall palms, perched on stilts and sported thatched roofs. I was reminded of Hawaii, but instead of ukuleles, reggae blasted out of the rooms. A surfer hotel! We loved it, and we did everything in Puerto Escondido we hadn't been able to do before, but I was itching to get back to Zihuatanejo, Zihua, where we could camp at retired ex-pat Frank's place on the beach for free and visit all my friends from my month at Pepe's Trailer Park in July.

We left on Thursday the 14th without checking our gas level. We made it to a Pemex Station in a place called Marquelia, just south of Acapulco and ran out of gas. Waking up in a gas station should have been strange or uncomfortable, but Fernando's scruffy face and bedroom eyes made up for the scenery. We filled up and stopped for some beach time and food in Acapulco before pushing on another five hours to arrive in Zihua in time to dine at Any's with Frank.

Zihuatanejo again proved to be a continuous round of parties, beer on the beach, dinners and breakfasts out with friends. Of course I wanted to eat at Rossy's and visit with bar owner Zocer and waiter Anibal, two acquaintances from my August visit. Sunday rolled around. Fernando felt the need to confess his sins. I was noticing a pattern: he had sex out of wedlock and smoked pot all week then dropped in to church to wipe the slate clean. Was that how it was supposed to work? His sins didn't strike me as serious. It wasn't like anyone committed adultery.

Frank and Fernando hit it off and we made a date to go to Guadalajara together for Christmas at Jean and Teddy Solomon's house, friends from home.

I can't remember what pried us off the beach, but we headed back to Mexico City late on the 19th, sleeping along the side of the road, arriving on the 20th after a stop for lunch in Cuernavaca. Now it was my turn to introduce Fernando to family. I was sure he'd charm my cousin, Marty, her family and my host, Pattie, and her crowd. How far off the mark could I get?

Chapter 11

La Capital

November 20-December 21, 1991

Mexico City had been my home for three months, but I attacked it *con mucho gusto* with my *guia*, Fernando. We spent days roaming the different *colonias*, eating, checking out stores, markets, museums. It was a private insider's tour. I remember catching my reflection in store windows and not recognizing myself. I looked healthy, relaxed, and radiating happiness.

When we weren't doing something else, we went to the movies. On the 21st we saw Mel Gibson's *Hamlet*. The Mexican movie houses played recent American films subtitled with the sound turned down. I improved my Spanish reading the subtitles, because the patrons talked and laughed and ate and moved around, creating a disturbance making it impossible to hear. I added to the racket every time the translation did not correspond to the dialog. "Hey!" I'd yell. "That's not what he said!" Fernando laughed and called me his little *chilanga*. I decided it was a compliment, although *chilango* or *chilanga* is a derogatory name for people from Mexico City. Movies cost about a dollar each and became a favorite inexpensive activity of ours. We saw *Regarding Henry* on December 6th at the Teatro Chino, an ornate Chinese-styled theater near Garibaldi Plaza, alone worth the visit, and many more all over the city.

Our favorite activity was going out for tacos: down the mountain to the Tacubaya Metro station for *suadero*, east to La Villa for *barbacoa*, north to Gil's for *alambre*. We traveled far for good tacos.

In late November, Patti bought her place on Privada de Roseleda, a large modern split-level house at the top of a private road with a security guard and gate. Halfway up the mountain to the west, it looked right into the forest of the 3rd section of Chapultepec Park. Amazing in the middle of a city of twenty-million people. I fell in love with it. Fernando and I took charge and organized Pattie's impending move in between our explorations of the city and trips to Tepoztlán.

I cooked, spending more time in the kitchen with Pattis's cook, Goya. She was a terrific, good-humored woman with great wisdom. I was honored she put up with me. Many of Fernando's and my sightseeing excursions included grocery shopping where I learned the supermarkets and how to shop in them. Mexican cuts of meat differed from American, and other differences made shopping interesting.

SAINTS AND SKELETONS

After the move to Privada de Roseleda, I resided in a comfortable carpeted room off the entry patio. It was large with lots of light and my own TV with cable. Fer and I spent a lot of time there watching movies. My accounting shows an increase in purchases of condoms in *La Capital*. We spent many nights together, but eventually Fer had to go home, if only for clean clothes. On days he left, I'd often discover a little love note tucked somewhere.

> *Para Ana de Fernando*
>
> *Amo tu sonrisa*
> *que me da vida*
> *al recordarte*
>
> *I love your smile/ that gives me life/ when I remember you*

We both liked music and listened to endless tapes of popular songs purchased from the street vendors, which Fer said were mostly bootlegged. I loved the pop rock of Lucero, Thalia, Cristian, Juan Luis Guerra whose romantic song, *Burbujas de Amor,* I'd learned in my Oaxaca language school. Fernando got a kick out of the translated meaning and blew a lot of bubbles on my body after that. *"Quiero ser un pez para tocar mi nariz en tu pecera*: I wish I were a fish to stick my nose in your fish tank."

Fernando preferred salsa tropical. Garibaldi was one of our favorites. I learned to *mover el cinteron.* Fernando was determined to train the rock 'n roll out of me, replacing it with Latin moves. That meant swinging my hips and moving my waist rather than hopping around flailing my arms. And salsa dancing? M*uy caliente*. Or, as Grupo Garibaldi sings, "*Hot. Hot. Hot.*"

November 30th was that. We went to a salsa club called Riviera. The orchestra filled the large club with lively brass, vocals, guitar, piano and rhythm. Some of the dancers looked professional. Both of us felt intimidated, but a couple dancing near us showed us some dance steps and *movimos nuestras colas*—we moved our tails. We ate pancakes at an all-night place. At home we shook our tails to our own thumping rhythms.

In the morning, we dragged ourselves out of bed to repent our sins at misa in the ancient Parroquia San Juan Bautista in Coyoacan. It was my first visit, and we spent the afternoon promenading arm-in-arm with the throngs of ciudadanos through the plaza and gardens. I met a living statue of the Archangel Michael. He was all painted in silver and could remain motionless for ages. Worth the thousand-peso note I gave him. It was in Coyoacan I acquired a taste for coconut ice cream.

The next weekend I was treated to a Christmas *Posada* at cousin Marty's. The neighborhood children reenacted the birth of Jesus with a procession, while everyone sang the *posada* song. I, of course, didn't know the words, but the kids in costume were darling and the traditional *ponche* made me grateful Fer didn't drink. My cousin liked lots of rum in her punch. Again he dragged me out of bed in the morning, this time for *misa* in Los Lomas. The man had a lot to confess.

I loved living in *La Capital*. There was plenty to do and learn. I had re-enrolled at my Zona Rosa language school for a two-week session. How did I manage to take a course with everything else going on? It makes sense Fer and I did so much in Zona Rosa, where the school was located on Hamburgo. School let out on December 11th. On the thirteenth I was back in Tepoztlán. I don't think Fernando went on that trip. Pattie and I spent much time talking about the possibilities of opening up Cuernavaca, Tepoztlán, and Cocoyoc for ex-pat relocation when the time was right. She may have been planting ideas in my brain. She knew how much I loved Mexico.

The rest of the next week, Fernando and I spent preparing for our Christmas jaunt to Zihua to collect Frank, and on to Christmas dinner with my friends. I spent a ton of money at my favorite upscale supermarket, Superama, and another wad at Gigante, the equivalent of Safeway, to restock the larder. My tally says I spent 150,657 pesos on Christmas gifts, then went on to buy a shirt and a new bathing suit for Fernando. I wrapped the shirt.

We planned a fabulous holiday—our first Christmas together. Joy to the World!

Chapter 12

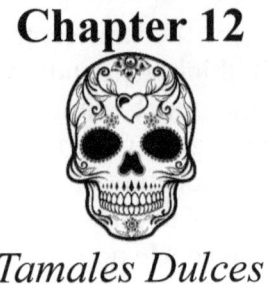

Tamales Dulces

December 21-25, 1991

We left Mexico City after dark. It took hours putt-putting along on the *carretera libre* to reach Taxco perched on the top of a small mountain. The main drag circled the crown of the peak, lined with silver shops. We looped around, looking for parking. A couple of passes later, we inched into a tight space between a taco vendor and a sightseeing bus. For dinner we walked until we found a *taquería* Fer liked the look of. Like most Mexican towns, the place was hopping after nine p.m.

Fernando had visited the famous silver town before and hurried me along. He didn't allow me shopping time in Taxco, the source of the country's gorgeous silver jewelry. I've always regretted that I never made it back to shop—the bargains on silver, even gold, amazed me.

"*¡Apúrate! ¡Apúrate! Estamos tardes,*" he nagged.

SAINTS AND SKELETONS

By then, I could understand much of what he said, and I bristled. Late for what? I wanted to shop and he wanted me to hurry up. The town glittered in the glow of naked bulbs reflecting off the silver and semiprecious stones. All the stores and street stalls had their doors thrown open. For a shopaholic, I'd reached heaven. I bought a silver and bronze choker chain for my mother and a pair of heavy silver earrings, rarely worn, but still in my jewelry case.

Anyway, if Fernando had been in such a hurry, why had we driven the slow, congested "free road"—stacked up in pods of noisy, canvas-covered trucks hauling chickens and vegetables that lumbered along spewing diesel exhaust—instead of taking the not quite completed *Ruta del Sol*, the *cuota,* toll road? So what that it cost about $35 dollars to drive from Mexico City to Acapulco—it only took three and a half hours. And I was paying—as always. We'd been on the road for at least four hours with a couple more to go. I turned cranky.

It was after midnight and we weren't going any farther.

"There's no place like home. There's no place like home," I chanted while Fernando kicked the tires of my VW camper with red hi-top sneakers, shoes found at the back of his closet.

My VW's clutch wouldn't clutch anymore. The parts stores and repair shops had closed for the night. Thankfully, we'd jerked to a street-lit curb high above Acapulco Bay. From between the rundown cinderblock homes and businesses lining the street, I glimpsed the lights of the glitzy hotel district in the distance. My dream of a cushy bed and hot shower evaporated into the tropical moonlit sky. Fernando, Parsley, and I locked ourselves into the bus and prayed we'd be safe for the night. What could happen on the street as the full moon eclipsed over a seedy district of Acapulco?

Christmas loomed four days away. My friends from Mill Valley expected us on the 24th at their retirement home in Guadalajara. Jean and Teddy had been like second parents to me; I looked forward to spending Christmas with them. I'd never been away from home for the holidays, and I missed the neighborhood holly trees ripe with red berries, the faint scent of acacia pollen in the air, and the hills, bright green with grass sprouting after the first rains. I missed the damp chill of the tule fog rising out of the ground in the wee hours, and the intense gold of the sun slanting from the horizon in the late afternoon. I missed the bare trees and the Christmas music. The veil of denial lifted for a moment at the curb in Acapulco. Deep down, I admitted I missed my dysfunctional family; I felt utterly homesick.

The Solomons would take care of that. I'd been planning this visit from before I left on my trip to Mexico in July. They'd graciously welcomed Fernando and ex-pat friend, Frank, to their celebration, as well as Parsley who was already great friends with their dog.

We planned to swing through Zihuatanejo, pick up Frank and visit some friends, doubling the length of our trip. Now we squatted on a crummy bit of real estate high above the glamorous Avenida Costera of Acapulco's hotel district, five hours from Zihua, and a couple dozen hours from our party. Fernando assured me we could still make it, but driving in Mexico—heck, doing *anything* in Mexico, could be an adventure. I needed to find a phone. Just what was it about Acapulco? This counted as my third visit and each had come with a story.

The first time I'd passed through Acapulco, on my way south to Mexico City in August, I'd landed at a motel recommended by my favorite Zihuatanejo waiter, Anibal. The place, next door to a throbbing all-night disco, rented by the hour. What on earth had he been thinking? I locked my room tight and slept in my sleeping bag, but the booming bass, the doors slamming, and the groans and screams penetrating the walls made for a lousy sleep. The second time I passed through Acapulco, I had planned to put us up at a nice hotel on the famous bay, but Fer and I ran out of gas and ended up camping out at the pump of a closed PEMEX south of the famous resort.

And now this.

They say God watches over children—and idiots. Fernando and I fit the idiot category. Morning announced itself with pounding on the outside of the bus. Fernando slid the door open and clambered out. Some thugs, dressed as cops, wanted money for parking in their neighborhood! Merry Christmas. Welcome to Acapulco.

Fer popped his head back into the cabin. "Lock the door after me. Don't open it for anyone but me."

"Where are you going? Take Parsley, she needs to go out."

"These guys are going to show me where I can buy parts. I'll get some *pan dulces* and coffee. Give me some money." Hmmm, from extortion to neighborly help. I guessed at what happened to Fernando's cash.

I can't say exactly how Fernando handled the situation, but eventually he and Parsley knocked. He carried a bag of fresh breads and two Cokes.

"No coffee, but the parts store opens at nine. There's a *fonda* down the street with breakfast and a bathroom."

I spent much of the day at the tiny fonda with my book. I also found a pay phone that worked and left three messages for the Solomons. Finally, around three o'clock, Fer had the bus running. We continued on toward Zihuatanejo. By evening, the full moon lit a bright path along the empty two-lane highway.

Back in Zihua, the clutch, probably held together by baling wire and chewing gum, decided to stop engaging second gear. There was *nada* we could do about it until Monday, except drink *cervezas* on the beach and salsa dance all night to a local band at my buddy, Zocer's, open air beach bar. I'd run out of cash—this was before ATMs became ubiquitous—and borrowed 200 pesos from Frank. Reflecting now, I wonder if I ever paid him back?

I applied the money to the new clutch Fernando negotiated at a *taller*, once again recommended by Anibal. While the installation of UYOLKAN's new clutch was speedily completed—we got the car back late on the 24th, setting set off for the long drive to Guadalajara in *la madrugada*, the pre-dawn, somewhere between three and four a.m. Frank decided not to go, but said if we drove straight through, we'd make it in time for Christmas dinner at four. Hadn't I heard that already? I thought at the time he bailed on our adventure because he thought he was going to be *my date*. He was a dear man, but older than my father! I tried again, with no luck, to telephone the Solomons.

Somewhere between Zihuatanejo and Playa Azul, the armpit of the Costa Azul, one of us noticed the bus running hot. Fer pulled over and checked the oil. Low. He added a liter. We drove on, limping into Playa Azul just after dawn. When I'd passed down Ruta 200 from Puerto Vallarta in July, the weather had been lovely, warm, blue skies, lingering sunsets. On Christmas morning, 1991, Playa Azul cowered under flat grey skies with 90% humidity. In my photos, few children play on the beach, fewer in the low surf. People wore shorts, not bathing suits. Not Fernando. He stretched out on a towel, clad in nothing more than his black and turquoise striped bikini trunks, too tired to care that it looked like rain.

"¡*Feliz Navidad*, Fer!" I gushed, and shoved a wrapped package at him.

He sat up and smiled, opening his present, a two-tone light blue and turquoise cowboy style shirt that perfectly matched the painted wooden chairs at the beach restaurant where we ate an unremarkable breakfast of *chilaquiles* and *café de olla*. I knew how good he looked in turquoise, and most of his things, beyond the suits hanging in the closet at his mother's, had been left behind when he returned home from Germany. Suits and ties he stored when he'd quit his pharmaceutical sales job, split up with his wife, and moved to Cancun. The tassel loafers came from the pill-pushing period.

Part of our intense connection originated from the similarities in our lives. We understood each other. We'd both felt trapped in relationships with people we didn't love. And we both had burned out of our jobs. We wanted freedom, adventure, love. Or at least a respite from adult responsibility. And we wanted to escape our families.

According to Fernando, Mexicans frowned on living together so he had married his *novia,* but he'd grown tired of her and filed for divorce. While married, he'd slaved at a job he hated to keep his wife, Claudia, in expensive clothes and a beautiful apartment somewhere in Insurgentes Sur. She demanded more and more of him. He walked out. That was his story, and he stuck to it through the bitter end.

I don't recall if he gave me a Christmas gift. If there was a photo of me opening a gift, it disappeared with all the other pictures of me from this time, and it's hard to tell in the snapshot of Fernando whether he actually liked his shirt.

At this writing, Christmas is three days away, and I'm thinking about the blessings that come with the season.

Christmas 1991 was no different, although I'm not sure I felt completely grateful at the time. In fact, I remember feeling tired and irritable as Fernando slept on the beach at Playa Azul. I was just as tired as he, but one of us had to stay awake and keep an eye on things. We needed gas and oil. Ruta 37, winding across mountainous Michoacán to highway 15 and Guadalajara, might not have an open gas station before Uruapán, over a hundred miles. Fernando should wake up and find a gas station.

I have a nagging sense that I'm forgetting the story, or perhaps re-writing history. For one thing, there's a niggling thought in my mind that the gas station wasn't open. For some unfathomable reason, I believe the owner came only to sell me gas and oil—a true act of kindness that I have not acknowledged. I picture us driving into the typical PEMEX station and me paying a woman. I'm wearing a sleeveless red mock turtleneck tee-shirt and carrying my half dozen liters of oil from the office to the *combi*. Fernando is in the office doorway talking with a dark-skinned man wearing a cream colored straw hat and gesticulating.

"We can make it by dinner—" Fernando slammed the door closed and turned the ignition key— "but the owner said it's going to be hard to find gas."

"You had the Jeep cans filled, right?"

"*Claro que si.*" He eased the *combi* onto the road.

"How long will it take?" I asked, as we made the turn onto the highway.

"Five or six hours. Plenty of time. We can get the

leak fixed in Guadalajara."

"Why is it leaking?"

"They probably didn't change the gasket when they installed the new clutch."

"Idiots," I muttered.

The slow, winding drive through the mountains of Michoacán took all day, in part because we had to stop and add oil practically every hour. The road remained deserted and the area appeared sparsely populated, desolate under the cloud cover extending in from the coast. I didn't find the scenery to be lovely or interesting, and had trouble staying awake. I amused us by translating my favorite songs, from the eighty cassette tapes I'd recorded before leaving for Mexico, into Spanish for Fernando. He liked American rock and pop, but he particularly enjoyed reggae and soca. I never have quite figured out how to translate "lively up your self and don't be no drag" but it was fun to try. Given the choice, Fernando would listen to mariachi bands, *salsa tropical,* and traditional Mexican music. He put up with Mexican pop music on the radio when we had reception because I liked it. He taught me the words to songs I liked. On the Christmas trip, he was teaching me singer Lucero's hits, *Ya No* and *Electricidad,* both repeatedly playing on the radio. As it turned out, Lucero was Fernando's first cousin, but he refused to take me to her Mexico City concert because, "I don't like her music." I later learned from Lucero's mother that Lucero didn't like or trust Fernando. But in the *combi,* we had fun singing her songs.

SAINTS AND SKELETONS

True to the Playa Azul PEMEX owner's prediction, we never saw an open restaurant or gas station. The one restaurant we passed with activity was closed to us. The owners' family held a private Christmas party and we weren't invited. We never found a functioning telephone and, pre-cell phones, couldn't call our friends waiting dinner in another state. My guilt meter went up. We should have left earlier.

Near dusk, the sky cleared and we stopped to view a watery sunset over steep mountains. We'd passed a huge lake that might have offered camping on its shore, but decided to press on in hopes that we could find food in the next city. The ice chest wasn't as well stocked as usual. We'd only planned a two-day run—Mexico City to Zihua to Guadalajara—no cooking, no camping. Only Parsley, who'd been fed on one of the oil stops, was happy.

Finally we descended the serpentine road through a pine forest along a singing river that freshened the air, and drip-drip-dripped into hilly Uruapán, one of the oldest cities in Mexico. Exhausted and starving, we drove up and down the main streets in *El Centro*, typically a tangle of one-way streets, and inquired at every hotel for a room. No vacancy at the inn, and NO DOGS allowed. I started to cry and Fernando swore (I learned to really rip off a string of Mexican swear words on Christmas night 1991.) Finally, we happened upon the central market and found Christmas: El Mercado de Antojitos, the market of little "cravings," or street snacks.

The building, square and open to the street on two sides, housed thirty or more vendors selling *tacos, quesadillas, tostadas*, fruit smoothies, *pan dulces,* fresh made potato chips, red and white *pozole*, *sopes*, *enchiladas,* and more—all at low prices. We'd spent much of our cash on meals and oil, and hadn't seen an ATM, or *RED* in Mexico. In short, we were almost broke. We wandered in, stomachs rumbling and noses twitching, Parsley too.

Christmas decorations glittered overhead. People thronged the stalls, laughing, talking, eating. The vendors sang out their offerings. A *cumbia* version of *Silent Night* blared. We bellied up to a counter for cups of hot Christmas *atole* made from ground corn, cinnamon, lots of sugar and water, Fernando explained. We inhaled tacos at another stall where the vendor gave a couple to Parsley for free. I slurped a white *pozole* while Fernando tried a regional beef dish. We ate our way around the room to the vendor of the very special sweet *tamales Navideños*, Christmas tamales.

"How much?" I counted the coins remaining in my pocket.

"Three pesos each." I only had three left. I looked at Fernando.

"You have it," he said. I handed over the coins.

The little round vendor in her blue gingham pinafore served us her last four tamales with a sweet smile and a warm, "*Feliz, Navidad, guëros.*"

Back in the bus, we cruised up and down, looking for a hotel. Finally someone told us about a motel a ways out of town. They said, if they didn't take dogs, we'd be able to sneak Parsley in since all the rooms were drive-up like a typical American motel.

Great! We'd try it out.

SAINTS AND SKELETONS

The motel we found with both a vacancy and dogs allowed, was dirtier than a stable, but the clerk didn't know how to run a credit card and told me to pay in the morning. He sent us to a room just vacated after a Christmas quickie—paid for the night, I read in the guest register. I re-made the bed with our own sheets, and we luxuriated in the hot shower then slept deeply. It was Christmas and through the kindness of strangers, the spirit of the season found us—low on luck and far from the friends in Guadalajara awaiting our arrival.

Chapter 13

*The Unkindness of Strangers—or—
Instant Karma*

December 26-Eve of New Year's, 1991

Our motel room looked pretty ratty in the light of day: worn carpeting, threadbare bedspread, and chipped grout, but the shower ran hot. By the time we dressed and returned my sheets to the VW, no one knocked to summon us to the office to pay for the room. Because some couple celebrating a Christmas tryst had paid for the room according to the register and we'd smuggled in the dog, I said "¿*Vamos*?" and gave Fernando a questioning look. He laughed, delighted with the idea of skipping out of the motel without paying for our turn at the dirty sheets.

Our room sat at the bottom of a small hill off a barren dirt drive. Gray dust billowed in our wake as we roared up to the entrance of the paved highway. UYOLKAN wasn't much for sneaking around, especially after Fernando had detached something he called the *"escapé"* which saved gas and caused the old bus to backfire sounding much like a jet taking off, pleasing him.

We laughed like naughty kids getting away with something as we backfired from our unpaid stay all the way down into *el centro*. Parking on a quiet street behind a church, we locked up, found a *RED* for cash, the went back to the Mercado de Antojitos for lunch. I was taken by the colonial architecture and the rabbit warren of narrow streets downtown. Uruapán struck me as the prettiest city I'd visited so far. In my photo album, I dubbed it "Lovely Downtown Uruapán," and I shot a few pictures as we made our way back to the combi, stopping at a payphone to try to call the Solomons, again with no luck.

At three o'clock after sightseeing, I unlocked the combi's side door, throwing it open to let Parsley back in. A mini-cyclone had hit the interior. A few photos lay on the seat, dirty clothes hung over the cabinet, the curtain lay on the floor, covered with most of the items I stored on top of the cabinet. I felt a punch to my gut, unable do more than stand on the cobbled curb and stare, dumfounded, grasping the sliding door for support.

"What's wrong?" Fernando came around the bus and leaned in through the door, assessing the situation. "*Ladrones*." Thieves.

I took inventory. The *ladrones* had grabbed my case of 80 cassette tapes, the bag of dirty sheets, both inconvenient but neither a crisis, and a hundred or more photos, with the negatives, from my first three months traveling in Mexico. I fell apart. I fancied myself somewhat of a budding photographer—a romantic notion of the traveler, recording the world for posterity, perhaps a future National Geo photojournalist. In August, I'd dropped my pre-digital Nikon SLR camera into Zihuatanejo Bay, ruining it. In Mexico City, I replaced it with an older, used model for way too much money. Now all the photos from both cameras were "disappeared".

I cried. "Why, Fer? Why would they steal my photos?"

He shrugged. He didn't have an answer. I inspected the bus and its contents while Fernando filled up the oil reserve. The odd thing about the break-in was that the doors had been locked and no windows were broken. I felt violated and hated Mexico. We'd parked in the shadow of a church, for Christ's sake. Was nothing sacred in this country? And the robbers could go to *misa* and get a pass.

"How'd they get in?" I asked, between sobs. Fernando remained silent as he shifted into gear, rolling is away from that terrible, lawless city.

We chugged out of town, up the mountains and east through Michoacán, stopping to top up the oil every ten feet. Arriving in Patzcuaro near five o'clock, we found the trailer park, claimed our space—not much of a problem, as there were few guests. Fer demonstrated how the robbers got in. The old VW busses had a wing window with a turning latch you could use to lock from the inside. But, if you banged on the window from the outside, the latch slowly unlatched; a robber could then reach inside and open the door.

SAINTS AND SKELETONS

The town lies in a broad valley between mountain ranges, and gently slopes down to Lake Patzcuaro. The old town is laid out in a perfect grid of high stucco walls, terracotta tile roofs, and cobblestone streets. As the sun sank down behind the western range, the air nipped crisp and cool at our skin, sending us to dig out our sweaters, which we donned over our jeans and t-shirts before wandering into the *centro* to find some food and bedding.

In the *centro,* I bought two thick blankets and a set of cheesy, flowered *matrimonio*-sized sheets for the pullout bed. In typical Mexican fashion, everything came in bright colors. I bought one blanket in aqua-green, yellow, and charcoal plaid, and the other in peacock blue, black, and fuchsia plaid. Made from a cotton blend with long twists of fringe on the ends, they reversed, the patterns changing from a tight plaid to an open box weave. I don't know what happened to the sheets, but I still use those blankets.

"You're crazy. Why are you buying that cheap modern Mexican shit? We don't need blankets. If you want blankets, buy the good traditional wool ones," Fernando advised.

"I like them. They'll be warm. It's cold here." I didn't carry anything but a cotton thermal blanket in the bus and already the evening air showed its teeth. I draped the blue one over my shoulders.

"Well, I like the traditional blankets better."

"Fine, when we see them, we'll get you one. We need food for dinner."

I wanted a hamburger—my medicine for the blues in Mexico.

We strolled the central plaza, the Zócalo, taking one of the diagonal walkways running from one corner of the plaza to the opposite end. The now-familiar Colonial-style plaza with its dotting of shade trees, triangular plots of grass, iron benches and statuary, reminded me of the parks in Coyoacan and Oaxaca.

Patzcuaro's central plaza was anchored with a large round stone fountain and pond in the center. We passed by its murky, dark water, following the scent of tacos. Surrounding the plaza, buildings formed a rectangle of white fronts topped in red tile, with an arched colonnade covering wide tiled sidewalks. Some vendors still crowded the edge of the plaza and the colonnade, selling many carved items, from wooden spoons to intricate wall hangings and brightly painted masks. I saw several blanket vendors, but no traditional wool blankets, to my relief. I wasn't really in the mood to shop.

I wasn't really in the mood for much of anything. I barely took any photos of the lovely town. A dark cloud hung over my head and I felt violated, lost. A deep longing for my family and the cozy houseboat I'd vacated in Sausalito settled into my bones. Why did I think I could spend Christmas here? Mexico didn't have eggnog. A call with the Solomons might have mitigated my blues, but I never reached Guadalajara.

Fernando carried our purchases, my handbag, his "man bag", and kept his arm around my waist, tethering me to the moment, as we promenaded past the vendors. He had heard that the area was known for its white fish and steered us to a *puesto* that looked clean. Knowing I liked fish and was in the dumps, he hoped to cheer me up with a good meal. The *puesto* had a table where patrons ate the fresh *charolitos*: small lake fish fried in a large flat pan and served with chili and lime.

Food, even if it wasn't hamburgers, improved my mood and lightened my load. We circled the colonnade, poking into shops, and finally hit a *tienda* for the grocery items we needed to restock the *combi*. By then, the day had lengthened into night. We needed to get back to the trailer park. Fernando held my arm to keep me from stumbling on the uneven pavement as we picked our way along the unlit streets.

Back "home" we set up camp, heated canned soup on the two burner Coleman stove, and snuggled down into our new blankets to talk. It was freezing! We made hot chocolate and watched the waning moon rise. Parsley loved the cool weather and complained in her doggie way when we closed the sliding door for heat retention. In the morning when we got up, we found the water in the dishpan had frozen, but we'd spent a cozy night together in our new blankets—the proverbial bugs in rugs. Fernando never complained about those blankets again.

Our trailer park sat on the edge of town where it was possible to walk down to the lake. Coffee in hand, we trekked through a pasture of black and white cows to admire the lovely views. In the watery sunshine of early morning, we passed a field of sprouted corn and a harvested field of hay. The hay "bales" lined the far boundary of the field, along the edge of the forest, but were tall cone-shaped piles like straw teepees standing fifteen or twenty feet tall. At the marshy shore, we admired the layer of ground fog hovering against the base of the far mountains that turned the island and town of Janitzio into a mysterious, shrouded place rising from the water. Only the top of Mexican Independence leader, José Maria Morelos's fist, triumphantly rising from the fog, shone in the sun. Later, we took a boat from the *embarcadero* over to the island and spiraled up the interior of the statue to peer from narrow windows in that same fist.

The island housed wall-to-wall tourist traps. Shrived indigenous *abuelas* sold embroidered doilies, tea towels, and napkins from woven baskets. The embroidery, bright colors on white cloth, varied in quality. The road up to the statue was steep and often turned into stairs. The vendors staked out the areas where the tourists had to slow down or stop then buzzed around like mosquitoes. Fernando batted them away with rapid Spanish, but I was taken by the work of a young girl and bought a square embroidered with red and green poinsettias—*flor de moche*, the Christmas flower—with tatted lace around the edges.

While I hadn't gotten over the break-in to my bus, Fernando's loving attention and playful nature distracted me. Still, I sensed a dark cloud building on our horizon. My Spanish couldn't support talking about it, or anything else beyond the superficial, yet I understood that his dissatisfaction, the gift of time and travel with the companions you loved—Fernando and Parsley, in my case—and money to last for at least a year, might not be his dream.

"Anita, I need to get back to *el D.F.* I don't have any

money. I've got to find a job," Fer said, while I fried fish over the Coleman stove for dinner.

"It's Christmas week. Relax. Let's explore the wood carving shops tomorrow."

He looked bored. I gripped him tighter—Fernando was the center of my universe.

Still in Patzcuaro, famous for its carvings of screens, lintels, masks, and statuary, I wanted to see as much as I could. if I distracted him with sightseeing, or traveling, or anything that kept the focus on me and his beloved *país*, he wouldn't leave me alone. I hated the idea carping behind my bliss that Fernando was eventually going to turn to a new passion—probably a job. It was his personality: intense and passionate. He needed a purpose, a cause, and I wanted to be it. Panic ignited in my heart. I changed the subject whenever he brought it up. What would I do without him? I clung to him, smitten and willing to put up with most anything to keep his full, loving attention on me. A wanderer lost in the cold of life, I'd found a fire and started to thaw. I couldn't get enough of his heat. I understood the hot part of Hot Latin Lover. Only my college beau had made me feel so approved of, so confirmed—so alive. I wasn't about to let that go in a hurry. But I couldn't admit this to myself for years.

"You can't keep paying for everything," Fernando said.

"You're making it possible for me to see more of Mexico than I'd hoped, Fer," I replied. "Tell me about Patzcuaro's history. Who was Morelos?"

So what that nothing had turned out as planned on this adventure. We missed Christmas with Jean and

Teddy, still had an oil-leaking engine, and Mexico City lay two states away. When we made a run for the city, we'd need a PEMEX about every two feet. Fernando agreed, we'd be better off taking our time. It was Christmas week, after all.

We strolled the broad, dusty boulevard that descended from *el centro* to the lake, lined with shop after shop of wood-carvings. Most of the *talleres* filled the patios of the wood carvers' homes. As in much of Mexico, Fernando explained, whole families for generations worked in one industry. Towns became known for that particular enterprise—a guild system. In Patzcuaro, woodcarving emerged as the principal guild, likely due to the surrounding forests making pine available.

I fell in love with the style: ornate columns carved with swirls and leaves, fat-cheeked angels, smooth-faced madonnas, and mermaids. Many of the masks and statuary were painted in saturated Mexican pinks, oranges, reds, blues. I fell in love with a room screen carved with mermaids emerging from clam shells on one side—a Mexican *Birth of Venus*, my favorite old master—and colorful birds perching in twining vines covered in red, blue, rose and creamy blooms on the other. I might have bought it, but there was no space to store it in the bus.

On December 28th, we pulled up stakes after breakfast and headed to the nearest PEMEX station. After filling the bus's tank and the two tanks mounted on back, we headed toward Morelia, about an hour away, at the speed of *combi*. Although the 28th was Saturday, Fernando felt the need to confess. His personal brand of Catholicism was a recurring topic of conversation. I struggled to understand how going to *misa*, made it all right to continue committing the same sins until the next visit, the big sin being me, or so I guessed. Luckily I liked religious art and architecture, because Fernando insisted I accompany him to church.

We followed my Michelin *Guía Turistica,* "Green Guide", maps into the historic city center, parked near the Plaza de Armas. Letting Parsley stretch her legs, we took a look around the central plaza. The hour rolled around for the mass. I poked through the trinkets and postcards in the stalls clustered in front of the cathedral. Fernando hammed it up for photos with some monumental statuary.

The cathedral was finished in 1744; its Baroque bell towers dominated Morelia's skyline. We approached the massive doors where Fernando dropped my hand. Typical. He was on his way to make peace with God for living with me out of wedlock. He insisted I tie a bandana over my head. As we stepped into the nave, he crossed himself with a little kiss flourish at the end, then we proceeded silently to a pew about two thirds of the distance to the altar. Light filtered through the stained glass clerestory windows, filling the soaring vaults with hazy swaths of colored light, visible holy ghosts that hovered and shifted above our heads in the magnificent church. Hanging below the layer of that God-stuff, the grand chandeliers' soft lights reflected in its many planes of crystal.

My recollection is of a light-filled, peaceful place. At first, I surreptitiously read my guidebook, but the intense silence, broken only by the soft droning of the priest and whispered response from the few attendees of the four o'clock communion, put me in a meditative state and I lost track of my secular world entirely. Fernando nudged me to take communion, bringing me back to the present. I didn't follow him to the rail. But when I noticed my grumbling stomach, I did start dreaming about El Mercado del Dulces, a nearby market devoted to sweets. At the service's end, we bolted for the door, my Green Guide staying behind on the pew, notes and all.

Fernando wasn't very interested in the Mexican candy. He loved dulce de leche candy when I bought it, but given the choice, he'd choose savory over sweet. Give Fernando tacos. Somehow I made it out of Morelia without even a photo of the amazing array of sweets: pink and white coconut bars, guava rolls, marzipan, *alfajores* with caramel and chocolate.

"We've got to leave. It will be dark before we get to Atzimba." Fernando pulled me away from the enticing sweetness overflowing from the market.

"Atzimba? What's that?"

"A *balneario*, water park. I remember it from when I was a kid."

"Like with slides and pools?"

"*Fuentes*."

"What? Fountains?"

"*Aguas termales*."

"In the fountains?"

SAINTS AND SKELETONS

"*Me confía.*" Just take my word for it.

I had begun to understand when Fernando said "trust me," that our communication had gone off track. Looking back, nothing was really what I'd thought at the time. I knew what I wanted to say—in English. All I *could* do was trust him. I sure couldn't trust our conversations. Anyway, he always steered us to the next adventure, so Atzimba with its hot-running fountains was sure to be interesting. It turned out the water was tepid, and dogs were prohibited.

We clambered back into the *combi* and motored out of El Centro to a gas station, filled up, bought oil, and got directions. Fernando wasn't opposed to asking for directions like Sam had been. In fact, he loved to ask directions, and enter into lengthy discourses on whatever subject he fancied with whomever would listen. Unfortunately, he seemed to have some trouble following the directions—or I did. I swear we turned north on the highway to Atzimba, although I thought we were heading south toward Mexico. The *carretera*, when we eventually found it, was a typical, wide Mexican boulevard, tree-lined and divided into two lanes in each direction. A *lateral* served the dilapidated-looking businesses lining either side of the *carretera*, mostly tire repair and muffler shops. It was also dark and jammed with cars moving fast. Rush hour in Morelia. We pulled over at the first PEMEX, added oil —again—then strolled to the nearby taco stand for some dinner. That's one good thing about car travel in Mexico, if you find gas, you find *tacos, quesadillas, tlacoyos,* or some other yummy street food. Food is everywhere. My kind of place.

Fernando triangulated directions, essential for finding a destination in Mexico, because the people will give you directions whether or not they know how to get there to be helpful. My experience of missed turns and dead ends taught me to always get a third opinion.

We chugged off into the countryside. I'm looking at Google Earth as I write. The *Parque Aquático* appears to be surrounded by city, but my recollection is of turning off the two-lane *carretera* onto a narrower road then driving into a wooded area, which opened up onto a large grassy triangle bordered by a break of trees on one side, a hill on the other, and the tropical-looking resort at the base. Groups of folks clustered in pods of cars, Suburbans (the ubiquitous middle-class station wagon), and pickups. I didn't notice any tents or campers, and certainly no campfires, but it was dark so I couldn't see well. We pulled to the farthest reaches of the area where I made camp then searched out the bathrooms and showers while Fernando went off to pay. I couldn't find them. As it turned out, there weren't any at the campground. I remember that Fer was paranoid we'd be robbed in the night, and we locked ourselves into the combi to sleep. Welcome to the great camping experience Fernando was so excited about.

The "campground" did not improve with daylight. The grassy expanse turned out to be dry, dusty, and soon filled to overflowing with vacationing families. It was, after all, the weekend before New Year's. Kids screeched and darted and giggled all over the place. Mothers and grandmothers gave us the evil eye, especially because their men cast envious glances our way. *UYOLKAN* wasn't very pretty, but she was *muy padre,* and, to a casual observer, Fernando had it all: the coolest camping vehicle and equipment, fair skin, a handsome face, a hot, devil-may-care *gringa*—and no responsibilities. Although Fer always worried that we'd be robbed, he couldn't pass on showing off the old camper. Luckily, the sight of Parsley kept most of the kids and men away. We left her on guard while we went to enjoy the thermal springs.

The *balneario,* waterpark, grew lush and green around the pools, but the water flumed down a brown scrub-covered hill that resembled so much of Mexico's landscape. I wonder now, if the dry, barren hills were once forested. Logging for firewood is common. I'm sure the area had looked lovely with its trees, flowers, and freshets of warm water cascading down the hill from the springs at the summit. As the day warmed up, we climbed the many steps to the *manantial,* following the flumes back to the pseudo-natural pond and swimming areas.

The resort had been well established and I realized it was considered a desirable family destination. Throughout Mexico I noticed entrances to *balnearios,* especially in the states of Morelos, Michoacán and México, where volcanic activity had been prevalent during prehistory. Thermal water parks made an impressive, relaxing attraction that offered therapeutic relief for hardworking Mexicans. Fernando talked up Atzimba as the queen of resorts. In fact, its name *is*

Reina de Atzimba, Queen of Atzimba. I enjoyed the palms with their white painted trunks, the mythological themed statuary, the thatched, palapa-shaded walkways, and ubiquitous white iron benches. I loved those Mexican benches. I found them inviting and cool in the shade of a towering tree and took every opportunity to sit and watch the world pass by.

Atzimba sounds like a little oasis. It might have been if the management hadn't busted Parsley. Fernando was convinced that one of the many campers tattled on us for the dog, for being foreign (and unmarried), but above all, for being sexy and free. A representative searched us out in the morning and told us to leave. By then, I'd discovered the tepid temperature of the pool and didn't have too much interest in swimming. I lusted after hot water. Fernando argued the point, and we somehow negotiated a stay of expulsion for the day, most likely through an exchange of cash, although I've lost the particulars under the burden of shame for being evicted from what I'd have considered a second-class resort.

We glided down a slide or two, lounged in the warm December sun—something remarkable for a Northern California girl—and ate unremarkable tacos at the restaurant since we couldn't cook at our camp—rules.

Fer and I had clicked two months before, becoming inseparable. Everything had turned out right, a situation I'd never experienced before. I'd floated on a continuous current of love energy, often reflecting on my incredible fortune. I'd felt invincible, able to go anywhere and do anything. I fit into my world perfectly, and my world fit itself around me like a spandex salsa-dancing dress. What a slap in the face. The universe decided to throw lemons into our bliss, and things began to sour from that high point of perfect sweetness.

Some might say that car trouble, robbery, and *perros prohibido* exemplified life's penchant for randomness, but I know better. These events augured disaster and I, already totally dependent on Fernando, dug in deeper. The Buddhists call it lust mind; I wanted to maintain the pleasurable feelings I had with Fernando and discover more of his fascinating country. At all costs. Hindsight always opens the hidden doors to possibilities, and, while I don't regret a minute of my experience—well, maybe a moment or two—if I'd only heeded the signs! That December 29th, the signs pointed to dancing in the pavilion at four p.m. and remembering the magic on the dance floor in Puerto Escondido. We went to the dance party.

A local salsa band played. We swirled and swayed over the tiled dance floor under the palms as the sun sank behind the trees and the lanterns blinked on. We'd changed from shorts to slacks and skirt and treated the spicy "tea dance" as a date. Parsley came too. She politely slept under our cocktail table while we danced. There had been something about the entrance price, we were cash poor, but I think the dog scared the ticket taker away. The magic was back.

Just before dark, we shoved-off in the already battened down combi, leaving a nasty pool of oil behind us.

All the guidebooks admonish motorists in Mexico to stay off the roads after dark, but that's when Fernando and I did most of our traveling. In theory, animals such as cattle, would be attracted to the warm pavement and, in the dark, motorists could hit them. Fernando's theory didn't concern animals. He claimed that drunks overran the roads like zombies once night fell, and we might run over one of them sleeping it off. Off the bottle, Fer lacked tolerance, and I think he secretly hoped to eliminate a few *alcohólicas* as we transited between our destinations in the night. I rarely saw cows, and never drunks, in the road, but I was surprised several times to be launched airborne when we hit a steep *tope* at 50 miles per hour.

Towns and hamlets had a tendency to cluster along transportation routes. In more populated areas, such as the state of Michoacán, city fathers built a series of speed bumps outside their towns to slow down the traffic. Some *topes* were indicated by yellow caution signs with a graphic of two round orbs resembling breasts. Others were painted white. But often the *topes* were not marked in any way and rusting vehicles with presumably broken axles crouched at the side of the road in testimony to the ferocity of the bumps. Vehicles had to creep along populated roads where *topes* cropped up every quarter mile before and after the every town. How UYOLKAN managed to weather the slings and arrows of Mexican driving, I'll never understand, but with the muffler disconnected, we roared along between speed bumps, emitting a sharp series of backfired *pedos* every time we slowed down. Reflecting, I wonder if the pits, pot-holes, *topes,* unpaved tracks, uneven pavement and debris-strewn roads, not incompetent mechanics, caused the oil leak and subsequent replacing of my "*monobloc"* as Fernando referred to the engine.

Eventually, Fer and I got hungry. I have no idea what the countryside looked like, or even what direction we headed. Mexico City lay to the south, but I have believed all these years we ate tacos in the *zocalo* of Zamora, and I see now that's impossible—Zamora was even then a city, and to the northwest. Because we dripped so much oil, we were headed straight back to *La Capital.*

We landed for dinner in a typical *zocalo* filled with food carts, balloon vendors, laughing children and friendly adults. Entering that plaza arm in arm, Parsley on a leash, suddenly all the tension and worry left me. Fernando relaxed and slung my bag over his shoulder after embracing me in a warm public display of affection. Why this town affected us so profoundly, I'll never know.

According to Fernando, this plaza, and this Sunday evening around nine o'clock, was typical of Mexico. Families out for fun and food. Young people all dressed up, the girls in tight pants and low-cut tops promenading in one direction, the boys in t-shirts emblazoned with rock slogans surging in the other—giggles and kisses and greetings and laughter. Old men on the benches playing checkers. Their withered wives knitting or watching the teens with eagle eyes from under dark shawls. Mothers grouped around stalls inspecting aprons or collars or clothing while their husbands nipped off bottles of beer and tequila, spotlessly clean and spit-shined, sporting silver belt buckles the size of luncheon plates and snakeskin cowboy boots.

Maybe the town was Acámbaro. Photos online show a pretty *zocalo* surrounded by trees. I remember trees. I remember tacos. After tacos, I remember a long, dark drive and ending up exhausted in a desolate area near a dammed lake.

Fer had turned the *combi* off Hwy. 120. We bumped over dirt tracks to a spot that satisfied him. Fernando's criteria for selecting camping sites remained a mystery to me throughout our trips together. I understood the need to be safe, but beyond safety, his choices were more divinely guided than thought out. Possibly the purpose of Sunday *misa*. But, *if* we were going to camp near a reservoir, why not within sight of the water?

"Vamonos cerca del agua," I suggested. I wanted to park at the shore.

"No podemos," he replied. We can't.

"¿Porque no?" I asked.

"No te preocupes—" Don't worry.

I'd learned *that* phrase, *bien bien*.

Parsley poked her cold nose in my face and I stirred from my slumber, cozy in our pull-out bed in the back of the camper. She whined softly, ears pricked up, tail wagging and her head cocked toward the no-see-um netting.

"Okay, girl, I get it." She needed to go out. I tugged my sweatshirt from under the bed and climbed into it, then pulled open the screen to take my first peek into the pre-dawn. It looked like we were on the moon. I let the dog out then climbed back into bed. I'd deal with moon-walking later—Fernando was warm and horny.

The next thing I knew, someone was shouting above a racket of strange voices. Fernando shot up and jumped out of the *combi*, returning in moments with Parsley. He yelled something from the doorway, waved his arm, then slammed the door shut. The strange noises got louder, closer, and I distinguished a bell—a cow bell. I sat up to look out the window. In moments, cattle surrounded the bus, driven by a *vaquero* riding a tough little donkey across the barely illuminated scrubby hills. Fernando held Parsley's collar as she strained to chase after the beasts. The cattle streamed around us, occasionally bumping the bus causing it to rock. They mooed and snorted and clopped past in a cloud of dust and eau de barnyard. The *vaquero* waved his thanks that Fer had brought in the dog, and they were gone.

It was still too early to get up so we drifted back to sleep as the sun rose. The morning of December 30th dawned chilly and overcast, enhancing the feeling that we were on another planet. In my early morning dreams, I listened as a swarm of demented sounding schoolboys descended on our camper. They morphed into aliens. They wanted something. One of them tinkled a little bell. They were looking for their mother, "Mmaaamma, maammmm, ma ma maa," a child bleated.

My eyes flew open to a gold toothed, mustachioed *campesino* grinning outside the window. "Mmaa ma maaa."

I grabbed the dog and slid open the door—goats!

Fernando had plunked us down in a main herd thoroughfare.

Unlike Atzimba where I didn't shoot many photos, I have several from this leg of our Christmas journey. I shot them in black and white and printed them sepia toned. Had I known then that these old photos would become my memory of the time? Hazy with little contrast? Did I shoot black and white because the color had begun to drain out of our romance?

I savored one of life's truly memorable breakfasts on that overcast morning in Tequisquiapán, and yes, it did involve tender, slow-cooked goat. The back of my photo says "Good breakfast" and is the only photo of a breakfast joint in my album—*Fonda Taquits.*

Fernando had introduced me to the *fonda* concept long before Tequisquiapán. We'd eaten our way from Puerto Escondido to Mexico to Zihuatanejo and almost back to Mexico, *taquería* to *fonda* to *puestos* in the *mercado municipio* and back to *taquería* in an ever circling sampling of regional, home-style cooking and conversation.

A *fonda*, or *comida económica*, also called *comida corrida* although I can't find an exact translation of this —is an inexpensive restaurant, most often a *hole-in-the-wall* establishment with a kitchen at the back, laden with blackened pots and pans, and *cazuelas,* clay stewpots, stacks of *barro* dishware crafted from low-fired clay, a couple of long tables covered in wonderfully florid Mexican oilcloth, with a hand-written sign announcing the three offerings of the day.

SAINTS AND SKELETONS

Most often *fondas* resemble a cement block garage, windowless, opening to the street by a wall-sized corrugated metal door. The *dueña,* usually a middle-aged woman, rolls her door open in the early morning. Then she and her daughters, or perhaps an aunt and aging mother, prepare the rice, beans, *sopa,* a plate of very lightly sauced spaghetti noodles, and three big main dishes, to serve people all day long as they gather at the communal tables for a meal or a snack through four o'clock, the hour of *comida*.

Picking your way along the notoriously pocked sidewalks in any Mexican town, you can determine the place to eat by nose. The savory aroma that pours out of these places is worth the price of admission. The next criteria, cleanliness. The tables and food preparation areas need to look attended to, and the cooked food has to be covered. In Mexico, flies can be a problem. We walked by plenty of places that smelled good but didn't pass the fly test. The third test—price. I learned that a good meal should cost about five or six pesos—two dollars. And Fer wouldn't eat anywhere he couldn't have a conversation. If the *dueña* wouldn't respond to him, he dragged me on to the next *fonda*. As I think on it, I'm sure these are always run by women because Fernando was quite a ladies man—he probably only stopped in *fondas* operated by moms and grandmothers, and Fonda Taquits was no exception.

Here's what I ate: first, a plate of the non-descript *sopa*—I never understood this tasteless, spaghetti-style noodle cooked with a dribble of thin tomato sauce served on a plate as an appetizer. Then came a large platter smothered in Mexican style rice cooked with tomatoes and *chile*, thick rich pinto beans slow-cooked with lard, *chile*, onion, and *epazote* in a clay bean pot until the beans had become tender and almost creamy, a pile of *machaca*, shredded beef stewed in the locally grown *chile guajillo,* topped with a poached egg, more sauce, and *queso fresco*, a portion of barbequed goat, and squash blossoms filled with soft local cheese and *huitlacoche*, a black truffle-like fungus that grows on corn, and is considered a delicacy. I washed it down with *horchata* left over from the feast of the Apostle John three nights before.

An important aspect of our food adventure was the opportunity to chat with other diners and, more importantly, the *dueñas* of the establishments. Fernando had a friendly word for all. He learned interesting facts about them, their families, businesses, and what they thought about the government and life in general. The sad thing was, I couldn't keep up with these conversations and relied on Fernando to translate the rapid exchanges into simple, noun-laden Spanish that he delivered slowly with much exaggerated gestures. Needless to say, I was left to savor the *mole* or *arroz* or *frijoles* in solitude. I played a little game with myself—identify the flavors and see if I could, in my mind at least, figure out how to make the dish.

After breakfast, we wandered around the dusty plaza, quiet on a Monday morning, and found our iron benches. Fer napped, a derelict crashed under the emblem for his beloved *país*. I read and observed women gathering to chat in the bright gloom. Were we tired? Bored? Was this the turning point? "*Huelle a tristeza... Ay amor, donde, donde estas?"*[2] How didn't I smell the sadness on December 30th, 1991?

Even as I chronicle these memories, waves of sadness wash over me. Could be that my *U Yol Ka'an,* Heart of Sky, playlist reminds me of every emotion, happy and sad, loving and angry—there's a song for each. We know how music transports us to the place and time we listened to it.

My mood lifts with the next on the list, Pérez Prado's *Que Rico el Mambo*. I see Fernando clearly in my mind, lurching, swaying stamping, abandoned to el Mambo on a crowded New Year's Eve dance floor.

After napping, we piled back into the leaking beast and continued south. Mexico City lay a couple-hour jaunt down the *autopista*; however, for some forgotten reason, possibly the cost of tolls, we took the *libre* through Pachuca, of all depressing places. Pachuca is the ugliest town I passed through in Mexico, grey, dusty, barren. Cement block buildings crowned with naked rebar. Probably Pachuca had looked especially awful because my *"burbujas de amor"* had developed tiny rents, and the sweet bubbles of love deflated slowly like balloons.

Fernando wanted to go home, get a job, and a life. Between scratchy sing-a-longs with our favorite radio tunes now that the cassettes were gone, we talked about

---
[2] ©1992 Maná, Donde Jugaron los Ninos, *"Huelle a Tristeza"*

what we would do next, the lyrics a romantic subtext to our conversation. Fer wanted me to support his work endeavors. He wanted me to commit to launching his career, to launching him. Fernando wanted me to stay in Mexico; he feared I'd go home.

"Anita, I can't travel around Mexico until you decide to go home."

"I'm not going home." *'Si no quieres mi amor, a mi no me importa. Te quiero a morir.*[3]

"You'll leave me. I know how this works. I came home from Germany."

I sighed.

"*Vamanos de fiesta esta noche ... no pensamos en la manana ...para mi que alegría ...¡vamanos! ¡vamanos! ...*"[4]

"That was you. Germany was cold and inhospitable. You couldn't work. I can work here. I'm not leaving."

" *... Por que sabes te deseo. Por que sabes te adoro....* "[5]

"How?"

"Teaching English, preparing taxes for ex-pats, working for Pattie in relocation. I've got skills." (That took some dictionary time to express.)

"*Te quiero, mi reina.*"

"*... Feeling hot, hot, hot ...* "[6]

"*A ti támbien, Fer.*"

"*... Por un amor me desvelo y vivo apasionada...* "[7]

---

3 ©1996 Cristian éxitos "Nunca Voy a Olvidarte"
4 ©1994 Garibaldi Caribe "Vamonos a Fiesta"
5 ©1992 Mana Donde Jugaran los Niños "Como Te Deseo"
6 ©1994 Garibaldi Caribe "Hot, Hot, Hot"
7 © 1987 Linda Ronstadt Canciones de Mi Padre "Por Un Amor"

Chapter 14

Happy New Year, Loca

New Year's Eve, 1991

Greater Mexico City, the *Distrito Federal* or *El D.F. (day eff éh)* fills the Valley of Mexico. Actually it's a basin, not a valley. It laps up the surrounding mountains and washes north and east, engulfing the townships of the State of Mexico along the Highway to Queretaro, and our route, the Mexico-Pachuca Highway 85. In contrast to entering *La Capital* from the south or west, there isn't any drama, no sweeping vistas from steep mountain curves, no sudden glimpses of high-rise islands floating on the sea of city as you emerge from the mouth of a tunnel—that is, if it's a rare, pollution-free day and you can see anything at all. New Year's Eve was one of those.

We pushed toward the city, passing the universal highway businesses: gas stations, shipping warehouses, brake and tire repair centers, rail sidings, plumbing, heating and electrical companies, and Mexico-style—

taco carts and sprawling treeless cement block and corrugated metal slums. It was a sand-colored blur passing my window, but Fernando pointed out the sights.

"Look, that's my exit. See?" Fernando pointed up a little hill to the east. "I live over there."

We'd arrived in Tlalnepantla, his hometown where I'd visited often, but still got lost trying to find. I did recognize, however, *Los Torres de Satelite* in the municipality of Naucalpan, the monument that loomed over the next rise and marked the town of Satelite where the Sanborns, with the best magazine selection, anchored one end of a huge shopping center. No slums here; the neighborhoods sported towering shade trees, pretty gardens, and plenty of iron grillwork. But soon we returned to the crummy blur of highway.

"There's the turnoff to Atzcapotzalco. Never take that exit," Fernando admonished me for the hundredth time. "It's the most dangerous area in *El D.F.*"

The scenery looked all the same to me, but I took his word that this borough had not only the largest population in the country, but the most crime.

I knew what came next: the arena and the military base—one of the prettiest spots in the city, filled with trees, lawns, tidy buildings with tile roofs sloping up the mountainside. Finally we roared up Paseo Reforma, cut through Chapultepec's forested third section, and arrived home at Privada de Roseleda.

Throughout our time together, Fernando drove. I paid more attention to him than I did the routes we took. I found Mexico City baffling. Streets ran north to south then disappeared at a dead end only to start up east to west somewhere else. Numbers ran consecutively—until they didn't. Streets started out with one name and, possibly in the middle of a block, became another name. I was happy to leave the driving to him. However, that caused a problem. He lived in Tlalnepantla in the *Viveros de la Loma* district, a good forty-five minutes north from my tony *Lomas Altas* address bordering the *bosques* of Chapultapec Park. When we parted company, one of us had to drop the other off and drive home. I was in love, but not crazy. No way was I leaving my VW in care of a boyfriend who lived somewhere in the Mexico maze I couldn't navigate, and couldn't find again.

On December 30th, Fer drove me home then took the Metro back to Acacias 88, a two-hour journey that involved busses, three Metro line changes, and blocks of hoofing it. He promised to return dressed for a night on the town, by nine the next evening.

True to his word, Fernando rang Pattie's doorbell just before nine on New Year's Eve. I tottered to the door in my black suede pumps and gasped. He looked fabulous in his suit and tie. For once, his shined lawyer loafers fit in.

He grinned and whirled me into his arms in the foyer. "Anita ¡*como bonita eres!*" He gave me a smooch and my heart pounded.

I'd pinned myself into my size 8 "little black dress" purchased in the spring for a fancy cocktail party and now a size too large. Dressing up in *La Capital* is *de rigeuer*, I embraced the opportunity to wear skirts or dress up my jeans with heels whenever we went out, but we'd been in flip-flops and tennis shoes for a couple of weeks. My feet rebelled against the black pumps. Where did I leave that shoehorn? No matter, my handsome date helped me into the *combi* where we called goodnight to Felipe and the guard for our *Privada*. "¡*Nos vemos en el año nuevo!*"

I had no idea where Fernando planned on taking me, but we would be the hottest couple out on the town. I slipped a wad of *pesos* into his pocket as we backfired our way down Constituyentes to José Vasconcelos and across the eastern tip of Chapultepec Park to Reforma.

"Fer, where are we going?"

"You'll see. It's a *sorpresa*."

"Are we going dancing?" I asked.

"Maybe."

We entered the roundabout under the Angel of Independence, or officially named, *El Monumento a la Independencía*. *El Ángel* was built to commemorate the centennial of the beginning of Mexico's War of Independence, celebrated in 1810. In later years, it was made into a mausoleum for the most important heroes of that war. Presiding over Reforma at the intersection of Rio Tiber to the left and Florencia and Zona Rosa's many restaurants to the right, I guessed we'd turn one way or the other. But we passed around "Winged Victory" promenading toward *El Centro Histórico* with the rest of the traffic on the eight-lane boulevard.

I cranked up some *salsa tropical* on the radio. Fernando grinned and crooned along with a popular tune. Again the electricity popped and sparked between us, adding to the festive holiday spirit illuminating the city. Mexico City puts on her best for the holidays, with boulevard decorations of colorful light designs woven into nets slung across the roads. Even in small neighborhoods, sparkling stars, deep red *flor de noche* and nativity scenes light up the streets. All the *espiritu Navideña* and city energy rekindled our passion. Or perhaps, a day apart had made our hearts grow fonder. I didn't care. Fernando and I were in love and ushering in the New Year together.

I recognized *Parque Alameda* as we cruised by. We were headed downtown. I didn't know much about the *Centro Historico*, but Fernando always surprised me with interesting restaurants, markets, stores, and activities. He should have been a tour guide for his amazing knowledge of *La Capital*. Driving, I usually got lost, but Fernando not only knew his way, he always found a parking space—a serious problem in the city. How he managed to stow the *combi* on a safe street within a short stroll of the *Tropicana* located on the edge of *Plaza Garibaldi*, remains a question. The surrounding neighborhoods of Guerrero and Tlatelolco had declined for years. The area was filled with drunks, thieves, and indigents, but I didn't feel unsafe with Fernando. We lived in a bubble of perfection, if one overlooked the *combi* break-ins. We reached Plaza Garibaldi, the legendary home of *mariachi* music, and even that was rundown with few mariachis waiting to play, and fewer clients needing songs.

Fernando hustled us past the *mariachi* lineup in the plaza then down some chipped steps smelling faintly of urine, into club Tropicana, a cavernous space booming with *cumbias*, gyrating with revelers for a hot, hot, hot *noche de alegría en Plaza Garibaldi*. We found our table on the main floor then ordered dinner, a *mole guajillo* with the usual trimmings, which I don't remember eating. But the margaritas—*¡qué rico!* And *¡qué fuerte!*—strong. Fernando drank Coke, but I was *borracha* before the meal was served. My apprehensions about my relationship with him evaporated, or drowned, as we danced into the wee hours. At midnight, the champagne corks popped. We toasted 1992. The *cumbias* resumed. I commenced the New Year in the arms of the man I loved. I tossed back another margarita, kicked off my too-tight shoes, and got my hips moving—*¡me mové la cola!* The sounds of toasting kept time to the Latin rhythms as the spotlights flashed off the cymbals and the ladies' jewelry. We gyrated and swayed in a press of skirts and bodies until four a.m. when the club closed.

Back in the *combi* I rested my head against the leather headrest, reflecting on my bliss. The year held so much promise. Fernando had hinted over dinner he wanted to make our relationship permanent. All the tension we'd experienced over the holidays had only been "deciding pains". It was a new year...

I woke up when Fernando set the emergency brake and the bus lurched sharply. Blue and white lights swirled throughout the cabin. My head swam.

"Where are we?"

"Constituyentes. Be quiet. I'll take care of this."

I closed my eyes to sink back into oblivion but a rapping on my window returned me quickly to reality.

SAINTS AND SKELETONS

A uniformed police officer peered through the window at me. I swung my head toward Fernando. "Wha—?" Another officer stood at the driver's side window. When Fernando opened the door, a current of sewer gasses wafted in with the pre-dawn stillness. He stepped out, gesticulating. I heard his voice, but he talked so fast, the words flowed together. I only understood, "No."

The cop by my window walked around to the street-side. I experienced the slow dawning of understanding when cash exchanged hands. Fernando got back into the driver's seat and started the bus, pulling carefully up the empty avenue.

"Wha'd they want?" I slurred.

"Money. Thought I was drunk."

"Bu' you don' drink. Wha'd you give them?"

"10,000 pesos."

"Por nada."

"*No se importa.*"

I nodded off, too tired and drunk to protest paying the extortion.

The bus stopped again. I opened my eyes to the architect's office, signaling our corner was just ahead, Avenida Roseleda. Why were we stopping?

"Wha's the matter?" I asked, then came fully awake. We were being pulled over again. How dare they? Fernando was sober and obeying the speed laws, as if that mattered. I wasn't shelling out more of my money to a greedy cop. I threw open my car door steaming with anger, poured out onto the sidewalk then wobbled around to the driver's side door as the cop arrived.

"How dare you stop us again! You just cheated us out of my money a few blocks back. I'm not giving you one dime more. Asshole," I screamed in English, poking my index finger toward his chest. He stepped back.

"Ana, get in the combi," Fernando commanded.

"No, Fer. He's got no right to stop us. I'm not putting up with this," I continued in English. I bared my teeth at the cop, who retreated another step. "That's right. Get in your car and have a Happy New Year. Asshole."

He backed up some more, projecting his voice over me to Fernando. I heard something about drunk Americans. I think it was Fernando speaking.

"Get in the *combi* and shut up," he said.

"Not until he's in his car and drives away. *Vete! Dejanos en paz.*"

Fernando's head hung in his arms. I saw his lips moving. Praying?

"Leave us alone!" I shouted once more. The cop sidled to his patrol car and sped off. I climbed into the bus and grinned.

Fernando was not amused. *"Estás loca.* Anyway, it was a different patrol," he said, as he eased around the corner and down the block to our *privada*.

"Wha'd he want?"

"Look, Ana, it's your California license plates. They see them and think they'll get money."

"I guess I fooled him."

Fernando shot me a dark look. "Happy New Year, *Loca*. We're home."

Chapter 15

Living on Roseleda

January 1992

Mexico City's temperatures dipped. Everyone insisted it was one of the coldest years on record. Days of chilly vomit-colored sky kept me huddling in my cheerful, many-windowed room at 11 Privada de Roselada. Between unsatisfying phone calls with Fernando, I shivered in front of the TV, sifting through my suitcases to find something warmer than shorts and sandals. Few homes in Mexico City came with central heating. When it was cold, the tile floors and stucco walls radiated the chill.

The weather matched my mood, and all my worries and fears re-manifested. It was the let-down after running on high excitement for five months. I wanted to crawl into the colorful blankets I'd bought and hibernate until the sun came out again.

Privada de Roselada was my second home-away-from-home. Pattie Hogan was a friend and business partner with my first cousin Marty—after Marty had moved to Mexico City through her job. Marty thought I'd be some company for Pattie since her divorce. Anyway, Marty's husband didn't want me and my dog living with them. Pattie lived with several dogs. In August, Parsley and I arrived at her iron gate on Roselada, two-thirds of the way up Constituyentes, the main commercial route from the Periferico to the highway to Toluca, the capitol of the State of Mexico. When a lovely home in the gated section of Lomas Altas off Roseleda became available during the fall, she worked her real estate magic to buy it. I inserted myself as her personal assistant, supervising Fernando and her staff to pack up the house and move down the short block to the *privada* in December.

The new house sprawled over a shoulder of the hill, dropping three stories from its rooftop *bodega*, storage room, to garden level office. The view was of trees, a rarity in crowded Mexico City. The long, wedge-shaped property fronted the third section of Chupultepec Park: the *Bosques de Chapultapec*, a forest of scraggly trees choking in Mexico City's pollution.

In that cold January, the pretty lawn and garden didn't beckon as it would later, but the brilliant red of the geraniums and flor de noches, poinsettia shrubs, made a pop of color against the dark green, olive, grey, and brown of the forest.

By January, I'd unloaded my gear from the *combi,* and stored it in the *bodega* on the roof of the new house. I'd moved my trunk of books and city clothes from my cousin's garage to my room. Fernando job-hunted. Between our lengthy phone calls, I didn't have much to do beyond mull over the path I had taken in life, and pine like a teenager over his absences.

He still left me love notes when he went home.

> *"Hola otra vez. Prepárate algo rico de cenar. Tu sabes prepara algo natural. Que tengas una buena cena Ana. Te Quiero."*

That one included a valentine heart with '*F y A*' inside. It read: Hello again. Make yourself a delicious supper. You know, make something fresh. Have a good supper. I love you.

But I wasn't so keen on reviewing my choices in life. I escaped into novels as much as I could. Pattie was a great reader who maintained a library of all the latest bestsellers. To avoid thinking about why I was staying in Mexico and attaching myself to yet one more unsuitable man, I happily exchanged the books I'd carted from California for her new ones. Pattie and I read *Scarlett* by Alexandra Ripley, and Tom Clancy's *The Sum of all Fears*. I caught up with Kinsey Millhone in *H is for Homicide*.

It was during the cold that I read *Desperados: Latin Drug lords, U.S. Lawmen, and the War America Can't Win* by Elaine Shannon, an exposé on the torture-murder of Drug Enforcement Administration agent Enrique Camarena in Sinaloa, Mexico, in 1985.

Desperados introduced me to the dangerous world of Mexican narcotics trafficking and hooked me on a line of inquiry that inspired me to write a series of novels set in Mexico against the backdrop of the war on drugs. But what an idiot I was! In complete ignorance I'd driven through Sinaloa en route to Mexico City only months before. I'd stopped for the night in Culiacán and "partied" with narcos (or wannabes) at the club down the block from my motel. Truth told, the narcos totally ignored a forty-year-old *gabacha*. I drank my drink and rejoined my dog in our tacky motel room without speaking to anyone. Was an angel watching over me?

When I was freezing or couldn't read novels any more, I moved to the kitchen to help Pattie's cook, Goya, prepare something, or pore through Pattie's library of cookbooks. It often was the warmest place in the house. I wanted to make myself useful in exchange for my room and board, so I chipped in for groceries, taking on evening chef duties after Goya went home.

Pattie and I dined lightly at night: salads or soups with quesadillas or dishes I'd learned in Oaxaca. Regardless of the meal, from the moment I'd arrived in Mexico City I'd steadily shed weight. By winter of 1992, I'd dropped about twenty pounds and toned up from all the walking I did. I attributed this fortune to the altitude and exercise, but eating the main meal in the afternoon was also a factor. For the first time, I could eat anything I wanted. In Mexico City, foul air and greasy tacos aside, I looked and felt better than I had since college, even as I embraced the culinary delights at every opportunity.

I picture myself that January draped in a blanket,

learning how to make *tamales*. Goya's tiny tamales were celebrated throughout Pattie's "ex-pat" world and Goya's part of town, where she ran a weekend tamale business. The Lomas Altas kitchen had been designed to accommodate a staff. Down the center ran a stainless island topped in black stone where we prepared the food. I loved that kitchen for its room to move and plethora of storage. Although I did not return to California a master of the *tamal*, I recall the time spent preparing food: the *caldos, sopas, albondigas*, and the *moles* I'd learned to make as some of the happiest time I spent at *Privada de Rosaleda*.

Eventually the overcast skies cleared and the sun shone on a city ringed with brilliant white-capped volcanic mountains. A white Ajusco presided over the southern quadrant of the city, and on the rare day the pollution index read low, Popocatepetl and his sleeping princess, Ixtaccihuatl glowed under a dusting of new snow to the east. Unfortunately, the air wasn't clean more than a couple of days that month because of thermal inversion, the "wintertime weather event that turns the air over *Mexico City* into a grayish-yellow pudding of pollutants,"[8] for which the city in a bowl is infamous. Some days I couldn't tell if the sky was overcast, or if the cold compacted a layer of pollution into cloud-like strata. Another reason to hibernate.

Lucky I lived next door to a forest. Tattered and gasping for air, it still gave off clean oxygen. I may not have survived otherwise.

Toward the end of January, Parsley became listless,

---

[8] www.nytimes.com/...he-world-mexico-s-political-inversion *Feb, 4, 1996*

fevered, suffering from a cough and runny nose. She wouldn't eat and panted rapidly although she shivered in the cold like the rest of the household. I bundled her in blankets, cradling her against my body, trying to keep fluids in her, but it looked like she wouldn't recover. Sadness overwhelmed me. I'd adopted her as a seven-week old pup from a box of eight littermates outside a Lagunitas store thirteen years before. She'd been my constant companion and protector. If she died, I had only myself to blame. I was frantic. Fernando had studied veterinary sciences during his several years at Mexico's UNAM, Universidad Nacional Autónoma de Mexico. He stayed over to care for Parsley and comfort me. "She needs a vet, Reina," he said.

Pattie folded her arms across her chest. "Fernando's right, Ana. You can't let her infect my dogs. Take Parsley to my vet. He's the best." It was an order.

She called for an appointment with Dr. Appendini, located about fifteen minutes down the mountain on Constituyentes. She wouldn't go anywhere else for her two dogs: giant Bouvier des Flanders, Cassandra, and a mop of a mutt, Algodón.

Dr. Appendini ran a *consultorio* in a run-down looking building on the main thoroughfare at a corner leading into what looked like a seedy neighborhood where we had to park. He kept the *consultorio* locked up and barred. I hoped these weren't signs of the service or the outcome of Parsley's illness. I shook slightly as I rang the doorbell; my stomach clenched and rolled. Fernando carried Parsley wrapped in her blanket.

The door opened. A smile warmed Dr. Appendini's

kindly face as he ushered us in then relocked the door. His gentle manner and tidy clinic belied the shabby grey sweater he wore (he was still wearing it sixteen years later when I visited) and the run-down neighborhood outside.

Parsley was dehydrated, not a good thing at any time, but life threatening to geriatrics. Dr. Appendini thought she had pneumonia. He gave her antibiotics, impressing me with his gentle touch and genuine love for animals.

The doctor and Fernando kept up a lively conversation, which I was unable to follow. Neither man spoke more than a few words in English, but I understood that my dear companion would not recover to her sprightly self.

He ministered to my doggie for a ridiculously low fee, saving her life. Was the bill paid by Pattie who couldn't abide animal suffering? As Dr. Appendini warned, Parsley's health returned slowly. She never gained back the weight she'd lost in the two weeks she was ill, nor did she fully recover her vigor. Another thorn to prick at me in those dark hours of torment and recrimination I actively sought to avoid: *it was all my fault; I was selfish; I never should have dragged a twelve-year-old dog around a foreign country in a VW bus*. But in my defense, Parsley had never been away from me for more than a couple of weeks, and then had stayed with loved friends. I couldn't leave her behind—*that* would have killed her, and killed me with guilt. I felt guilty enough over abandoning my kitty, Zaxxon, to the cat sitter. The agreed six months was about up and I knew I wasn't going home. At least Parsley stayed with me to her last breath.

Chapter 16

You Have to Move

January 1992

The earth turned; the sun warmed the city, but the dangerous smog levels continued. Fernando insisted that the factories in the north of the city, unregulated and pumping God-knows-what into the air, or worse—buying off the inspectors and belching toxic waste into the bowl of Mexico—*"era cupable"*. The news blamed the ten million cars congesting Mexico's thoroughfares and spewing leaded gas exhaust. I was convinced it was the lead that gave street tacos their flavor edge. Regardless where the pollution, *contaminación,* originated, the problem was so bad that winter, the city government instituted a no circulation plan, *Hoy No Circula,* to prohibit driving one weekday, removing about one fifth of the registered vehicles from operation every day based on the last digit of the license plate. My *combi*, UYOLKAN, was off the road on Friday with the plates ending in nine and zero. To enforce, vehicles sported a colored sticker for the cops to see. Mine was blue. But I wasn't going to work, and didn't need to keep to any kind of schedule. I wasn't greatly inconvenienced.

You've gotta love the *chilangos*, denizens of Mexico City—besides swapping plates with the day's sticker from one car to another, during the winter of 1991/92 there was a rush on car sales. Everyone who could, bought a car with a different circulation day to never be off the street. So much for taking 20% of the emissions out of the air. Pattie bought a new car, adding a sedan to the garage where her hulking Bronco pawed the pavement, ready to race over the mountains to her weekend home down valley from Tepoztlán.

My Spanish still lacked fluency. I didn't quite understand what Fer described as an "underground" car swap taking place within the population, or how it applied to me. I detested driving in the city: the crazy drivers, the honking, the incomprehensible starts and stops to streets, and direction of circulation. I'd learned how to get pretty much anywhere I wanted using the French-built Metro and the *peseras,* boxy mini vans that ran routes everywhere throughout the city, stopping about every three minutes. Fernando preferred driving, coming alive with the challenge of insane city traffic. It wasn't a secret he loved my VW bus. I fully understood he wanted to officially get Mexican plates on it: "*legalizarlo*"— legalize it.

"*Reina*, my uncle knows a guy in the government. He can legalize it and we won't get pulled over anymore."

"I don't know, Fer. The law says I have to take it

out of Mexico when my visa expires."

"But you aren't leaving. Aren't we getting married?"

I balked even as butterflies swarmed in my gut. Married? "As long as I'm on a tourist visa, *amor*, I'm out of Mexico every six months. How would I get it into the US with Mexican plates?"

"We'd put it in my name. We'd have to."

How disingenuous—he'd always wanted my *combi*. I smiled. "Yeah, sure. I'm giving you my bus, Fer," I said in English, the sarcasm lost in the syrupy tone of my voice.

Luckily, neither Fernando, nor Mexicans in general, acted fast. If he ever made the calls he said he needed to make, nothing came of it. In the spirit of *mañana*, the *combi* remained in my name. But between the pollution, the day off the road and changes at Pattie's, we got out of the capitol as often as possible.

Pattie had been dating the president of Yamaha Corporation Mexico, Rick Johnson, who moved to the city with Yamaha when NAFTA ratified. Rick loved to enjoy life. He worked hard and *fiesta-ed* hard—just like Pattie. Rick distracted her from the sadness she felt surrounding her divorce. In no time they were an item, and he was moving into the house at 11 *Privada de Roselada*—into my pleasant room off the courtyard. I was relegated to a curtained-off alcove in the hall outside Pattie's garden-level office. It was cold, damp and lacked privacy. I had to be up, dressed and out by the time Nora Campos, Pattie's assistant, showed up for work. No one was happy with the arrangement. Fernando was no longer welcome to stay over. Pattie really didn't want another woman in-house while she was having her fling.

She owned and operated a relocation service that put ex-pats into homes then helped them settle in to life in Mexico. With NAFTA, her business boomed. Prior to the new trade agreements, she had worked primarily with couples or singles coming to town through international companies. With the flood of corporations into the capitol, whole families were arriving. Pattie hoped to solve two problems with the same stroke of genius: she would set me up in her house in Tepoztlán, 40 kilometers northeast of Cuernavaca, an hour southeast of Mexico, to open up the Cuernavaca region to housing rentals for *extranjeros*, foreigners. Cuernavaca, Tepoztlán, Coyococ, and even Oaxtepec, had high-end housing districts in clean air. Families with kids could live in the State of Morelos while Dad, or in rare cases, Mom, commuted two to four hours daily to *La Capital.* Pattie wanted me to find the properties. While I developed an inventory, I could take over running her weekend place, now called *Hacienda Clemente Jacques*—managing the *velador y la criada*, the caretaker and his wife, the housekeeper, writing ad copy, advertising weekend rentals, preparing for the guests, and eventually catering the rentals.

"Ana, you love it there," Pattie said, in her Texas drawl.

"I'll have to think about it, Pattie."

A wide grin spread across her face. "You'd be a natural at it."

"I failed at selling encyclopedias and Mary Kay."

"You won't have to sell the families. They want clean air for the kids. Lead stunts children's growth. Everybody knows that."

I shrugged. "I don't know, Pattie. I'm so bad at that kind of thing."

"I'll pay you a commission just like I do all the rest of the agents."

I raised my eyebrows. *You mean you weren't going to?*

"Think of how you'll improve your Spanish."

"Well, maybe."

Her voice hardened. "Think fast. You have to move."

Pattie was right. I wasn't doing anything: I'd stopped taking Spanish classes. I'd stopped traveling. I spent my time at home either whining about Fernando, or as a dervish preparing to meet him. What I needed was something constructive to do.

Even ex-pat Americans are obligated to pay Uncle Sam, and we'd entered tax season. Pattie arranged several little tax-related accounting jobs for me then brought me into her business sphere to begin training. I spent more time in her office and less time moping after Fernando. My cousin Marty bought me a pad of three-column accounting paper, headed *en español.* I was back in business.

The office spanned a narrow space running the

length of the northern wing under the bedrooms at garden terrace level. The picture windows faced into the *bosque*. In the morning, sunlight swam through the low hanging pollution, brightening the ground floor space with a filtered cheeriness. Packed with desks, files, worktables, books, telephones, etc., this was where Pattie's pretty assistant, Nora Campos, presided.

Nora came to work early, enjoying the quiet and the dappled light. Many days she caught me still zonked out in my "closet"—sometimes with Fernando crammed into the twin bed with me, and always with Parsley close by. Nora did not allow dogs in her domain. Like many Mexicans, she was afraid of them. Only little Algodón got a pass, and only because she came with *la jefa*. Fer and I chuckled seeing Nora's face when giant Bouvier des Flanders Cassandra bounded into the room, and more so when Fer was caught out wrapped in a towel. But she was a good sport, accepting the *bohemia gringa* graciously. I was quite fond of Nora.

Now and then Nora brought her little boy, Danny, to work, generally when her daycare fell through. He and I played on the patio while he taught me more Spanish. Nora, however, spoke English fluently. She served as an excellent source of information on Mexican culture when she had time to talk to me. She had attended UNAM, and was using her background in sociology to suss out the American community, profiting from newly ratified NAFTA.

With the free trade agreement, international companies swarmed into Mexico. Pattie's business skyrocketed. Nora didn't have much time to talk due to the tide of families needing homes, services, schools and hand-holding. She coordinated paperwork, agent site visits, inquiries, and appointments. Pattie's job grew with the migration of corporations to *La Capital*. She worked long hours managing the myriad details and staff. I understood her wish that I'd stop fooling around and start making myself useful. She felt my Spanish had improved sufficiently and my grasp of Mexican culture broad enough to support training me as an agent.

Although I don't recall the exact number, Pattie's relocation agents filled a room with women, both American and Mexican. Were there any male agents? If Pattie contracted with guys, they weren't memorable. At meetings, we strategized how to sew up the market before rival companies had a chance to grab much of the NAFTA share. Well-dressed and prosperous appearing, the agents exuded an image of confidence I didn't share. I doubted I'd be effective selling landlords on the idea of renting to corporations, or prospective clients on our services. I had a suitcase of business attire dragged 5000 miles from BookWork, my bookkeeping service in California. My good ol' vintage Saks Fifth Avenue label black cashmere skirt and the charcoal herringbone jacket I'd found in the dumpster outside my Sausalito office, worked in the big city.

Pattie pressured me to come onboard, to open the Cuernavaca area to International Relocation Services. Dutifully I took notes in meetings, learning what the business was all about. I attended cocktail parties with Pattie for a taste of how business was transacted between captains of industry. One thing was certain, these people could drink! I hated the cocktail parties. I didn't know how to make small talk, and I couldn't hold my liquor, a fact that never stood in the way of my consuming plenty. Damn Fernando and his stupid idea of opening a dog training service. Where was he when I needed him? Out of my element, I yearned for my comfort zone. In the corporate crowd, I felt like a kid. Unfortunately it was true—if cocktail parties signified adulthood, I was not a grown up. I didn't fit in.

The new international crowd might have been a goldmine for guard dog contracts had Fernando made himself available. He loved opportunities to chat with anyone about anything, and could sell with the best of them. And he owned a suit. But Pattie never included him in the plan. I avoided thinking about why as actively as I avoided thinking about taking up Pattie's offer to open the doors to relocation from her *quinta*, house in the country, in the State of Morelos. But as she'd said, "You've got to move."

Chapter 17

Olvidar a Todo

February, 1992

As part of the plan to move me to Tepoztlán, Pattie invited me "down" for weekends with her inner circle. Regulars included Rick, her boyfriend and head of Yamaha, David, a thirty-something Brit and the head of Barclay's Bank, Susan and husband Pete, retired from the Mexico City bureau of the CIA. Pete now operated a Latin American hostage negotiation and crime consulting service to combat the increasing violence and kidnappings taking place as, unbeknownst to me, the Mexican drug gangs coalesced into the Federation headed by the Sinaloans and eventually run by the infamous *El Chapo*.

Chapo was never invited, but other guests might include one of my favorite relocation agents, Amparo, today a partner in the firm, and any number of Texans, friends of Pattie's in town for a visit, including the late Ann Richards, a former Texas Governor.

One particular party comes back in all its humiliating detail. The usual posse attended: Pattie, Rick, David, Susan and Pete, along with their bride-to-be daughter, Jennifer, and her betrothed. Pattie had friends in town. She wanted to show them a good time and had pulled-out all the stops. The house was full, the bar stocked. Even Fernando and I had been invited.

At that time "Hacienda San Clementito" as it was called, consisted of a main house, which slept up to fourteen in six bedrooms cobbled into a three-story stone tower resembling a child's stacked block castle. Narrow hallways and staircases twisted through the upper stories, uniting bedrooms and baths.

Every uniquely appointed room looked out on a magnificent view. Some featured *muebles rusticas*, a typical style of wooden furniture where the wood is first buried for a period of time to weather and look worm eaten then fashioned into headboards, tables, wardrobes, and any manner of furniture. Other rooms brooded under the weight of Spanish colonial antiques. All displayed brightly colored textiles and *artisanía,* handmade crafts and art objects. I particularly loved the Talavera tiles hand-painted in colorful patterns and shapes adorning bathrooms and the country-style kitchen. Talavera was everywhere, in tile and flowerpots and even dishes.

I was in love with the house, from its buffed to gleaming terracotta Saltillo tile floors to the heavy dark wood-beamed ceilings. The iron grated pane-over-pane windows set into the rough finished white stucco walls enchanted me. I loved the over-stuffed grey-blue couches in the living room and the rough-hewn dining table that sat sixteen people, set with heavy, carved leather-seated chairs. Pattie's art collection hung throughout the house, and I often could be found admiring the works—a private art gallery.

Double sets of French doors invited guests to the patio, tiled in terracotta and stone, and screened with thorny vines. The eaves along the living room were deep and shaded groupings of *equipal*, pigskin, and split wood, the chairs and sofas making this a popular place to congregate. Along the northern side, the bougainvillea-covered pergola-shaded another giant table with thick hewn benches. Running down the south side, the bougainvillea created a dark green wall flowering in vermillion, red, apricot and white, separating the lawn and pool from the patio. Giant clay pots of geraniums circled the Moorish influenced fountain in the center of the courtyard as did whimsical driftwood sculptures made by the previous owner, Clemente, heir to the Clemente Jacques canned vegetable empire.

To the east, the vines traced a picture window overlooking the wild hills sloping to the verdant but hazy, volcano-ringed valley below. At night, the towns winked and twinkled, reflecting the starry sky above. It was everyone's favorite place to party.

Pattie's studio cottage on the grounds became a refuge for me when she wasn't using it. Perched on top of the five-horse stable, it overlooked the cliffs of Amatlán. Closing the triangle between the house and cottage squatted the caretaker's house, which connected to the laundry, maintenance shop, and a roofless shack used for storage. The driveway bisected the triangle to separate the servant's quarters from the *hacendado*. A six-foot adobe wall ensured guests wouldn't be troubled by the servants.

On the south side of the house, Pattie built a swimming pool that butted up nearly to the bulk-headed drop—almost an infinity pool. At the opposite end of the green expanse of neatly trimmed flower borders and lawn from the pool area, nestled a non-consecrated chapel in a stand of tall trees. This was my favorite spot on the property and later became my sanctuary from the heat, the drinking, the loneliness, and the skeletons I carried in my back pocket.

Fernando and I arrived on Saturday, so we'd missed the Friday night boozing. I assessed the group from my perch inside the chapel door for familiar faces assembled around the aqua-colored pool, talking, laughing, and popping open another Corona pulled from the cooler. That weekend the pool area was crowded and the plentiful beers chased away the hangovers. We wandered down to say hello and I grabbed my first beer of the day. Housekeeper Belen would be serving lunch soon.

Since the house was filled, and my *combi* had a bed in it, that's where we were staying. Pattie let us use her bathroom, but she was embarrassed by my old VW camper and wouldn't let us park in the main compound. Fernando, with no English language skills, wasn't unhappy about what I took as banishment. He needed a retreat when the Americans, Brits, and Canadians overwhelmed him. Luckily, Hacienda Clemente

SAINTS AND SKELETONS

Jacques' five acres sprawled over the shoulder of the hill, dropping to the irrigation ponds below a leveled field used for soccer matches. Sheltered by the lime orchards and invisible from the house, the field was our perfect get-away. We set up camp.

I'd picked up my fluency in Spanish since meeting Fernando and loved listening to the radio for both the enjoyment of the music and the practice. I'd become familiar with quite a few songs. That February my theme song was *Sopa de Caracol* and its flipside, *Fiesta*, by Banda Blanca. I'd learned the words to *Fiesta: ¡Fiesta! Fiesta! Yo quiero más fiesta: quiero divertirme, ovidar a todo*, Party! Party! I want to party more; I want to entertain myself, forget everything. It became my weekend theme song and I played it full blast from my *combi's* stereo system over and over while drunkenly salsa dancing, first with Fernando under the Saturday night moon, and finally alone.

I drank too many margaritas during our Trivial Pursuit game. I enjoyed playing on Pattie and David's team. We excelled at the literature questions and won many rounds. But Fernando didn't drink, nor could he understand much of the conversation. That evening he felt left out, bored, and not a little pissed off that I was having so much fun making a fool of myself. He dragged me out of the party and half-carried me down the uneven stairs past the tennis court and around to the soccer *cancha*. Parsley trotted ahead of us, thrilled to finally get away from the noisy party. I imagine the look on her face when I cranked up "Fiesta" and sang at the top of my lungs. I remember laughing hysterically as I twirled across the silver-illuminated turf in

Fernando's arms. Salsa dancing was sexy and easy when I was lubricated. Fernando was *muy caliente* when he danced and soon, after a dozen or so repeats, he was able to draw me into our *combi* bedroom for a hot, noisy romp. *"Fiesta, fiesta—olvidar a todo..."* all night long.

Exhausted, my head pounding, I finally sacked out with him curled around me, and Parsley snoring softly from under the bed as dawn broke over the valley,

The pungent smell of dust and dried herbs rose on the heat radiating up from the parched *cancha.* I sneezed awake, jostling Fernando as I rolled out of the VW wiping the sweat off my brow. It smelled like tequila.

Parsley was already up, keeping tabs on the architects whose house perched just below our soccer field, or *fútbol* as it's called in Mexico. She looked over her shoulder at me and twitched her tail. Something had her attention—lizards? I searched around for a good place to pee but the field lacked cover. I looked up at the house. It emanated stillness so I guessed no one was up yet, although, judging from the position of the sun, it had to be around eleven. I'd use the powder room up there.

"Buenos días, moñeca," Fernando said, from our bed.

Good morning, doll. I didn't feel much like a doll, but that was part of the appeal of Fernando. He was so sweet-talking! "Morning. My head is killing me. I'm going to the bathroom."

He sat up and dragged on his jeans. "I'll make coffee."

SAINTS AND SKELETONS

Bless him.

After a few Tylenols and plenty of coffee, I felt more or less human again. Pattie hadn't appeared yet when I went up, so I sat in the shade of the bus's canopy waiting to hear sounds of life from above. Fernando inspected the water collection system. I'd taken the tour several times and knew that the cistern and the storage area were part of a large, covered structure we called the *bodega*. Fernando was fascinated with the elaborate system. The cistern could hold a million liters of water collected through a system of gutters and troughs running from the roofs of all the buildings on the property. When the cistern was full, the overflow ran down into the three collection ponds, which were used for irrigation, or the house when we ran out. The house commandeered most of the cistern water, in fact, by the next year, we were buying *pipas,* truckloads, of water to accommodate the guests and keep the pool filled.

I was bored and ready for a shower or a swim. Although almost February and two months away from the hot season, the weather was already warming. Temperatures in Tepoztlán, even though the town perches along the cliffs at 5600 feet, never dropped like they did in Mexico City, which hung at 7000 feet above sea level. Pattie didn't heat the pool, but most of the year the sun took care of it. In February, it would be chilly water and Rick was sure to throw me in. He was a real kidder. Maybe a shower would be a better choice. But the lure of cook *Melones'*, named for her ample bosom, *huevos Mexicanos,* eggs scrambled with fresh tomato salsa, and bacon, with a frosty limeade, or better yet, a couple of Victorias, was strong enough that I tugged on my swimsuit and grabbed my towel.

I'd been in Mexico for six months. Mexico-style agreed with me. I walked more, I ate differently, and since I lost weight, wearing a bathing suit had become a pleasure rather than an embarrassment. After my wardrobe was stolen from my bus in Oaxaca, I'd bought consistently smaller sizes. I flaunted my new figure in tight jeans, short shorts, and skirts, and of course in my bathing suit without a cover up. Andy Warhol said everybody gets their fifteen minutes of fame—well, I take that to mean everybody gets their fifteen minutes of thin!

I popped onto the patio to find breakfast still in progress and the early birds already stretched out on lounges by the pool—Pattie, Rick, and all the people whose rooms faced north. The south side guests glared at me, yawning.

"What were you doing in the field all night?" Susan asked.

Her daughter, Jennifer, added, "If I ever hear *Fiesta* again I'll scream."

"I bet your head is hurting," her boyfriend commiserated. He looked a bit haggard.

Fernando got the gist of it and grinned. He fired off some explanation in Spanish too rapid for my sluggish brain to comprehend; everyone laughed. He looked rather pleased with himself. The boys at the table eyed him with a new respect. Ah, they all had heard us in the *combi*. Well, bully for them. I felt the heat rising up my neck and shrugged. "I'm going to the pool." I grabbed a heaping serving of the steaming eggs Melones had just clunked onto the table then wiggled off across the patio in my flip-flops, balancing my plate, a glass of limeade and another cup of coffee, knowing that Fer and his new friends watched every sway.

"Good afternoon, Ana, how'd you sleep?" Pattie asked, no hint of irony in her voice.

Good. She and Rick were doing their own dance and didn't hear mine. Their bungalow didn't have windows on the south stable-facing side.

"Nothing like sleeping in a field under the stars." I put down my plate, dragged a chair off the lawn into the group, sat down, then dug into my breakfast.

Rick, who was well tanned, the effects of demonstrating his products—Waverunners—hauled himself off his lounge to fish in the cooler. He popped two Coronitas and held one out to me. "You look like you could use this."

"Thanks, Rick. I shouldn't try to keep up with you guys. You're the pros." I swilled back half of the Coronita, the 7-ounce cousin to a regular Corona. It tasted like maybe I'd survive the day. I slathered on some of Pattie's sunscreen.

I blotted sweat from my face. It didn't taste of tequila anymore, but I was beginning to think I'd be more popular if I went to the bungalow for a shower. I got up. Rick sprang from his lounge. Before I could react, I was cannon balling into the pool. I guessed I wouldn't need that shower after all.

Melones cleared the breakfast dishes.

Eventually Fernando joined us, sleepy eyed, and adorable in his faded Hawaiian baggies, Parsley in tow. I knew it must be near lunchtime because he was most likely to show up where Pattie was if food was involved. Fernando feared her. I remained blind to his failings, but Pattie, Rick, my cousin Marty, Susan—everybody—saw Fer for what he was: Ana's Mexican gigolo. I shoved over to make room for him on my lounge.

In hindsight, I clearly see that Fer gave me ample warning that he detested being a kept man, yet the temptation to take all that was offered was too great and the task ahead—growing up—daunting. He wanted to stand on his own two feet, but on his terms, not those of his family. He had completed two years of a veterinarian program at UNAM and nurtured a deep love of animals, part of the attraction for me, a confirmed animal lover. Parsley loved him. I never quite got the full story as to why he left university, more than it had something to do with the woman he married. According to Fer, his Claudia was an over-spending social climber, and she and their families pushed Fernando into the corporate world of pharmaceutical sales—he was a natural salesman—and it paid well. He hated the job. He hated the expensive apartment in chic del Valle, the suits, the game; he bolted when his wife talked about babies. That's when he moved to Cancún and worked in a hotel. I can only imagine what he did there, but he jumped at the chance to move to Germany with his fräulein.

Fernando had only returned from 'cold' Germany a month or so before we met. He'd left his cold climate clothes behind and arrived at his mother's house with moderate fluency in German and what was on his back. But the closet in his old bedroom still contained all his suits from his corporate years. And the tassel loafers.

His mother, his aunt, the mother of Mexico's beloved singer Lucero, and older brothers pressured him to go back to the corporate world. Uncle Beto encouraged his entrepreneurial leanings. I urged him to spend his time with me.

I'd made it too easy for him, opening my purse for everything in exchange for his chauffeuring, protection, and guidance through the language and culture. He also played my arm candy and hot lover. By this time, we'd started talking about making our affair permanent, but I knew deep down, I'd be going home to start my own (second) career. Although I couldn't admit it to myself, I dangled Fernando on an emotional/financial string—I couldn't let him go. He was my conduit to *"olvidar a todo"*.

Chapter 18

Ruta Maya

February 1992

My six-month visa had expired on the 24th of January. I needed to leave Mexico for at least a week before returning on a new visa. The next trip was overdue, and while Fernando was itching to get going on his dog training project, the promise of adventure was an irresistible lure. Fernando and I both swallowed that baited hook. Back at Pattie's, we planned our next trip. Even Parsley perked up her ears at the mention of the *combi* and shot long looks toward the door.

This time we'd make my pilgrimage to Honduras to visit the now-designated UNESCO site, Copán. A ruin we had visited together north of Cuernavaca, Xochicalco, included a ball court built to the exact specifications of that in Copán, which had been constructed centuries earlier. I couldn't wait to see the original. After all, I'd come south to Mexico for this pilgrimage. Hopefully we'd cross the border before anyone noticed my visa had expired.

In the early eighties, I had taken a class at College of Marin in past life regression where I'd been introduced to a Mayan stone carver, presumably myself in another lifetime. That sculptor chipped his way under my skin. I took up the study of ancient Mesoamerica and eventually started writing a novel, *Stonecarver,* about him and his world. I named him Eb Zotz after the day he was born, a common practice in the Mayan region. For years Eb Zotz hovered on the periphery of my sight, pointing the way, while I dreamed of making the trek to see his birthplace.

The trip would take days of driving, but we'd stop to see the sights, camping along the way to Punta Gorda, Belize, where we'd catch the ferry to cross the Gulf of Honduras to Puerto Cortéz and drive to the ruin. We'd be gone for at least a month. The only date we needed to keep was the equinox at Chichén Itzá. No way I was missing the plumed serpent *Kukulkan* slithering down the great pyramid late in the afternoon on March 21st. We had plenty of time. This was a dream come true. This was life as it should be: love, time, money, and adventure.

On February 16th, as the moon grew almost full, that bothersome little thought in the back of my mind from the night of *Fiesta* had become exigent. It was official —I'd missed my period. Nah, just stress and excitement for the coming trip, wasn't it? That day, in preparation of taking off to Honduras, as I passed through Zona Rosa to return books to the free American Benjamin

Franklin Library on Liverpool Street, I ducked into the pharmacy at the Insurgentes metro station for a home pregnancy test. Later, I confirmed the bad news. I carried Fernando's child.

Dread paralyzed me. I wasn't ready to be a mother. Besides that, I might be too old to safely bring a child into the world. Babies weren't part of my plan. I was sure to suffer debilitating morning sickness. I'd gain weight. Would Fernando stick around if I got fat? We were about ready to leave for Honduras. How would this affect our trip?

Fernando's first reaction was to terminate—another reason for those Sunday confessions? I wrote, *F and I went to Naucalpan to the OB/GYN hospital he knows, where his ex-wife, Claudia, had her five abortions. Cost me fifty thousand pesos to talk to the doctor. There were two; the younger was a naco, and the office was dirty. His examination table was covered in a dirty cloth and his manner was too eager.* I wouldn't ever go back, I said as we ran out of the clinic and proceeded to get lost in dangerous Naucalpan, only to be stopped by the cops. *¡Siempre la mordita!* We didn't pay "the little bite" but got away and drove to colonia Del Valle to the Toshiba repair to drop off my computer for servicing, then filled the combi's tank before finding the ABC lab to drop off my urine sample. I noted, *We're both dragging our feet and very unsure about this baby.* We agreed we'd keep the news quiet until we figured out what we would do.

While we finalized our sorting, stocking, and packing of the combi, Fer and I had conversations about the pregnancy and our futures. At times he strutted around like a proud *gallina* while formulating a plan to get married, move out from his mother's, and find a place with me where we would launch his dog training business, and have the baby. Oh, and live happily ever after. Now my future foretold both Eb Zotz and a mini-Fernando. I wasn't so sure about all of this—the money would run out and I couldn't imagine living in Mexico "on the economy"—but Fer was so cute, and what a lover! We had two months to hash out a real plan. Who was I kidding. I was forty-one and hadn't wanted kids before. Why would I now?

The week was fraught with anxiety, arguments, and accusations.

"You didn't check the oil," I nagged.

"You haven't bought it."

"Are you ever going to get the trunk out of the *bodega*?"

"I can't go away, I need to get my *negocio started.*"

"You promised! What are we going to do about this problem?"

"You don't even want it. Don't you love me?" he asked.

"Don't you love me?" I asked.

But somehow we managed to pack up on Fernando's thirty-third birthday—February 22nd. Mexico City was cold, gray, and raining. Parsley, agitated from all the packing and her illness, really showed her age. I worried about putting her in the bus for an extended trip. We were due to leave for Veracruz, but Fer didn't want to spend his birthday driving. Pattie, Rick, and friend Jennifer had spent the day drinking beer. I finally joined them. Immediately Fernando bitched to leave. What he really wanted was to go home and get stoned. At five, we headed north to Tlalnepantla to pick up his luggage., e.g. his stash. I might have been the queen of picking Mr. Wrong, but I'd never considered living with an alcoholic or drug abuser. Traveling was one thing—he made it possible for me to see and do things I'd never enjoy on my own, but why was I thinking of having a baby with him? At the time, I called it love.

We hit the free road toward Tlascala, stopping once to eat some lousy *tacos al pastor* at a roadside dive. I was cranky, tired from the pregnancy, paranoid we'd be stopped and be arrested for entering the country illegally, adding to the stress of the trip. We drove mostly in silence. I slept fitfully, waking up as we started the descent through the Veracruz's capital, Xalapa. We arrived in the port of Veracruz at three in the morning then spent the rest of the night in Hotel San Martín. The same hotel, in the same room, as our first trip while escaping Sam. Now I wondered if I'd made a huge mistake, even as I tried to convince Fernando we should keep the baby during a fit of maternal instinct. Panic—*is it my last chance?*

My memories of the stop in Veracruz are sepia-toned. I remember Veracruz as overcast, softly gray—as though seeing it through an opaque lens. We woke up late and made love. I'd noticed there was *a certain new feeling to love making with the baby.* At mid-day we left the hotel for brother Victor's and wife Ana's house to greet the entire family, but Fernando immediately got lost. We bickered, circling the district where he thought his brother lived until I convinced him to call. I talked with Pilar, another sister-in-law, about her pregnancy, and played with his little nieces. Fernando doted on his *sobrinas*, something I found charming. When we went to the market for ice and food, we showered them with sweets.

As always, the family greeted us warmly, but I knew I was a tolerated guest, not a welcome one. Blanca, his mother, had always been kind to me, going so far as to warn me about what a scoundrel her kid was, but I never believed her, and never quite understood her anyway. Blanca, the grandmother, wasn't as kind to me because she was convinced I was leading her darling grandson astray. His brothers, Diegito and Victor, nicknamed Toto, took a more pitying attitude as if they had the secret information—the poor deluded *gringa* dreaming she'd make a life with Fernando—but they always acted pleasantly toward me. Not so with Fernando. They loved telling him how he was ruining his life and needed to get busy. I remember hearing talk of marriage and wives and family, and what was he doing running around with foreigners and not taking care of his responsibilities. I took it to be hypothetical: they didn't accept Fernando's non-traditional life choices. If they only knew we were in the family way and thinking about marriage. In hindsight, I'm almost laughing out loud—the joke was on me.

Victor's and Ana's place was an apartment or townhouse constructed of cement block and re-bar in a new development on the flats in suburban Veracruz City. The area was devoid of trees and, while new, looked bleak and shabby like tenement housing.

Everything appeared shadowed in muted shades of gray: the buildings, the sandy ground, the overcast sky and the murky gray-green Gulf of Mexico. I recall the requisite crucifix over the table and ubiquitous Maria serenely watching us, but not much else. Aluminum and Formica dinette. Brown upholstered sofa. We slept in the combi in the parking lot.

Parsley refused to eat. She had trouble walking. I was anxious, not made easier by the fact I felt Fernando and I moving apart. He hid it well around his family, masked by a display of loving attention.

On February 24th we celebrated the Leon Torrens family reunion at the shore. I'd gotten up too late to take a shower at Toto's before everyone left for the beach, then the *combi* wouldn't start. Finally we got going and passed several hours on a boring beach, but what a cheerful, loving bunch—at least for the day. I struck fashion poses with Carla, Chareni, and Fabiola. They loved having their pictures taken. They and Fernando radiate joy in the photos. I was charmed, led by tiny hands to inspect a snail shell or piece of oil crusted driftwood. Their seven-, five-, and four-year old Spanish I could understand—if they spoke slowly. I connected with the youngest of Blanca's siblings, Uncle Beto, his wife Pilar, and little Chareni. I viewed Beto as a potential resource for information about Fernando. He certainly understood his nephew and gave the impression he supported Fernando's path. Another bonus was, he spoke a bit of English.

Although the day looked cold in the photos, Veracruz is in the tropics and our picnic and play on the beach was enjoyable. The Leon Torrens family

SAINTS AND SKELETONS

reminded me of my family, everyone having fun, talking, eating, getting along, but with a dangerous current running below the good will. I understood more Spanish—I'd had seven months in country and four of them with Fernando—but I still relied on intuition for understanding. I could tell Blanca Torrens and her clan were pissed off at youngest born Fernando. I wanted to ask what was so terrible about his lifestyle? Back at the house the dust-up erupted into accusations, denials, and angry shouting with Fernando at its center.

I understood plenty of the family's hot words, but call it denial, I remained oblivious to the underlying issue: his ex-wife. No one bothered to tell me. I could have solved the Leon family's problem right there by leaving Fernando and driving away, but instead I excused myself, fleeing to my bus with Parsley shortly before Fernando stormed out of the house. I felt alone and awash in despair.

At some point, Fer knocked on the door. I let him in. We headed out to Villahermosa. I can't remember saying goodbye to his family.

Ruta 180 skirted the Gulf of Mexico at times on the edge of the salt marshes, but more often, inland. The occasional views of the Gulf revealed kelp-colored water with ghostly outlines of oil platforms on the far horizon. I picture the two-day drive as colorless and overcast like my black and white photos. Fernando put on a good face, talking incessantly about his usual topics: politics, the economy, his dream of making a success and creating a prosperous life for himself—and me, of course. I knew the visit with his family had unsettled him although he waved it off. I didn't have the energy to draw him out. I felt tired, and deep conversations sapped my energy because we had to stop to search for words so often.

"*Fer, ¿porque sientas malo? ¿Qué pasó con tu familia?*" (Fer, what's the matter? What happened with your family?)

"*Dijieron que estoy perdiendo tiempo. Tengo responsibilidades. Debo que regresar al trabajo. Estan enojados que no cuido la niña ni la ex-esposa. No quieren prestarme ningun centavo más ni pagar mis errores. Me proponían—*"

The family accused him of wasting time when he should be going back to work, taking responsibility for his daughter and his wife. Blanca cut him off: no more cleaning up his messes.

"*—¿Que quiere decir 'proponian?*" What does *proponían* mean?

"*Que necesito considerar mudanza a Veracruz. Pude trabajar con la familia.*"

"*¿Mudanza a Veracruz?*" I repeated. "I don't understand. Let me look it up in my dictionary. How do you spell it?

" *M-U-D-A-N-Z-A*"

I flipped through the pages searching for the word. "*Esperame.* Ah, *aqui es: Mudanza*—Move? Leave *el D.F.?*" My voice rose as my stomach rolled.

"No *mi amor*, the family wants me to come to Veracruz. Mom is going to move to be closer to my brother. She said she can't help me anymore."

"Okay, so what does *acercar* mean? How do you

spell it?"

By the fifth word, we were both tired. We rode in silence, the grey-green coast slipping past the windows with the uneasy thoughts circling my mind. Fernando's wife? He claimed to be divorced. Why would she be an issue? I knew about the daughter with his long ago girlfriend and pestered him regularly to go visit her. Blanca was helping them? Fernando better do what his mother said. I certainly wasn't going to get any help from her.

The sign for the turnoff to Catemaco, the town of the *brujas,* witches, loomed and I brightened. "Let's go!"

I'd heard about the annual convention and wanted to see it for myself. My curiosity for Mexico's *brujos* and *brujas,* fortune tellers, and healers had grown with my increased fluency in Spanish and visits to the local markets. I always found the aisle devoted to strange healing herbs and minerals mixed in with Tarot readers, and suspicious looking bottles and jars filled with mysterious insects or fetuses or unidentifiable elixirs. I wanted to know all about this thriving subculture.

"The convention is on the first Friday every March. That's only eleven days away. Should we stay?"

We have a long drive to Copán. If you expect to be back to Chichén Itzá by the 21st, we can't stay."

It was over 300 miles from Veracruz to Villahermosa in the State of Tabasco on Ruta 180 Libre. In my slow VW camper on two-lane highways, the drive took hours. We'd passed through Covarrubias, a town with nothing memorable beyond its name, which offered good practice for trilling the double *r,* Jaltipán,

Minititlán, and soon Coatzacoalcos choking in the smoke from the huge PEMEX refinery, which we skirted as the highway jogged 90 degrees to avoid crashing through its gates as it descended the Coatza Bridge. I didn't realize at the time, the city resembling a rundown version of any oil city, but Coatzacoalcos in *Nahuatl* means *the place where the snake hides*. It was an apt name for the location *Quetzalcoatl*, the plumed serpent of Mexican lore, departed to the sea in approximately 1000 C.E. after promising to return and hence, unlocking the door to invaders arriving by ship. Hernán Cortez would sail through that portal in 1519 and destroy the Aztec empire.

I woke up at the toll plaza for the bridge at Alvarado. A slate-colored bay spread west. We were nearing San Andreas Tuxtla, the beginning of the official oil region. Although we traveled south on the free road, toll bridges not included, I saw prosperity in the region through shiny new pickups, luxury Suburbans, sedans, and oil tankers. The buildings we passed looked maintained. The houses, many large, showed signs of additions and expansion.

"We're almost at the big PEMEX headquarters and *refinería*."

"What's that word? How do you spell it?"

The blush was off our communications; my language limitations had worn thin—for both of us. True, my Spanish was more and more fluid, if not exactly correct, and he remained tolerant, remembering how dreadful it was for him in Germany. Regardless, to avoid the struggle, I lapsed back into a half-sleep as we turned inland again.

SAINTS AND SKELETONS

We arrived in Villahermosa around ten p.m., spending the next two hours circling, looking for a nonexistent trailer park. We ended up at one of those *expensive and smelly motels out of town—Costa del Sol.* Costa de mosquitoes would have been a more apt name. The maids jabbered outside our window until I went out and told them to shut up. But the drive through the State of Veracruz was pretty, despite the gray skies.

I don't think the sun shone until we crossed the arching drawbridge across Rio Grijalves into Villahermosa the next morning. Golden rays beamed into the city, illuminating it into Cíbola—one of the seven cities of gold the Spanish explorers sought. Or maybe it looked so shiny because the rest of the Gulf coast journey had been so dull. Although I was still shooting in black and white, the abundance of trees, exuberant vines, and flowers color my memories. In Villahermosa, my Ruta Maya took on new excitement. We began by searching out a *RED* to get some cash. Fernando had to stop in the street to repair the bus and immediately we were hassled by the cops. Once he wriggled out of whatever the problem was, we continued toward Parque-Museo La Venta. We had giant basalt heads to greet.

I hated leaving Parsley in the *combi* while we went to the museum. I opened windows, made sure the solar powered exhaust fan spun in the ceiling, and the cooling fan was turned on. It was before nine but already warming up. The heat and worry had me feeling a bit queasy. We said goodbye and locked her in. The museum was an outdoor park, tree shaded and lush, boasting over 400 kinds of flora and fauna, with sandy paths meandering through. Each bend revealed a new marvel of sculpted antiquity: altars, stela, monoliths, and the colossal Olmec heads carved between 1300-200 B.C.E, found at a site called La Venta in the '40s.

Between the artifacts, crocodiles, and the sightings of coatimundi cavorting in the trees, I felt better. *We always have a close time when our minds are stimulated,* I observed in my diary. Or did puking behind a bush help? Fernando treated me kindly, teaching me the term for morning sickness: *nauseas del embarazo.* I had plenty of mornings to look it up in the dictionary, but I was no closer to making a plan. We flipped and flopped, fish out of the stream, when it came to choosing a course of action.

We packed up and moved out as soon as we finished at the park, crossing both the Rios Grijalva and Usumacinta as we continued south. Parsley was happy to see us. She liked traveling as the cabin of the bus cooled down with the rush of wind streaming through the windows. I didn't have air conditioning, but I don't recall ever needing it, at least not when the *combi* was moving. We stopped beyond the Palenque turnoff for lunch at a truck stop. Fer enjoyed talking to the truckers while I fed the dog and suffered diarrhea.

Our next stop was a small archaeological site in Campeche, Becán, the place of the serpent. I'd stopped there with Sam on the way home from Belize in the '80s and had been impressed with its rough but excavated appearance and lack of policing. We set up for the night. Parsley wasn't feeling well.

SAINTS AND SKELETONS

In the very early morning we were awakened by workers, but we slept in and ate a leisurely breakfast before wandering into the ruin. Not much had changed in the five or six years since I'd visited, except now the Briseno Hernandez family lived at the site as caretakers. That meant for a few pesos we were able to set up camp within the ruin and let Parsley out while we explored every niche and cranny with experts: the four Briseno children. They, and an archaeology student, showed us every wonder of Becan, the unusual carvings, wooden beams, secret passages, blood stained altars (or so they said), the plazas and houses, and the archaeologists' slag heap. I smuggled home painted pot shards and a carved clay snake head, probably a piece of a footed bowl, from that discard pile.

We may have invited the student to dinner that night, I can't recall. I do remember, to maintain harmony, Fernando and I avoided touchy subjects. After dinner, we read. I was nearing the end of Pillars of the Earth. The jungle and the antiquity surrounding us worked magic. The day had been relatively cool and both Parsley and I felt better. Energetic even. Under the last quarter of the waning moon, the ruin woke up with the calls of night birds and rustles in the underbrush. Wasn't that when the priests walked the stones, and the shadows in the plaza turned to people talking, laughing, eating, praying after the day's toil? It was eerily beautiful in the silent jungle as the magic rose, lifting the antiquity of humanity to our awareness. It was also a little frightening. I heard the yowl of a jaguar.

The experience of primal Becan and exuberant children momentarily sparked joy back to our relationship. We breakfasted and had many hugs and kisses with the kids before leaving. Fer liked kids and got on well with them. I'd observed him playing with Julio and Lisbet, even toddler Jose, and realized he'd be great with a child. He was dropping suggestions about keeping the baby. Maybe I'd reevaluate the pregnancy plan. Again.

We sang along with Pink Floyd, Fernando's famous cousin, singer Lucero, and the mariachi songs only he knew the words to playing on the tape deck, as we made the last hop through the jungle to the border with Belize. The two-lane highway ran straight much of the way, dipping down into depressions bordered by seasonal swamps called *bajos,* Fernando volunteered, then climbing up small rises. In places, the highway was built on causeways cutting through densely vegetated dry scrub. It wasn't lush or jungle green, but patchy with golden grasses and groves of palmettos. The ground was the white of limestone; here and there horizontal outcroppings jutted up through the forest. The only water was the muck in a *bajo,* often nothing more than a puddle pierced by black tree trunks stark against the cerulean sky. On the rises, we saw other hillocks dotting this arid forest.

"Look at the shape of that hill, Fer. It's kind of rectangular."

"They aren't hills, they're temples."

"How would you know? They have trees all over them."

"Quintana Roo was densely populated and no one

has enough money to excavate all the ruins."

Well, that sounded plausible. I tended to believe what Fer told me. My texts and teachers hadn't specifically said this, but once Fernando pointed it out, I started counting the odd-shaped hills. I also spotted places with dark vegetated hummocks rising from light colored lower ground set out in moderately ordered rows. Ancient raised bed farms! I was stoked. I'd studied anthropology and archeology for this. When we stopped to stretch and shop for ice and water in Chetumal I grabbed my copy of *The Ancient Maya 4th edition* from the storage trunk on the roof. Later that night I read up on the Southern Mexico and Belize Maya. Fer showered under a hose in a parking lot. Too self-conscious to shower in public, I stayed grimy.

We went to the Guatemalan consulate to get our visas for the stop in Tikal and talked to the clerk for some time. It wasn't busy, but for some reason lost to memory, we had to pay a fifty peso *multa,* fine, and had a big hassle, to cross the border. My diary note: *shitty Mexicans.*

Chapter 19

Reggae and English

February 27-March 4, 1992

It was just about dark when we finally entered Belize on February 27th. No hassle on that side. I hadn't realized how much I missed English until we crossed. The sounds of my own language buoyed me. What a difference it made to fully understand what was going on around me. We had driven into *my* territory and I took charge. Finally. I was happy to stop being dependent on Fernando; for a short time I'd been an independent, adventurous woman whose wings were clipped, and I hadn't even known it. I felt like myself again. Now I got to decide where we went and what we ate, what we saw and where we slept. Of course, I'd always had the final say, I had the money, but I tried not to hold that over him. I said we'd continue on to Corozal Town and Hotel Caribbean, where I'd read there was a trailer park.

SAINTS AND SKELETONS

Unfortunately it was behind a restaurant and hardly qualified as a trailer park. The bathroom was dirty and the shower ran cold. I was too tired to care, and it only cost eight Belizean dollars a night, about four dollars. I crashed early and slept late.

In the morning we went to the bank to change pesos into Belizean dollars. The Bank of Belize was jammed with people from the sugarcane industry, so we tried Atlantic Bank also in Corozal. Flush with the currency we chugged south toward Belize City where we found our way to Mom's Triangle and *I ate horrible conch. Rubbery. Old fish taste. Puke.*

The plan was to visit Coxcomb Wildlife Preserve and Jaguar Sanctuary after lunch. I'd met a wombat in Australia, now I wanted to see a jaguar in the wilds of Belize. We parked downtown to buy camping supplies in the crowded center. The city, perched at the edge of the Caribbean on a spit of swampy land surrounded by mangroves, appeared to be the antithesis of orderly Chetumal. And all that English and Garifuna and Caribbean patois! Fernando couldn't understand anything except the snatches of reggae spilling from stores and restaurants. He looked visibly uncomfortable as I relaxed and allowed the bustle to imbue me with energy. Although he nagged to hurry us through the shopping, I managed to meet and converse with several people, learning that I couldn't take Parsley into Coxcomb.

Instead of seeing a jaguar in the jungle, we found JB's Roadhouse. Mike, the owner, was a friendly, garrulous type. He introduced me to other travelers, and a guy named McNutt, an archaeologist who talked me out of going to Caracol. Fernando held his own court with the few Spanish speakers and all the potheads. As it got late, people started to leave and Mike sent us out behind the Roadhouse on the edge of Monkey Bay Wildlife Preserve to park for the night. No monkeys, no jaguars, and not much else there in early 1992 beyond the owner's vision of something great. I bathed in the Sibun River. I needed it.

After a hearty breakfast and a walk, we skedaddled late-morning, March 1st, to head out the Western Highway en route to Punta Gorda via Belmopan, Belize's capitol, and the turn-off to the scenic Hummingbird Highway. PG was the southernmost city in Belize, and the terminus for the ferry to Honduras, our final destination.

A late winter sun shone with low-beam intensity across the scrubby jungle landscape as it rose toward its zenith. We passed small farms, swaths of grassy savanna, and stands of towering jungle forest, remnants of primordial times. The highway slowly rose from the swampy sea with the sun; by lunchtime we'd arrived in La Democracia near the western edge of the Belize District and about halfway to Belmopan in the Cayo District. We stopped to eat in a typical roadside restaurant, a one-story clapboard and cement building abutted by an open, thatched porch crammed with rusty, paint-chipped tables, many populated with loose-limbed men and fleshy women colorfully dressed and joyfully eating, chatting, and laughing. I found Belizeans a happy people, be they the stocky Garifuna descendants of Caribbean Islanders and African slaves, petite Mayans, fair-skinned British decedents, Central

Americans, and the multicultural flotsam washed up from distant shores—geologists, archaeologists, hikers, divers, sailors, and tourists. People in Belize loved to socialize, and because it was a warm Sunday, the neighborhood had turned out for good food and Punta rock blasting from the jukebox.

By the interior door, a swarm of skinny kids, barefoot and sprouting out of their clothes, pawed through a leaking Coca-Cola cooler for favorite soda flavors. At the edge of the stony parking lot, an aproned chef in an iconic white hat that set off his glowing blue-black skin, tended the smoking grill. The enticing aroma of charring meats and fish made my mouth water.

Drifted into food heaven, I dug into my beans and rice with a side of potato salad, and a plate of grilled spiny lobsters. After all, we were only 49.5 kilometers from Belize City so the lobster was fresh.

Fernando ate chicken. Both meals tasted delicious, made more so by the friendly staff and patrons. That's how we learned about the Belize Zoo, then a mere nine years old, built on twenty-nine acres of pristine jungle land. They had a jaguar. I wanted to go. Fernando's dream had been to become a vet. He loved animals and was all for a zoo visit.

We said goodbye to our new friends, loaded Parsley back into the bus then followed directions to the rustic turnoff to the zoo. The place looked homespun with hand-lettered signs, bamboo shacks, and enclosures, but our guides were proud to be a part of something so exceptional in their country. They devoted the next couple of hours to making us welcome and informed.

No one else visited that afternoon. We saw the toucans, met Tyra, a bush dog, petted a coatimundi, and Danto the tapir. The collection of rescued and preserved species was smaller then, but I saw a jaguar and a jabiru stork. Fernando was in his element as I translated. Thirty-two years later, I still think of my experience at the Belize Zoo. Friendly, informative, somewhat wild!

The sun had dipped by the time we finished our visit and drove the remainder of the distance to Belmopan. While Belize wasn't reputed to be dangerous, we agreed the lonely jungle highway would not be a good place to travel after dark, and looked for somewhere to stay.

"Ana, is there a trailer park?"

I opened my guidebook. Belmopan barely warranted a page. No trailer parks were listed. "Not that I can find."

"Do you want to keep driving?" Fer asked.

I wasn't about to go knocking on doors to rent a spot in somebody's yard as we'd done in Zipolite. "Not really. We could go on to Dangriga, but hotels were hard to find three years ago, except for the Stann Creek Inn. Too expensive and we'd never sneak in Parsley."

We circled Belmopan's downtown area on Ring Road and found a community of gray, official looking buildings completely lacking in charm or character. No wonder. In 1970, the capitol had been moved from Belize City to Belmopan, fifty miles inland, presumably for hurricane protection. Nothing was more than twenty-one years old and, except for two blocks of government buildings built to resemble Mayan architecture, the architecture looked boxy and modern

SAINTS AND SKELETONS

The town appeared semi-inhabited. We saw few people and few businesses. I was sorry to have missed the Monday, Wednesday, Friday tours of the archaeology vaults at the Belize Archaeology Department, but we'd be off before it opened in the morning. I checked my guide. It indicated there were three hotels and three restaurants.

"Here's the convention center hotel." I pointed to a place across from the bus station.

"No."

"The guide says there are two more on Half Moon Avenue."

"Maybe we should camp in the jungle," Fernando said. "It's a long drive tomorrow. We should get an early start."

"Turn. Turn here!" I shouted, shaking my hand toward the turn. I'd seen a sign for the Bull Frog Hotel. The book said it was cheap and had a good restaurant. Fernando turned left onto Half Moon Avenue.

"Let's try this one," I said, as we entered a neighborhood of palms, green patchy lawns, and one-story cinderblock homes on lots encircled with low chain link fences. The tallest building, the Bull Frog Hotel, loomed three stories over the neighborhood. It resembled a truncated pyramid with cubbyhole rooms recessed from the face of the building and outlined in orange like a pyramid base of orange boxes stacked upon each other. Boring architecture striving to be brave and exciting. Sort of how I was feeling. It was only twelve dollars, had shiny red tiled floors, and it was safe to park on the street.

We asked for a ground floor room for Parsley's

access and ate at the Bull Frog Restaurant. The food was good but nothing stood out about Belmopan. It was like how Fer and I were getting along—kind of blah, but I felt grateful we weren't antagonistic toward each other. The zoo had been a brilliant detour, renewing us both. By then I'd started feeling puffy and tired all the time. I didn't have the energy to add discord to my day. In hindsight, it was a kind of truce. Fer and I found common ground in sightseeing, and the forward momentum of travel gave us the illusion of connection and deepening relationship, at least for a while.

On the 2nd, we headed south on the Hummingbird Highway. Belize is a tiny ribbon of jungle clinging to the edge of the Northern American continent between mountains and sea. From northern to southern border it's only 170 miles, but we took our time, stopping in the tiny Garifuna village of Seine Bight for the night and camping on the beach. We stopped again the next day in seaside Placencia for traditional *salbute*, fried tortillas with shredded chicken, pickled cabbage, and tropical salsa for lunch. Fernando felt right at home with tortillas and salsa.

Back on the two-lane highway, we dipped and rose between swampy lowlands and forested hills; we wound around cornfields, farmsteads, and tiny hamlets dotted across flat valleys; and twisted through the dense jungle that hadn't been cleared. We forded a river at one crossing, Fernando driving slowly as I waded, testing the depth, but most of the small rivers—they were more like creeks—were bridged.

Just like the ancient Maya huts depicted in my textbooks, the homes were stone and thatch built with high peaked roofs, probably to shed rainwater. Where we saw fencing, farmers had constructed it with irregular lengths of tree branches. The further south we went, the more banana groves we saw.

Few northbound vehicles passed us, and we didn't overtake anyone driving in our direction once the turn-off to Dangriga disappeared behind us. Had the highway not been paved, we might have been the first 20th century travelers. The handful of people we waved to herded animals, rode horses, or hung laundry. They wore light-colored, loose-fitting clothing and sandals and resembled the agrarian peoples we'd encountered in southern Mexico. These people were taller and more angular than those same round-faced, diminutive Yucatecan Mayans. I wanted to stop, but the wary expressions on the men's faces told me this population wasn't interested in tourists. I examined the jungle and the turn-offs to ruins instead.

Fernando requested a continuous stream of reggae on the tape deck—appropriate Caribbean travel music. We both loved Jimmy Cliff's *The Harder They Come* and we sang along, belting out *"You can get it if you really want... you must try, try and try ..."*

The positive message, *try hard enough and you'll succeed*, spoke to us. Unfortunately, Fernando and I had different measures of success. We should have spent a little more time listening to the other songs' lyrics, like "Sitting here in limbo..." because that's what it was— a kind of limbo. I was pregnant knowing I'd terminate; I clung to my disintegrating relationship, knowing I'd go home anyway; Fernando knew he was avoiding the inevitable leap into adult responsibility of job and family. Both of us were aware that soon the money and fun would run out. But with true denial, I felt certain we'd make it; I'd learn everything I needed to write my book; Fernando would make a success of his dog training business, and we would solve our problems and end up together. I don't know what he thought, but he enjoyed learning the lyrics to the songs he liked and was quick to pick up English. Neither of us could carry a tune. I pity anyone who heard us braying.

We arrived in Punta Gorda in time for an early dinner. Our weather-beaten hotel overlooked the wharf. It sported cheerful red gingham curtains in the restaurant windows. It was actually a converted home, which a family owned and operated. We stayed two nights, during which time I made the acquaintance of the proprietress, a large, warm woman of African descent who spoke in the lilting patois of the Kriol English. Oh, yes, she cooked a mean conch stew.

Fernando and I were the only guests and our host welcomed Parsley, too. During the day of March 4th we explored the town, a fishing village with low wooden buildings fading from turquoise to blue grey in the tropical sun and a clutch of kids waving to us from the windows. We stopped in at the ferry office, discovering the ferry was for passengers only—no vehicles and no pets.

"How did you miss that, Anita?" Fernando snapped, his anger sharp. "What do you want to do?"

Mortified, I double-checked my information. Nowhere did it say the boat was a passenger ferry. I'd even telephoned Triple-A to make sure it was a car ferry before leaving the US. Had it stopped carrying vehicles in eight months? I tried to explain in my still rudimentary Spanish and ended up apologizing.

"I'm sorry, Fer. I tried to have accurate information."

"Maybe we can pay the hotel to take care of the *combi* and get to Copan by bus."

"But we can't take Parsley."

"Why not? They take goats, pigs, and chickens on Central American busses," Fernando said with a little sneer.

"They told us dogs aren't allowed on the ferry. I couldn't leave Parsley anywhere. Anyway, this is Belize. We might not have a *combi* to come back to," I snapped at him then took a breath to calm down. Why was he so interested in going to Honduras? I was the one who wanted to see Copan.

"Let's have dinner and we'll head north tomorrow. We can go to Tikal," I compromised.

I wasn't in a hurry to return to Mexico. I wanted to get back into that magical state of blissful love Fernando and I had shared traveling during the fall. And we had reservations in a week at Chaa Creek Cabins in the northwestern part of Belize, where I was going to take a workshop in Mayan medicinal herb identification and usage. Maybe I'd find herbs to turn us back into the adoring lovers I'd fallen for.

Chapter 20

Danger

March 5-8, 1992

The ruins of Lubaantun rise out of the jungle above the village of San Pedro Columbia. On March 5th, 1992, the human population was thin and the forest thick with vegetation, birds, and insects. Flowers brightened dense pockets of green where the brilliant shafts of sunlight struggled to penetrate.

As usual, we breakfasted and checked out of the PG inn at a leisurely pace. We'd argued again, about what I don't recall specifically, but our fighting continued into the afternoon as we chugged north on the Southern Highway, the only road back to "civilization" as Fernando had begun to call Mexico. The distance to our turnoff at a place called Dump was about thirty minutes away from Punta Gorda. I was too busy fighting to notice if it was a village or actually a dump.

Somehow the day had warped into later afternoon

by the time we arrived at the entrance to the ruin, a cloud of dust billowing behind us. We were met by a middle-aged man dressed in the typical white shirt and loose trousers of Belizean jungle folk. His close-cropped black hair and lively obsidian eyes gleamed in the sunlight, warming his wide grin. I guessed, by his diminutive stature and broad, sloping forehead, he hailed from Mayan ancestry. We stopped and I greeted him as the dust fell and the sounds of birds rose.

"You will need a guide," he said.

"A guide?" I echoed and smiled my warmest smile, as I leaned over Fernando to negotiate through the driver's side window. "But we've come a long way to visit Lubaantun. Isn't there someone to show us around? Perhaps a caretaker?"

"I'm the caretaker," he said, through his grin.

While in country, both with Fernando and with Sam in the '80s, I'd studied the Belizean character. Call it a bureaucratic national personality, people adhered to the rules of officialdom. Hard to get around.

"¿Qué le dice?" Fernando asked.

"We need a guide," I responded in Spanish.

Fernando brightened up, a gleam of triumph in his eye. Did he think he was getting out of exploring the ruin? No way was I missing this wild, overgrown, and nearly forgotten site. Touted as an anomaly, Lubaantun was built of black basalt instead of the local sandstone. It lacked the decorative marking used to date most ruins. Archeologists guesstimate the ruin was active between about 700 and 870 C.E. and may have served as a military outpost for its strategic location at the confluence of two tributaries of the Columbia River, a feature I couldn't discern. What interested me—I was still pretending to research my unwritten novel, *Stonecarver*—were the three ball courts with hieroglyphic texts and depictions of the game. But what really drew me were reports that Lubaantun was the site where one of the infamous crystal skulls had been found. In New Age lexicon, believers assert thirteen crystal skulls exist, and when brought together, will unite humanity and heal the world. It couldn't occur soon enough.

I'd always been into magical thinking—why else would I cling to the belief Fernando and I were destined to be together? All we had to do was work out a few cultural bumps in our road. ¿*No?*

It looked like we had to manage a cultural bump here, too. I fished my handbag from the floor, pulling some bills from it. "Is it possible to hire you to show us around?"

The smile broadened, then he pointed up the road and told us to park.

We scrambled over the talus of stone rubble admiring the beauty of the jungle as we swished away billowing clouds of gnats in the brilliant rays of sunlight and mosquitoes in the deep shade. Much of the site remained unexcavated, although I noticed through the trees, workers clearing swaths of jungle. Juan, our guide, showed us how to write messages on false banana leaves. He named the flowers, many I recognized under other names such as a profusion of pink begonias spilling out of the shadows at the edge of a clearing. I shot a photo of the false banana flower that reminded me of a ginger stalk.

The tallest pair of pyramids stood about forty feet high and were made of hewn stone set ends and sides in what is called an "in and out" pattern. From the top of the pyramid, the jungle swept down to the village and beyond, reaching to distant peaks and a clear blue sky. Cook-fire smoke rising in columns dotted the landscape. The raucous calls of parakeets and parrots rose and fell on the breeze. Another time warp to the past. Fer and I stood together, the first humans, with the world spread out in front of us. What we could achieve!

On the ground, Juan guided us through what may have been one of the ball courts. Everything was so overgrown and falling down, it was hard to identify what the structures might have been. As the shadows deepened, we decided we'd better get going. But where? We needed to figure out where we to stay for the night.

As we talked with the caretaker of Lubaantun, a few of the ruin workers gathered. One of them invited us to camp in his yard in Columbia, the closest village, on the Sitee River. We followed him down from the ruin to a grassy knoll dotted with modest stone houses dwarfed by their steep-pitched palm-thatched roofs. We saw a barn, several long, low buildings, and a small flock of turkeys scratching for bugs in the grass. In the distance, a woman and her dog traversed the expanse of green and disappeared into a structure. We putted along a weedy track toward the river, where we set up camp and got ready to prepare our dinner.

The shadows lengthened into dusk; stars began to

twinkle on as night fell. The compound lacked electricity, which made the stars appear across the sky in profusion. Stars also glittered in the trees and in the grass, accompanied by mellow guitar and singing coming from the Mennonite church across the commons. The magic astonished us. It didn't matter that the winking grass stars were beetles; the peace and beauty of San Pedro Columbia affected us to our hearts. We relaxed, our arguments forgotten, and reveled in being together, to bearing witness to paradise.

In the morning, little kids came out offering fresh tortillas and gawking at the oddity of two foreigners and a dog living in a VW camper. I felt the unseen eyes of mothers, also curious about us. Fer and I made and ate breakfast, chatting amiably, soon proving uninteresting to the villagers. The children ran off, jabbering in Ketchi, a Mayan dialect, to play in the park-like setting. We changed into bathing suits, and joined the women, who pretended not to watch us, in the river to wash our dishes and bathe in the cool, clean water.

My journal reports: *This is truly paradise. Even the bugs are benign.*

Again by midday, we cast ourselves out of paradise to hit the Southern Highway. Our stores of water and food dwindled. We needed to restock before we ran out. My diary is inscribed: *Bank PG*. Did we return to Punta Gorda for more cash before heading north? I'd noticed few markets on the way south, but we could make it to Dangriga in a few hours and be okay. It turned out we wouldn't need to rush.

Periodically along the highway, water pumps jutted

up out of the ground. At first we looked quizzically at each other, wondering what they could be. Soon we spied a group of Mennonites clustered around a pump at a pull-out with their water bottles. We stopped. I asked if they were pumping potable water. A woman in her white cotton gown and white headscarf assured me the water was provided by the Belizean government free for the taking and was pure. We should fill up because we wouldn't get such good water anywhere else. Now, I'd normally be leery of agricultural-looking water supplies, but the Mennonites were renowned for their cleanliness and purity—just look at those spotless white dresses—so I jerked my head toward the bus and nodded. Fernando gathered four containers. We pumped as much as we could carry. I said our thank-yous and we jumped back into the VW.

A few miles up the road we came to Nim Li Punit, little more than a gas station and crossroad for the ruin of the same name. We stopped to ask for directions, being observed by a group of rough-looking men hanging out by the drink cooler. I didn't give the encounter another thought as we turned left across the highway to creep up the track to the ruin.

A group of children saw us head up. Soon they'd chased us to the parking area, carrying baskets of trinkets, woven bracelets, tiny carvings, all for sale. I bought a bracelet and engaged the oldest in conversation, a girl of about eleven. She wore a too-small faded green dress decorated in rickrack, and dark hair in a knot on the top of her head. The kids were brothers and sisters, cousins and neighbors, ranging in age from about five to the girl who was the leader.

When it became apparent we weren't spending any more money, a couple of the girls foraged into the jungle, came back with a long vine, and got a game of jump rope going, chanting the same rhymes I'd chanted as a child, although theirs in Maya.

"I like coffee, I like tea, I like Rosita to jump in with me ... "

One of the things I admired about Fernando was how much he loved kids and was willing to play with them. We spent a delightful hour or so playing and learning about their lives in a round robin of Kechi, Spanish, and English. Fernando patiently turned the "rope", taking his turn jumping—joining in as we all laughed at what a lousy jump-roper he was.

The time came for our new friends to go home to supper and we started our good byes. At that moment, three of the laborers from the gas station appeared in our clearing. The atmosphere changed. These men didn't speak much English. They spoke incomprehensible Spanish. The kids said they were Hondurans illegally come to pick bananas. I was afraid. So were the kids for us; they dawdled with us until dark and one of their fathers coming off his *milpa* led them home to eat.

But the men hung on, chatting with Fernando, who had a worried crease in his forehead. I sensed his apprehension and my own fear escalated. Why wouldn't these men leave? It was full night. We wanted to eat. Maybe if I fed them they'd leave. I invited them to dinner.

We had little food. I had no idea how I'd feed five of us, but I sent one man off to get sugar and set to the miracle of turning provisions for two into loaves and fishes. When the errand runner returned, he brought two more hungry men. Did they plan to rip us off? Seven men would easily overpower us. How could I feed seven hungry migrant workers?

Here's how: I rounded up every comestible scrap in the bus, and it turned out to be a delicious smorgasbord of pork simmered in tomatoes, zucchini, purple potato, corn, and peas; a salad of cucumber and jicama with lime dressing; the Mayan ladies' fresh tortillas; and *agua de tamarindo* made with our newly pumped water.

Sated, we pulled our chairs and a log around the picnic table and leftovers, and talked for what felt like all night. One of the newcomers was an English-speaking college student working to pay his tuition, so I was able to learn much about the hardships of being an illegal *ag* worker in Belize. Although I relaxed as we got to know one another, the convivial conversation and breaking of bread didn't dispel Fernando's apprehension.

Finally, after a polite thank-you by the gang-style tattooed man, the group's putative leader, they left. It was late; I was tired and wanted to go to sleep. Fernando flipped-out ranting in rapid fire Spanish and started packing up. We threw everything into the camper and drove down the hill as fast as we could toward a gravel quarry Fernando noticed coming in along the Sitee River. We would be hidden from the highway and safe from prying eyes. We locked ourselves inside the camper for a stuffy, too-hot night of little sleep. This was not paradise.

In the morning, we returned to Lim Ni Punit to see

the ruin. Awaiting our return was gang-man with a (probably stolen) freshly cut stalk of bananas in a brown carton as a thank-you gift. I was shocked and ashamed. We'd feared this man because he looked different and was poor. We, and the neighborhood, had been certain the men would rob us, possibly killing us for our camp stove. We said goodbye; the man went to work.

We explored the mostly unexcavated ruin, visiting with the kids when they arrived with eggs, tortillas, and more trinkets. They asked if the "bad men" had hurt us. The little girl said they'd prayed for us because her dad had heard the bus drive off in the night. I gave them the bananas and bought the food and a tiny finely woven basket.

Over eggs and tortillas, I pondered my fear and automatic distrust of the farmworkers. Later, driving north, Fer and I discussed our prejudices. It had been a recurring topic. Fernando explained his system of Mexican societal stratification. First you had the Europeans, the highest caste: Spanish and French because his grandfather was of Spanish descent and his grandmother, French. Next were the *güeros*: light skinned, fair-haired and often blue eyed. This described Fernando. Following that were a parade of mestizos, mixed indigenous and European—the *morenos* (light colored) and *prietos* (dark colored) down to the lowly *indio* (*el negro*, black) who was surely a *campesino* (country person), ignorant and uneducated, a *naco,* the lowest of the low. African descent blacks, a tiny segment of the population, counted higher in Fernando's social strata, as did the growing Asian population, all he called *Chinos* regardless of descent. Anyone with money placed high in his ranking, but also elicited his disdain.

Of course, it took months before I fully understood this system, and I made many *errores*, according to Fernando. I forgot to use the appellation, *doña*, when addressing vendors in the market and other women providing services, using *señora* instead. I was friendly and polite with people to the degree I spoke Spanish. He tutored that I was not supposed to actually engage with lower classes beyond using them for services, and *campesinos* only as *burros*. My problem was, I didn't see myself as "higher". I just was luckier to not be struggling as much as they were at that time. He called me naïve. Maybe he was right. At least I didn't turn obsequious around the higher ups.

At first Fernando had conniptions when I treated the lowly the way I'd treat anyone else. Eventually, as my Spanish improved, I was able to make him understand that I viewed everyone as deserving the same friendliness and respect—or so I thought, but my fear of the farmworkers, especially the gang-looking one, pointed out I wasn't above prejudicial stereotyping.

"But Ana, the *campesinos* aren't the same," Fernando argued.

"Why not? They bleed just like you or me or *Presidente Salinas Gotari*."

"They're stupid and ignorant. Small-minded. They are like *burros*. It's their nature."

"You mean, they lack education."

"They can't learn. They are inferior."

"You're full of shit, Fer. Given opportunities,

anyone can rise."

"God didn't give *nacos* a brain, Ana."

Grrrrrrr. Could I really stay with a man who believed this? He'd been to school, but that little voice in my head said he wasn't really my peer. The doubt leaked into my thoughts now consumed me.

One thing was certain; our philosophical debates filled much time driving. We chugged past the turnoff to Dangriga, forded a stream or two, swollen from the afternoon rain and topped up the tank in Belmopan as we turned west toward San Ignacio at the border of Belize and Guatemala, locating a camping place called Cosmos, owned by two brothers, Bing and Juni, on the Mopan River, where we camped for the night of the 8th.

Chapter 21

Tikal

March 9-11, 1992

I was hot to stop on the way to Tikal and explore a Belizean ruin I'd read about, Xunantunich. Although it was first documented in the 1890s, it was under excavation at the time and had a reputation of being haunted by the Stone Woman, a ghost dressed all in white, with glowing fire-red eyes who appeared descending the stairs in front of "El Castillo" and disappeared into a wall. Right up my alley.

"Anita, there's no such thing as *fantasmas*, ghosts," Fernando commented as I translated from my guidebook.

"Sure there are. Mr. Palmer haunted my grandparents' house after he built it and died."

"*Eres loca.*"

Crazy? Probably. I planned to experience a ghost in an ancient Mayan ruin. Surely this would liven up my book, *Stonecarver*. I couldn't wait to see her.

We'd planned to explore the site in the afternoon and journey on through the border at Benque Viejo into Guatemala before dark, and our date with magical, mystical Tikal where we'd booked two nights of camping and entry into the famous ruins.

Except Xunantunich was closed to visitors in March of 1992.

Overlooking the Mopan River on a ridge, Xunantunich perched near the border with Guatemala in a then unpopulated western section of Belize. Like the fiasco of the car ferry, we didn't find out the ruin was closed to tourists until we'd made the winding trek from the turn-off at the main road, slogged through the jungle on a muddy track, to arrive at the closed gate. I was disappointed. From points along the road, we'd seen the ruins peeking through the trees and ogled the magnificent vista spread below us. To the east, the silvery Mopan flashed through the green carpet of jungle spreading toward a hazy coastline. To the west lay the blue shadow of the cloud-ringed mountains of Guatemala. Fernando argued we wouldn't have made it to Tikal if we stopped.

We'd never have made it to see Tikal on March 8th anyway. While the distances weren't so long, travel was slow, and I hadn't considered things like siesta at the border. We arrived in Benque Viejo in the early afternoon. After refreshing the ice in the cooler, picking up a few supplies for two days in the park from an under-stocked market, and having a bite to eat, we proceeded to the border. It was closed! We could leave Belize, but we couldn't enter Guatemala until the border personnel came back from their two-hour lunch.

SAINTS AND SKELETONS

Benque Viejo was not a town to while away the time over beers and tacos awaiting backwater bureaucrats. There was nothing there beyond a pig or two lounging in the dust, a few tiny food stores, and several auto insurance offices, auto insurance being a big moneymaker for the Belizeans, which I'd learned when we entered from Mexico.

Eventually, we passed through customs, obtained our 72-hour visa to visit Tikal and got underway for the last two or three hours of our day's journey. I remember it was a warm afternoon with brilliant blue skies appearing through the canopy of every shade of green. The two-lane highway, more of a tarmac ribbon, wove through the trees past occasional sunny clearings of maize, a thatched house or barn, corralled goats, pigs, and cows. People were few and their faces resembled those of the stone carvings I was so interested in. I breathed the loamy smells of forest rushing on the breeze as we putted along at about 35 mph.

Fernando's mood lightened at the border when we resumed speaking Spanish. He dialed in a patchy radio station playing Ranchero music. He felt as excited as I to visit Tikal. I sensed the current of electricity building up between us again. Things were finally going right.

"What's that?" I pointed ahead as we came around a bend. A uniformed youth stood in the road waving.

"I don't know, *Reina*, it looks like a soldier. This isn't good." He shifted into second gear.

The boy, who couldn't have been much over sixteen, held a rifle pointed at the *combi*. Fernando braked to a stop in the road at the entrance to a military base. The boy leaned into my window.

"*Buenas tardes, ¿que pasa?*" Fernando greeted the kid.

"*Papeles*. Papers," the young soldier demanded. I handed over our visa and the boy squinted at the seal. "Where are you going?"

"Tikal," I answered.

"Where are you coming from?" he asked, although it was clearly marked on the travel visa. "*Pasaportes*."

Fernando didn't bat an eye. "*Belize por Mexico*." He flashed his passport while I fished mine out of my purse.

The soldier eyed my bag with a hungry look. I dropped it to the floor.

"You need to pay. Get out of the vehicle." He pointed the rifle at me.

Fernando and the boy had a rapid discussion, something about how we'd taken care of everything legally at the border, *frontera*, and this was robbery—he was going to get into a lot of trouble when we reported him.

His hands shook slightly and his eyes shifted. Looking for witnesses? We were alone in the jungle with a twitchy teen toting a gun and trying to rob us.

They say you can smell fear. The kid reeked. Parsley smelled it too. She barked from the back. The boy flinched and stepped away, Fernando gunned the accelerator. I jumped out of the bus. Fernando thought he'd kill us.

"Put that gun down," I said in my most authoritative, mom-like voice. "What would your *abuela*, think if she knew you were robbing tourists?" I towered over him, menacing. He stood a good foot shorter than me.

The boy soldier lowered his head along with the rifle, and shuffled his feet. "*Pasale, pasale,*" he said, motioning his hand with the enthusiasm of the tail on a dog that has been kicked.

I got back into the bus, gave the kid a little lecture, and a bottle of Coke, before we drove off. I trembled all over. Now I felt my fear as relief washed over me.

"You know the soldier couldn't read," Fernando said. "He was on guard duty at the gate and wanted money. The army doesn't pay much."

"I got that. I wonder what his superiors think about it. Isn't he too young to be in the military? I know Guatemala is pretty corrupt, but how old could that kid have been?" I asked.

"People are poor here. His family probably lied about his age to get his pay."

"Or he was conscripted, no questions asked. I heard the military is still killing off the indigenous population."

"Or he's just a highway robber with a stolen uniform. Wow, you really got to him! Good thinking, bringing in his grandmother. *Le diste verguenza, Anita.* You shamed him."

We laughed for the rest of the trip into Tikal.

The region near Tikal was marked by the pueblo of Flores on the shores of Lake Petén Itza, approximately forty miles southwest of Tikal. I recall the lake looked vast nestled into the dense green of jungle. We stopped for more supplies and putted on to the park. None of the few roads we'd traveled in Guatemala were anything to shout about—paved, narrow, winding, or bumpy. We'd passed tiny stick and mud huts, cornfields and corrals hacked into the jungle, the ubiquitous burro and short folks, many in colorfully embroidered *huipiles*. In contrast to the country folk in Belize, the Guatemalans smiled at us, expressions that lit their faces. I'm sorry I didn't stop to chat, however Fernando said it was likely many did not speak Spanish. In Flores we heard plenty of the indigenous Mayan I thought might have been Quiché.

It was getting late. Fernando insisted on going straight through town to the ruins. We needed some fresh vegetables, but he insisted we'd find a store at Tikal. It wasn't far, at least in comparison to the journey we'd already made from Mexico City to the tip of Belize. Now we drove into the northeastern corner of Guatemala, the Petén, but the narrow jungle road kept our speed down. We arrived in the park in the late afternoon as the sun angled sharply and the shadows deepened between the trees. We were directed to a grassy strip along the main road, which had been designated as the campground. It had a few other "campers" and no amenities. As I'd found throughout my wanderings in the region, we were on our own. I again blessed my foresight in equipping the VW bus. We'd be almost self-sufficient—once we found the store. We pulled across the clearing near the trees, parked and clambered out. Parsley hopped down, shook, stretched into a deep downward dog pose and grinned. I offered her a bowl of water. After a slurp she sniffed the air and trotted toward the edge of the woods.

I didn't need to worry about her; she wasn't a biter or a food thief. She would checkout the area then "introduce" us to the other visitors as we trailed her. I met many people through my dog.

This time I met a squat woman wearing a drab hued shirt tucked into khaki pants, stout boots, an impressive billed hat, and carrying a woven bag. The park ranger.

"*Señora, las mascotas deben estar atadas,*" she commanded, a little too officiously.

I looked at Fernando questioningly and mouthed, *atadas*? He nodded. "*Anita, átala—*" pointed toward Parsley, nosing around a pickup with a camper on the back near the edge of the road. Pets on leash. I got it.

"*Sí, señora, ahorita ponemos una correa.*" He turned his most irresistible blue-eyed smile onto the park ranger. She frowned. He leaned into the bus and shuffled through a pile of stuff on top of the cabinet, looking for the leash.

"*Hay tienda cerca, señora?*" I asked, hoping to solve our food shortage.

She looked up at me through narrowed eyes, her lips pursed. "*No. No tienda. Flores.*"

No store in Tikal? What tourist area didn't have a store? I tried to look friendly and asked, "*¿No hay restaurante tampoco?*"

"*No, no hay.*" Her frown deepened. She drew herself up to her full height, which probably didn't top five feet, and pulled a booklet from her bag. With a disgusted look at Parsley, now sniffing along the edge of the grass, she said, "*Atade usted el perro o page la multa.*" She started to write the date on her form.

I knew that word, *multa*. No way I was paying a

fine. I whistled for my dog. Parsley's ears shot up. She tottered back to me, panting through her toothy grin and scaring the little ranger. Good dog!

Fernando pulled out of the bus and clipped the leash to Parsley's collar. The booklet disappeared into the bag. She said, *"No se permita mascotas en la zona arqueológica,"* and marched away.

My stomach tightened. Parsley couldn't enter the ruins with us? No way could I lock her in the bus all day. For one thing, the heat would kill her. Fernando and I looked at each other.

"¿Que vamos a hacer? What are we going to do?" we asked in unison.

The day waned. I needed to get dinner cooked. We set up the kitchen together. I screwed the legs into our roll-up table then positioned the camp stove on top, pulling the long flex tube from the propane tank tied into the roof rack and plugged it in. Meanwhile, Fernando opened the tank's valve then tented over our "kitchen" with the canvas on tent-poles. I'd taught him the truckers knot—one pull and the canopy popped up into place. Parsley picked at her bowl of kibble as I rushed to unpack some pasta and bottled red sauce. The cooler yielded up a sad looking onion and a not quite limp grey squash. It would have to do. Without a store or a restaurant, we'd eat creatively. I closed Fernando into the VW's cabin when I sealed the door opening with no-see-um netting. The mosquitoes hummed around me as the sun dropped into the jungle. Bloodsuckers had always found me tasty. I lit several sticks of incense and set them around our camp.

"Fer, find the bug spray."

He handed out my last can of OFF. I stepped away from the stove to spray my shorts-clad legs, rubbed repellant on my bare arms, and the skin exposed by my tank top, then washed my hands in the dishpan. A nightly ritual in the jungle.

After our spaghetti dinner, we had nothing to do but read and listen to the night sounds. Strange calls echoed out of the jungle across the road where the growth was thick, hiding the ruins. Before dark we'd taken a stroll to find the entrance to the archaeological zone where we discovered a parking lot set amid the trees, which would have to be suitable for UYOLKAN and Parsley the next day while we explored.

The shadows cast by the rising sun angling through the dense jungle surrounding our clearing kept us cool as morning progressed into day. Fernando, typically an early riser, popped out of bed. He got us going with coffee, greeting other campers doing the same. He pushed through the no-see-um netting with a steaming mug of black coffee. Of course we were out of milk.

"Anita, get up. We have a lot to see today." He grinned. Tikal was high on Fer's bucket list. Mine too.

I sat up and took the mug. "*Gracias mi amor.* Do you want breakfast? We need to move into that shaded lot before it fills up. I could make it there. Toss me my shorts." I pointed to the top of the cabinet.

Fer complied while I wedged my coffee between pillows, wriggled into my green pants, and swung off the bed to stow the bedding, folding the bed back into the benches and table formation before finishing dressing. I wouldn't take a shower in this turnout alongside the main road.

"How hot do you think it will be?" I asked when I noticed Fernando had pulled on jeans.

"Warm. Like yesterday," he replied with authority.

I fished around the tiny closet until I found a clean white v-neck tee-shirt. I would need my boots for clambering over ruins, meaning I'd need socks too. I dug in a bag and found a pair. "¡Muévete!" I ordered, squeezing into the doorway alongside Fer to put on the shoes and finish my coffee.

We made another pot, greeting campers from our sheltered "kitchen" as they emerged from their tents and vehicles. People were already packing up.

"*Apúrrate*, Anita. People are leaving."

"What time do the ruins open?"

He shrugged. I tipped the muddy grounds out of my mug into our garbage bag then washed up the coffee service. I needed a bathroom, but couldn't remember one in the camping area. Fernando and Parsley walked around; he chatted with people as they packed up to leave. In a few minutes he returned. "It's eight now. The park opens in an hour. Are you ready?"

"Just need to wash my face and brush my teeth." I dumped the dishwater and poured hot water from the little kettle over my washcloth. Fernando disconnected the stove then folded it closed.

In five minutes, we had the campsite torn down and the *combi* ready to roll.

The parking lot was a flat section of jungle thinned

to park thirty or forty vehicles between the trees. We found a shaded slot between two trees and pulled in. Parsley would stay inside—always a deterrent to *ladrones,* thieves—with the fans blowing and the exhaust fan sucking hot air from the interior. I fixed her up with a pan of water after walking her around the parking lot. For a Tuesday in March, the spaces filled quickly.

Soon we locked Parsley in then made our way to the entrance with the assembled throng to wait for the gate to open. I carried a water bottle and a sitemap in my fanny pack. Photos show us grinning, tanned, trim on top of temple VI with famous temple VII towering above us in the background. In 1992, visitors could scramble all over the ruins. We climbed, exploring everything.

Entering through the east portal, we walked a broad, dusty track bordered on either side by dense growth. Overhead the chatter and whistles of parakeets, the growling chants of howler monkeys and the thud of our footfalls filled the damp, earthy air with a jungle soundtrack. The trail terminated at Plaza de Este, which we explored as we continued toward the Central Acropolis, the heart of the excavated ceremonial center presided over by Temple IV to the northwest. We explored the crumbling moss and lichen covered structures, plazas, stairs, ramps, passageways, marveling over the masonry, the antiquity, and the echoes of voices from the past. Tikal means "the place of the voices" in *Itza Maya.*

We climbed the pyramids in the Plaza of the Seven Pyramids and snapped happy-looking shots of each other. Other than worry over Parsley, I remember Tikal as a carefree day. Fer and I were tuned into each other like we'd been in our early days. He engaged in our explorations and didn't harp about needing to get on with his life. I forgot my inconvenient, unwanted pregnancy as we held hands, kissed in secluded plazas, and shared a grand adventure.

Around lunchtime, we headed back to the *combi* to check on Parsley and eat tuna sandwiches. The temperature had risen significantly; she looked distressed. We took her out for a walk and sniff then refilled her water bowl with cold water, keeping her drinking until she rehydrated. Fernando re-positioned the vehicle into deeper shade. We opened it up to let cooler air in. When Parsley returned to her seat to nap, we returned to the ruins. We had half of the park yet to visit.

Buoyed by our happy vibes, we tramped off to a couple of remote sites far from the crowds. At Zona Norte, a remote raised plaza, mostly overgrown, we found a secret sunny spot and made love amid the profusions of orchids growing on the trees and stumps, the soft grass sprouting between the stones, colorful flowers filled with bees. I picture the day as bright cerulean blue and kelly green splashed with red, orange, and yellow. I felt certain our future was rosy.

I drank in the jungle growth: purple wandering jew plants spilling down walls, thickets of trees, and fruiting bushes trimmed with low palms. A green paradise dotted with colorful birds and flowers. I saw a toucan from the top of one of the pyramids, flying high over the jungle, shot an image of a wild oscillated turkey hen, a brightly plumed scarlet macaw, and one of the howler monkeys up in the trees, but I never saw the famed Quetzal. Awed by the beauty of the jungle and the marvel of the architecture, we pretended to be Mayans, early explorers, and jaguars.

As the shadows grew, employees circulated the park announcing closing time and ushering visitors out of the archeology zone like town criers from olden times. We headed in the direction of the track back to the parking lot, but slipped through the "net" to checkout one more set of ruins. After all, this was our chance; we wouldn't be back. But we had to be quick. Tropical twilights are fleeting and we found ourselves on an unfamiliar track in the dark with the sounds of the jungle enveloping us. No, we didn't see any jaguars, but picking our way back to the *combi* after the sun went down, we heard one growl.

"I hope we see a jaguar," I said.

"*I* hope it isn't hungry."

"It wouldn't attack two humans would it?" I grabbed Fernando's hand.

Alone on the, thankfully groomed, dirt track, we stumbled and laughed to cover our fright, but we kept going. Crickets and mosquitoes made the base line of sound—not scary at all—but sudden eerie cries and frantic flapping made us jump. At one point in the long walk to the *combi,* a barrel of spider monkeys rolled through the treetops, making a chilling racket. Something rustled out of the trees and crossed in front of us. Our blood pounded and we clung together until it disappeared. It barked or grunted once then shambled back into the jungle. In the dark, sounds amplified and distorted. Fer made creepy sounds to scare me. I tried to imitate the sounds we heard, but when that jaguar growled, the night went silent. We really were terrified.

Near the entrance, a ranger found us and kicked us out of the park. We made our way to the *combi* and an overjoyed dog then headed back to the camping area. The next day we had to cross into Belize. We had less than twenty-four hours before our 96-hour visa expired. Well, we wouldn't dally. We were pretty much out of food and water.

In the morning, we spent a little time checking out the Tikal amenities. We found some food, but it smelled atrocious and we drove back to the Camino Real Tikal on the shores of Lake Petén Itzá to enjoy an overpriced American breakfast of scrambled eggs, bacon, sausages, hash browns, fruit and toast with jelly, on the balcony overlooking the lake. I remember being delighted with a familiar breakfast. Maybe it was the barometric pressure or something but I felt depressed. The pregnancy was a heavy anchor around my neck. I didn't have morning sickness, but it was getting harder to ignore.

"Where are the tortillas and salsa?" Fer asked.

"We don't usually have those with eggs."

"We need to buy some tortillas." Fernando was obviously cranky. Maybe he caught my mood.

The lake was huge, a soft grey-blue under high cirrus clouds. I saw flat rocks offshore and thought they would make a great sunning platform but the waiter explained the flat rocks were the local "laundromat". So much for sunbathing. We walked around after breakfast, taking some photos as the sun burned through the haze and the lake turned blue.

Further along the lake, we passed through Flores again. Since we needed food and ice, we stopped and stocked up. I made sure to buy tortillas, but they weren't the nice thin one of Mexico. These were smaller, about 3-4 inches in diameter and quite thick. We bought them from a *doña* in an apron with a bucket full, a familiar sight, but neither of us liked them. We stowed our food and headed back the way we came, crossing to Belize in the afternoon.

Benque Viejo bustled as before. The highway coming in from Guatemala lined with auto insurance agencies, tour busses, expensive food, and gift shops. We stopped for gas after passing through the border and pushed on. We needed to get back to Cosmos to camp before dark, but we had some time to explore before our next scheduled stop: Chaa Creek Cottages. We stopped again at a market for fresh food and ice to last us to check-in the following day then blasted out of town, ignoring the plethora of auto insurance sales rooms. I already had insurance for the U.S., Mexico, and Belize.

The trip today takes about sixteen minutes to drive the ten or so kilometers to Chaa Creek Lodge. At the time, the turnoff from the highway was a barely paved road, and it felt like, we drove for hours through the jungle before we found the track leading onto a sunny knoll sloping down to the river.

Chapter 22

Chaa Creek Cottages

March 12-13, 1992

I was excited to visit Chaa Creek Cottages. Fernando dreaded two nights in an English speaking resort with nothing to do, but that wouldn't deter me. I'd signed up for the guided Mayan herb walk where I would learn about the flora of the region and its culinary and medicinal uses. I still thought I'd write *Stonecarver,* the story of an eighth century architect/sculptor who left Copan to travel to Xochicalco, In the Place of the Flower House, ruins just north of Cuernavaca famous for its ball court with architecture remarkably similar to the one in Copan and Mayan style carving on the main buildings. My premise: Eb Zotz brought the Mayan style to the Aztec world. We'd visited Xochicalco on our way to the missed Christmas Party and planned to go back for its Tropic of Cancer mystery in July. My guidebook said the sun would reach its zenith at astronomical noon and a beam would shoot down a chimney into a cave under the main ceremonial center, creating an image of itself on the cave floor. No way I'd miss that!

If the site of our campout the night of March 11th had an address, it's lost to time. Fernando perked up when we found Spanish-speaking campers carrying *mota*. He bounded down to the river with his new friends, spending the rest of the afternoon getting high and playing in the warm, slow moving river. I knew he liked to smoke pot; we'd gotten high together now and then, but I couldn't partake if I were to keep the baby. It was one of our ongoing arguments. We'd traded hours of driving and discussing everything under the sun with arguing about getting married and having the child. It was a feel-good idea, but I was forty-one. Did I want a baby? To be safe, I stopped drinking and smoking *mota*. But I knew the answer was NO.

The longer I avoided making a decision, the more we argued. Fernando pulled away. The truth of the matter should have been clear on the banks of the Mopan. Parsley and I ambled down to discover Fer and four or five others sunning, passing a joint. He jumped up and pulled me aside.

"Anita, do you have any *lana,* cash, I can get some of this *mota* for cheap—fifty pesos."

I was watching my money pretty carefully as banks in Belize seemed to be scarce. Besides, why should I support his pot habit?

"I don't know, Fer," I said, "we're pretty low right now. We won't get to a bank for a couple of days."

"*Pues,* let's go to the bank now."

I looked at my watch. "We'd never make it."

"Then come swimming." He pulled me toward the nearly naked group passing another joint. "*Oye, mi novia, Ana,*" he introduced me. He was acting nice in front of his new friends, but I could tell he was angry.

Someone handed up the joint. Fernando grabbed it. I said I'd go get my suit on, which I had no intention of doing, and fled. No way was I putting on a bathing suit, now that I'd started to gain weight, to sit around with a bunch of stoned bathing beauties.

It was getting dark, Fernando finally turned up wanting some food. "Did you eat?"

"No, I waited for you."

"Why didn't you come back for a swim?"

"I don't fit into my suit."

He grinned and cupped my stomach with his hands. "You look great. What's for dinner?"

"Quesadillas or tacos with the Guatemalan tortillas? You can make salsa."

"Quesadillas. *Un momentito, Reina.* I'm going to put on clothes. Where's the mosquito spray?" he asked. We were both slapping away bloodsuckers by then.

I nodded to the table. "Use it outside."

He stepped away from the bus and doused himself. "I'll light some incense after I get dressed," he volunteered and climbed into the bus closing the no-see-um netting behind him.

"Bring me the cheese and salsa stuff from the cooler," I said, pulling open the netting to reach into the cabinet for a *comal*, a bowl, the grater, cutting board and my Chinese vegetable cleaver before re-velcroing the net in place.

Fernando popped Bob Marley into the tape deck

(I'd bought some, probably bootleg, tapes from a street vendor) and rooted around inside like a pig for truffles. He came out looking preppy in ratty jeans with his loafers on sockless feet, topped by a clean, pressed shirt. Where did that come from? Or maybe the question was, who was he trying to impress? He dropped cheese, chilies, an onion, and a tomato onto the table and popped open two Fantas.

I accepted the soda. "You look good. Got a hot date?"

"I want to look good for my Anita." He grinned and kissed my neck. "We're invited to a fiesta with the folks from the river." He pulled one of the sling chairs around and plopped into it.

I pictured the golden bodies sunning on the bank and wondered which one he was attracted to. The one with the dope, probably. "I don't know, Fer. I can't drink or smoke if we're keeping the baby." I rammed the cheese through the grater.

"You don't need to. It will be fun talking. They're nice."

I hacked the onion into bits then scraped it into a bowl. "I'm sure they are," I snarked. "What are their names? Where are they from?"

"I don't know. One of the girls said her name was Maria. I think they're from the coast." I smashed a garlic clove and chopped the jalapeño. "We were talking about the Bajada at Chichén Itzá on the twenty-first. They plan on going."

I crushed the tomato and tipped the running mess into the bowl with the rest of the veggies then whipped it into a thick salsa with a fork. "Which one was

Maria?"

"The skinny girl with the dreadlocks. Come with me and you can find out for yourself." He gave me one of his warm smiles. "Come on, Reina, it will be fun. Parsley, want to go to a *fiesta*?" My traitorous dog grinned, tottered to him, then pressed into his leg wagging gleefully. He leaned over and gave her a hug. "Your dog wants to meet new people." Parsley was feeling better. I attributed it to the evenly warm weather.

I liked meeting new people too, but not hot chicks with *mota*. I was a decade older, starting to pooch out, or I felt like I was getting fat, and I didn't feel up to par. No way I could compete with pretty, fluent Spanish speakers for Fernando's attention. And I wanted it all. The bad angel on my shoulder whispered, "You're paying for it all." I maimed the cilantro and started toasting the quesadillas.

"That smells good. I'm starving."

"You have the munchies," I mumbled.

"What? Speak Spanish."

"I said, I can't keep up in a group speaking rapid Spanish."

"I'll translate and ask them to speak slower."

"Let's eat and figure it out later." I doused my quesadillas with salsa then passed Fernando a plate and the salsa bowl.

Maria and one of the men trotted down the sloping path, calling out as they passed, "See you later."

Fer waved. "*Adios. Más tarde.*"

"Who's the guy?"

"I think he's her husband. Jose or Javier or

something like that."

That angel snickered. "Jose and Maria, what a cliché. He's conning you."

We ate in silence. Bob Marley admonished me to "lively up yourself and don't be no drag" while my better sense analyzed the situation. *He wants dope. He's bull shitting you about wanting to get married. It's just his macho attitude. He's flattered to have impregnated you. And you know you're going home.* After dinner, I hid my cash.

The Coleman lantern glowed, a bright beacon to lead my *novio* home. I read Patti's copy of the *Sum of All Fears*, but found myself straining to hear the party going on down the slope near the river and losing my place. I finally went to bed.

Fernando climbed in late, reeking of pot. Was this some sort of instant karma for how I'd treated Sam? I pretended to be asleep, but brooded until I drifted off again. When I awoke, Fernando was already making coffee.

"*Buenas días, Reina.* Come swimming with me today."

"We're going to Chaa Creek."

"Later, right? Let's enjoy the river before we go."

"With your new friends?"

"They left. They're going to Tulum."

"Too bad," I said as I poured myself a cup from the insulated carafe. Fernando missed my sarcasm. "Sure, let's take a swim."

We spread a towel on the grassy bank above the

water and sat down to soak up the sun. It was a brilliant, warm morning. Fernando rummaged in his man bag, pulled out a baggie of pot, rolling papers, and rolled a fat dube.

"Where'd the *mota* come from?"

"*Un regalo,*" Fernando grinned.

A gift. *In exchange for what?* "Great, so you didn't need any money after all. *Qué suerte.*"

When we returned to the *combi* I checked my secret stash, . Fifty pesos short. I'd counted the cash after we bought food and again when I hid it, worried we wouldn't have enough to see us back to Mexico. Gift my ass.

"Let's pack up and get going. We can check-in in an hour," I said.

"No lunch?"

"We'll get lunch there." I had no idea if it were true.

Back on the road, we wound up the ridge and over the crest to Chaa Creek Cottages for the nights of the 12th and 13th. It wasn't far from our campsite. I remember little of the ride except the fight.

"You stole fifty pesos from my purse to buy that *mota*," I accused Fernando as soon as we got underway.

"It was a gift, I told you. They want us to meet them in Tulum. I have to sell some of it for them."

"*No me mentiras,* Fernando. I counted the money yesterday after buying food."

He kept his eyes on the narrow road. "Maybe somebody stole it."

"*No creo*. I was here last night. And who would take only fifty pesos? *You*."

"I didn't steal your money."

"Then where did the *mota* come from? I'm not an idiot."

We drove into a clearing in the thick jungle finding an assortment of thatched structures rambling down the slope. We had arrived. In 1992 the term "glamping" hadn't been coined, but Chaa Creek Cottages qualified. The lodge was open to the air with a small wood hewn restaurant and bar where we ate breakfast and dinner overlooking the jungle. Our host showed us around, pointing out the cottages, sixteen of them tucked into the trees, until we reached ours: a wooden lap-sided lookout on stilts with a thatched roof. From our green deck chairs we could look out over the property and catch a glimmer of the Mopan flowing toward the sea. The cheerful decor in the open-air room, consisting of local weavings, ceramics, scenic paintings, and a grass rug, were handmade. I reveled in the charm. Even Parsley liked her eco-resort digs, making herself comfortable on the edge of the deck where she could watch the comings and goings of the few guests and staff. I know she waited to see a tapir or a *coatimundi*, a raccoon-like jungle creature.

The queen bed turned out to be supremely comfortable, possibly just because of its roominess after the tiny bunk in the *combi*. I forgot about our problems for a while.

Fernando did not. Everyone we encountered spoke English, and he felt left out. I'd come here to learn something, which meant he had to take care of himself for the day while I took my medicinal herb tour.

"What am I going to do while you go on your plant walk?"

"Take a walk with Parsley. Go swimming. Read a book. Sleep. Hey, there's horseback riding. Do you ride?" I remember regaling him with stories of my riding adventures with my cowboy cousins.

"I haven't had much experience with horses."

"Then let's go check out the stables."

"I'd rather go swimming. Get your suit on."

"Okay. But let's go by the stables first. I might want to ride with you."

"Let me smoke this joint."

"Don't smoke up your profits." I plopped into a chair and opened my book. He took a hit.

Parsley's ears shot up. An animal scurried across an open space, disappearing back into the trees. I gave her a pat. "You wait 'til tonight girl. You'll have plenty of smells and sounds." She grinned.

"Aren't you getting your suit, Anita? Parsley thumped her tail on the decking. "Parsley wants to go too. Come on." He got up, held out his hand and blinked those bedroom eyes at me. We didn't go swimming.

Later, we went to the corral where Fernando was able to talk to the stable manager who assured him the ride through the jungle, which included a picnic lunch, would be well worth his time, and the trail leaders would take good care of him. I remember I was impressed with the horses. I didn't peg any as nags. In fact, they all looked fresh, spirited, and well cared for. I half wished I could go too, but it probably was better we take a break from each other. At least he wouldn't spend the day getting stoned.

Coming back from the stable, the dinner gong sounded so we ambled over to the dining room and seated ourselves on the rail to watch the sunset and the lights around the property come up. Chaa Creek had only had electricity since 1985, and plumbing since 1987. While we ate a delicious dinner of homegrown vegetables, a local freshwater fish marinated in lime butter and cooked in Maria Santa leaves, we learned the cottages had a makeover in '91 when they gained the local handiworks. The other guests we met: an archaeologist, a nature enthusiast, students, all enjoyed adventure. I felt at home, wishing we could stay for more than two nights, but even then Chaa Creek Cottages fetched a premium price. It was a place for young, educated, well-to-do hippie-type adventurers. I thought I fit right in. Strolling back to our cottage, we smelled pot drifting from more than one room. Fer had started to think he fit in too.

"*Reina*, thank you for bringing me here." He pulled me in for a hug.

The sounds of the jungle crescendoed. We kissed. Parsley sighed and thumped down onto her spot on the deck. Fernando and I left the lights off as we fell to the bed.

After breakfast, we got ready for our respective tours. I left Fernando at the stable after taking a photo of him on his horse. Except for the sneakers instead of riding boots, he looked like a pro. Someone directed me to the correct trail, and I ambled off for my medicinal plant tour at Ix Chel Farm. Ix Chel was the Maya goddess of healing. I was blessed to have Dr. Rosita Arvigo, founder, lead the tour along the Don Elijio Panti Medicine Trail, named for Don Elijio Panti an aged Mayan traditional healer. The walk fascinated me. I scribbled notes and thoughts about my Stonecarver book. I'm sure I could unearth the notebook I carried that day, but Dr. Rosita has now written a book on the jungle medicine—with photos. I arrived back at our elegant hut tired but intellectually stimulated. My only photo was a perfect image of a blooming Black Orchid, the Belizean national flower.

Fernando was also stimulated. He jabbered non-stop about his day, the things he saw, the people he met. And riding a horse. At dinner he introduced me to his new acquaintances. It included a woman I'd met on the medicine trail. We gathered for drinks and dinner, sharing stories in English and Spanish into the night. This was why I'd come. To learn about people, places, and cultures, to excite my mind and imagination, to revel in a kind of freedom only jimmying yourself from your daily life can offer.

That night in bed, we listened to the symphony of jungle sounds and dreamed of the adventures to come.

Chapter 23

He Got What Was Coming

March 14-17, 1992

We slept in on our last morning at Chaa Creek then ate a leisurely breakfast of locally grown tropical fruits and homemade yoghurt before returning to our room to pack up. We planned a leisurely drive back to Chetumal, Mexico with a stop at a small ruin called Altun Ha northeast of Belize City on the way. Did we somehow decide on another night camping at the river? Looking in my 1992 datebook, I see notations we camped at Cosmos, but maps show no such place exists in the Cayo district of Belize. I notice I used the same notation, *nite cosmos*, for the night of March eighth as well. That night we camped along the Sitee River, not the Mopan. A secret code lost to time?

I'm not surprised I've misplaced certain facts over the thirty-one intervening years, but some things are hard to forget. We visited Altun Ha, a few miles north of Belize City in Belize District on March fourteenth.

The park sat off Old Northern Highway in a green clearing of a wooded area. It consisted of two well-excavated and maintained main plazas with temples and buildings surrounding them on three sides. Although the scale of architecture isn't grand like Tikal, the ruin was maintained, and imbued with a sense of peace and immortality. Again we me little kids who happily guided us through Altun Ha's attractions and lore. We tarried longer than we planned, and as the sun angled lower through the trees, we saw more birds and possibly a white tailed deer, as the otherworldly sense of calm filled the atmosphere. Fer and I connected again. Love and calm surrounded us. I remember considering camping in Altun Ha. Possibly we did. Altun Ha's magic turned the experience into a dream, but the reality was, the caretaker shooed us out and we continued on toward the border.

Belize is small and distances are short. We drove through Orange Walk and on toward Corozal. Shortly after the sun sank below the horizon, we came to a slowdown on the highway.

"There's an accident ahead," Fernando said.

I craned forward to see, and in moments, realized we were in line to be inspected at a checkpoint. Not unfamiliar with immigration checkpoints around the borders, I said, "Get your passport, it's *inmigración*." From the hidey-hole between the seats, I fished my passport, our entry papers, and the vehicle permission.

It took about five minutes to reach the officials. I did the talking.

"Your papers," the man said.

I passed them through. He looked them over then

asked Fernando where we were going. Fer looked at me. I said, "I speak English. We're on our way back to Mexico." It was less than ten miles to the crossing into Chetumal.

He persisted. "Where have you been?"

I listed our itinerary.

"You exited Belize to Guatemala?"

"Seventy-two hours in Tikal."

"Where is your automobile insurance?"

"I handed it to you."

He held up a paper. "This is expired."

"Maybe it's too dark to read. I bought fifteen days of insurance in Corozal when we came in from Chetumal. That was on the 28th."

"You left the country and came back. You needed to buy another policy."

"What?"

"You're under arrest for driving without insurance," the officer told Fernando.

"What?" I screamed. "Why are you arresting him? Let me pay you for the missing days and we'll leave the country."

"He's the driver. He's broken the law."

From zero to hysterical in two seconds. It didn't matter; the man was implacable. He wouldn't listen to reason; he wouldn't let us buy insurance; he wouldn't take a bribe. Fernando was put into a patrol car. I was left to trail the police car to the Corozal jail in my uninsured bus.

I can't believe I don't have any photos of Fer in jail. I picture a yellow and green two-story cinderblock building set back from the street curb a short distance.

There may have been a small lawn in front. To the right of the main building, a cyclone fenced courtyard with picnic tables ran between the offices and cells. The main office door opened into a grungy waiting room and reception. And what a reception I got: stonewalled.

"I'd like to pay my fine and bail Fernando out. We're on our way to the border." I plunked down my credit card.

The cop eyed my card. "No bail until he goes to court, and it's cash only."

I checked my wallet. I didn't have enough to buy dinner, let alone whatever extortive price the Belizeans put on Fernando's head. "Court? For what? Let me pay the penalty and let us get on to Mexico. Where's the nearest bank?"

"The judge doesn't come until Monday. The banks are closed."

My blood pressure skyrocketed. "Where can I buy the insurance?"

"Closed until Monday."

"What the hell am I supposed to do until Monday?" I shouted and started to cry.

Meanwhile, I'd pulled the bus right in front of the Corozal Town Police Station and parked. Several officers peered into the windows, checking out UYOLKAN. I stormed from the office, slamming the door and yelling at the cops to get away from my bus. They stepped back, but didn't go. I was sobbing and needed my dog. I unlocked the door and wrenched it open to let Parsley out. She'd been inside for a couple of hours, and bounded to the curb, startling the police who retreated quickly. I calmed down, fed her on the sidewalk, and started unpacking my kitchen to make dinner. I'd make myself at home and drive the Corozal police crazy.

Of course, the men all came around to see the bus and hear about our travels. Belizeans are friendly. We got along fine until a superior showed up , telling me I had to leave.

"Where am I going to go? I don't have any cash and your crummy banks are closed until Monday. Let Fernando go and we'll leave your curb."

"He has to see the judge, whose docket is filled. It might be a week before his case is heard."

It had worked before…I went ballistic, screaming and crying, making a scene until most of the station had gathered outside.

"I'm not leaving until you let my boyfriend out!"

"I can arrest you."

"For what? Because you're so officious you can't find a way to solve a small problem and be rid of us? You'll have to arrest my dog too." On cue, Parsley growled.

The men I'd talked to agreed with me. "Let them go, Sir."

He ordered the men to get to work then retreated into the station. I stayed parked at the curb for two days, making the police's lives miserable, invading reception, tying up the bathroom, and making a scene as often as I could.

On the Saturday overnight shift, one of the policemen tried to enter my bus. I stormed into the office yet again, and shouted accusations. The officer was reprimanded. I slept soundly after that with a guard sitting outside. They let me go in and visit Fernando on Sunday, perhaps in compensation for the intruder. I brought him some clean clothes, told him what I'd learned, and asked what he needed.

Fernando was not at all unhappy; the food was good, and he didn't need anything except money. What was new there? I felt more irritated than before seeing him. As usual, he'd gravitated to the addict, an old Mexican alcoholic in his cell. A repeat offender, sobering up for a couple of weeks in jail. They played chess and chatted. The inmate was pleasant with me and assured me Fernando was not being abused—except that he was in jail for what I considered a clerical error and may have to stay for a week. The other inmates checked me out, made a few rude comments, mostly about hanging around with Mexicans —Belizeans were better lovers—but generally kept their distances. The old Mexican leveled an evil eye at the cat-callers. We all got along minding our own business after that. Maybe Fernando intuitively knew who held the cards in the clink. Or maybe he'd been in jail before. I didn't know, and never found out. The guards chased me back to the curb at dinnertime a couple hours later. Parsley was glad to take a walk, and I made another ruckus at the station desk. Why did Fernando get a nice dinner served to him and I was punished by stupid police, banking laws, and lazy judges?

Early Monday morning, I took a sponge bath, put on a dress, then made my appearance in the police station, hounding them to get the judge going, and hear our case. I'm sure news had traveled through the law enforcement community, as a bunch of people were anxious to see me gone. The police had the liability of keeping me safe and were getting tired of it. I took up time and resources. Although Fernando didn't seem to be in any danger, it was only a city jail, not a prison, the police couldn't let anything happen to him either. We were foreigners legally entered into Belize and if I, especially, went to my embassy, they'd have bigger problems than an annoying woman camped on the doorstep. I got someone to tell me the amount of the fine, found the bank, and an insurance vendor, taking care of things as soon as businesses opened, before court.

Anyone who has been in court knows how long things take, but by the middle of the afternoon, Fernando was released and we were on our way again. Of course the judge made sure I knew he'd made a special effort to get Fer on the docket. Hoping for a bribe? Fat chance. I'd been told in Belize, if it wasn't nailed down it would be stolen, but my experience said Belizeans liked to follow the law, so maybe he just wanted to be thanked, which I did. Obsequiously.

Fernando put another tape into the deck. We belted an off-key version of *Mexico Lindo* y *Querido* to Ana Gabriel's throaty rendition: *"Vos de la guitarra mia. . quiere cantar su alegría a mi tierra Mexicana ..."* My guitar wants to sing of its happiness to my Mexican land. We didn't have a guitar, but we had the vast and varied landscape of Mexico as we crossed the border. What more could we ask for?

The sun was sinking beyond Chetumal, a compact city laid out in a tight grid with wide, palm lined boulevards and white-washed houses on the Bahía de Chetumal. We didn't have any information on trailer parks, and after several days without a proper shower, I wanted to stay in a motel.

"Let's get a room tonight," I said.

"What about the dog?"

"What about her?"

"We'll never find anything. I'm going to ask where the trailer park is."

"I'm dying for a shower, Fernando."

"I'm hungry. Let's find some *mole*."

I checked my watch. We needed to get a place or we'd be sleeping by the side of the road. I'd had enough of that, and it wouldn't come with an armed guard.

"Look. There." I pointed to a motel called Hotel Boston, that should have been in the Swiss Alps, not the southernmost city of Mexico.

Fer pulled into their palm-shaded courtyard. We piled out. After the jail adventure, We had reconnected. Everything was happy and perfect again. Yes, they had a room. Yes, Parsley was welcome. A long shower, whether hot or cold, and clean clothes were just the ticket before a delicious *mole* dinner. Our knotty pine paneled accommodation had a lovely hot shower and lacy, ruffled curtains on the pane-over-pane windows. I can't find the receipt, but I'm betting we didn't pay more than fifteen dollars for the clean, comfortable bed we made long, lingering love in on March 16th.

We should have stayed in Chetumal.

Chapter 24

Chasing Ku'kul'kan

March 18-21, 1992

In the morning, after walking Parsley and enjoying a hearty breakfast of my standard, eggs and *mole*, we meandered the four hours north to Tulum. The campers we'd met on the banks of the Mopan had described this lovely area where we could camp and enjoy the nude beach. Of course Fernando was all for it. Not so much me, although when we arrived, after chugging through the dry jungle, along the banks of a vast lagoon on a hard-packed sand track, I was taken with the sunny, clean beach and vista of ruins facing the aqua-colored Caribbean Sea.

The one-lane road led us for some distance along the back of a twenty- or thirty-foot dune between the sea and the lagoon. Eventually the road turned, skirting the shoulder, to the beach below a restaurant, El Mirador Restaurante & Bar, perched atop the sand dune.

As we drove out to the sand, we saw campers with vehicles, tents, and makeshift structures. The place bustled with uniformed military amid nearly naked hippie bodies. We claimed our patch of sand, reasonably near the outdoor showers, the restaurant/store towering above, and unpacked, setting up camp. Everyone passing stopped by to meet us, and checkout the camper. Fernando was in heaven, making friends, gathering information—mostly where to score. I met all the dog lovers while gleaning my own information. Everyone ogled the bathing girls on display in the shower.

Our section of beach lay north of the point housing the Tulum ruin, a unique walled city on a bluff above the sea. Unusual for its emphasis on trade, Tulum was built at the intersection of land and sea trade routes. The city had been a major distribution link for jade and obsidian, hence the wall for protection. None of the Mesoamerican people had been known to use seafaring vessels, but Tulum proves that wrong. I couldn't wait to explore, but first we had our immediate surroundings to learn.

The restaurant/store was a casual affair selling things like tacos, tortas, tortillas, beer, soda, water, and good coffee. I remember suntan lotion and knickknacks like shell necklaces, and cheap imitations of the antiquities dug up during excavation. The store was where we paid for our camping and showers, which I'm sure was a total rip-off. I refilled a *garrafón* with water and bought ice, which we lugged back to the *combi*.

Parsley was supposed to be on a leash but, as usual I ignored the rules. She really didn't like beaches but was a good sport lying in the shade under the bus while we swam and lounged around in the sun chatting with everyone stopping by. I don't remember seeing the Mopan campers, but I did meet "Mexican hippies" I recognized from Tepoztlán. They invited us to come to a bonfire down the beach later that night.

Fernando was back in his element. Everyone, other than a scant handful of Americans and Europeans, spoke Spanish. Fer loved to talk. He had a brand new audience to socialize with. This was one of the reasons I loved him. We easily met people and had interesting conversations. I continually learned new things, especially more Spanish. By Tulum, my listening Spanish was pretty good, although my speaking was still simple and only moderately grammatical. But it got me through most topics. I could have had an amazing time on the Tulum beach. Unfortunately, besides feeling fat and self-conscious, morning sickness made me feel crappy and tired.

Fernando towed me a step behind him through the sand on the way to the bonfire. With little energy, and less desire for a night of bacchanalia, I wasn't up for the beach party. Parsley stayed in the bus to protect it. I didn't trust all these beautiful people.

We arrived at the beach party after full dark. It wasn't late, but the night had settled warm, humid darkness over the beach and lagoon. Away from the fire, a multitude of stars glittered against the black. The party was getting going. Bottles and joints circulated. People played guitars and bongos. Some sang, many danced. Somebody cranked up a tape deck and played familiar tunes from the '60s. It was the Fillmore

Auditorium Quintana Roo style. And as in the '60s and early '70s, the electric Kool-Aid came around. Not being a stranger to psychedelics, I was tempted, but my better sense prevailed. I wasn't drinking or smoking because of the pregnancy—acid or mescaline or whatever unknown drug laced juice circulating was probably a bad idea. I'd given it up in the '70s. I don't recall seeing anyone taking cocaine—that was still an underground, back-alley kind of drug in Mexico in the '90s. The cartels had only started selling Columbian cocaine in 1985, and most of it went to the U.S.

As the evening wore on, people got drunk and the vibe turned sour.

"Fer, let's go back."

"Soon. This is fun."

"I'm not feeling so well."

"*Ahorita nos vamos.*"

Yeah, we'd leave sometime between now and never. I trudged back to the camper and my dog. Fernando remained ensconced with the Tepoztlán hippies, clattering in late.

In the morning we took a swim, wearing suits, then went up to El Mirador for breakfast. Over eggs and chorizo he told me about the *marineros* coming and breaking up the party the night before. He said some people were arrested. Great. I'd probably have to bail him out again.

After eating, Fernando dumped our trash. He filled my sun shower bag while I hung my shower curtain off the open back window. It was designed to encircle a mast, but I'd devised a tricky way of getting it up with a wide enough circle for me to properly bathe. The bag held two gallons of water, which took about thirty minutes to heat up to quite hot under a tropical sun. Again, people gathered around to admire my gear.

"*Muy padre, Ana, pero ¿porque no te bañas alla?*" asked one of the Tepoztlán hippies, jerking his head toward the beach showers where a sea nymph bathed.

I felt the color rise in my cheeks. He thought it was cool, but wondered why I didn't use the shower. Well, that was why.

Fernando cleared it up. "She's modest because she's pregnant. She thinks she's fat."

The group surrounding us laughed. Fernando laughed. I boiled with *verguenza,* shame, but showered in privacy. I had two gallons under which to stew. Fernando had turned on me, ridiculed me. I wished I'd left him in the Belize jail.

While I showered, Fer put together a little group to explore the lagoon, including a couple of the women from Tepoztlán. The apple-cheeked one looked enviously at my shower while the dreadlocked blond laughed at me when I came out wrapped in a beach towel.

"Fer, fill the bag again," I ordered, handing it down from its hook. I looked at Xochitlicue or Tonantzin, or whatever her name was, and said, "You're welcome to use it when we get back from our walk. The water will be hot." We smirked at the other woman and chatted as we trudged over the berm to the track along the lagoon.

As we walked, she told me about the resurgence of interest in the ancient cultures and how people were naming their babies after the gods and goddesses. Her name meant something like Earth Mother (Tonantzin) or Goddess of Fertility (Xochitlicue), but her birthname was more prosaic. Probably Maria. I guessed the bitchy dreadlocks' name was <u>Malinalxochitl</u>, goddess of snakes. I knew something about this because my friend in Tepoztlán, Lupe, had named her twins after Aztec goddesses. It turned out the earth goddess and Lupe knew each other, and my new friend was actually a secretary on vacation. The Tepoz crowd was in their thirties; none of the women ever showered in the public shower.

We gathered again at the site of the bonfire that evening for a potluck meal. This was more fun than the stoner party the night before. I was feeling pretty good. The crowd wasn't so young and naked, and the conversations ran the gamut of topics: politics, religion, food, culture and the coming equinox at Chichén Itzá. Our hippie friends drew a map in the sand. of the free camping outside the park where they. and most of the Tulum crowd. would be camping. Fernando was excited. He acted solicitous toward me. I think he knew how awful he'd been and wanted to make up. Or maybe he was just horny. He got a lot of admiring nods from the men when we got up in the morning and went to eat.

The beach around El Mirador buzzed with activity. People were filling water bottles, buying supplies, packing up. The equinox was in two days and the herd mustered for the move. We planned to visit Tulum then move on to a partially excavated ruin on a lake, Cobá.

Tulum was completely excavated. It offered great seascapes. A couple of the guys from the bonfire walked over with us. They inspected the temples, what might have been a customs house, and the many stele, some reputed to date from 564 C.E.—imports from somewhere else. The ruin was in its heyday between the 13th and 15th centuries. It was abandoned in the 16th century after contact with the Spanish. I translated my guidebook as we wandered around, pointing out the important buildings and speculating on life in the trading fort. Interestingly, no graves were unearthed during excavation. How could there be no people? Theories abound, but the one I espoused, claimed the good folk from Tulum ascended en masse into another reality and still live in their lovely Tulum. Fernando accused me of sipping the bonfire juice. But more believable: measles, small pox and syphilis decimated the population.

We were a cheerful foursome. I was sorry to say goodbye to our companions when it was time for Fernando and I to pack up and get on our way to Cobá. I don't recall the men planned to meet us in Chichén Itzá.

Cobá, whose name means "waters stirred by the wind". for the sea breeze rippling the nearby lakes and lagoons, was only about an hour away, but our late departure meant we arrived with limited time to explore. We found a path and wandered through the jungle until we came to one of the famous roads, a *sacbe*, "white road", a raised stone pathway leading to the ceremonial center from the residential area we passed, and the lake. At first, I didn't realize we passed ruins of dwellings for the jungle growth subsuming the structures.

"Look at the map, Fer. It says these are houses." I swept my arm toward the lumpy hillocks paralleling our stroll.

He trotted over to the nearest mound and started pulling away undergrowth. "Anita, come. It *is* a structure!"

I joined him. We clambered over hewn stones into a squared-off area overgrown with trees, shouting, "*¡Mira, mira!,* Look, look!" as we found indications of human habitation—a fireplace in one abode, potsherds in another. I smuggled home the foot of a tri-footed bowl with a face molded into it. The maker? Eb Zotz, my stone carver, I liked to imagine. Again, time warped to the past, and we found ourselves in states of giddy excitement, sharing wonder, the silk that originally bound us. But traveling through the overgrown rubble was difficult, slow and dangerous, although we weren't thinking about snakes at the time. We trekked back to the *sacbe* and on to the main pyramid, *Ixmoja,* and it's 120 steep steps to the 138-foot summit. It was comfortably warm out. By the top, our legs had turned to rubber and we were dripping in sweat. We sat on the flat top to dry in the soft sea breeze as we breathed in the rich aroma of growing things laced with salt, awed by the magnificent view. We were surrounded by a sea of emerald jungle, with the deep-blue Caribbean, and the immense swath of deep-blue sky blending at the horizon. We might have been the first explorers discovering Cobá for the total absence of human noise. Only birdcalls and the soft susurrus of wind through the treetops. Fernand grasped my hand.

"*Gracias mi amor.*"

SAINTS AND SKELETONS

"*¿Para qué?*"

He held his arms over his head to encompass the universe. "*Para esto.*"

My heart did a little flip as he smiled into my sunglasses and pulled me into a kiss as deep as the blue of the sky.

For some mysterious reason, I thought we'd be able to camp within the park. An attendant said Cobá had no accommodations as he ushered us from the Nohoch Mul group of structures. Visitors exited the park. We asked about camping. No dice. The few tourists were on tours from the Mayan Riviera resorts. Finally we ran into a ruin worker who agreed to let us park on his land next to Macanox Lagoon. As the sun set, we watched fishermen standing in the lake casting their nets and hauling in their catch. The workers' children charged us four hundred pesos, about twenty-five cents, to take their picture. A windfall for a six-year-old girl wearing baggy white underpants, and her four-year-old brother in jeans. Both came topless because the weather was perfectly warm and still. Unfortunately for us, it was also the hour the mosquitoes poured out of the marshy edges of the lake, and a lot of slapping began.

The kids' dad came to collect them for dinner. He gave us what he said was a fresh *mojarra* to cook. I made the fish fried in garlic—*mojarra mojo de ajo*. We put on long sleeves and pants then got out the incense and DEET, ate, and watched the reflection of nightfall in the lake. Fernando jabbered on about our new friends, the marvel of Chichén Itzá, and the Bajada. As if he knew. He's never been to the ruin. I let him talk—we were getting along. It felt like the giddy early days of our relationship. He didn't mention his need to get his business going or unreasonable dreams of marriage and children. We were together and had a fresh fish to eat. What more could we want? To get out of the bugs! We climbed inside the *combi*.

After the noise and activity of Tulum, it was peaceful, the stridulating of insects overlaid by the chirrup of frogs, and the soprano whine of mosquitos, blending into a perfect new age meditation soundtrack. We spooned in silence behind the no-see-um netting, letting the natural world envelope us. New sounds emerged: a honk of a night bird or a crocodile, a splash, flapping of wings. We relaxed until we breathed as one.

I woke up early, whipped up coffee and *huevos mexicanos* with a stack of tortillas. We planned the day over breakfast. I wanted to explore more of Cobá. My guidebook said it had had a long history and had been important to the region until the political climate changed when the Puuc states and the power seat shifted to Chichén Itzá. We'd missed the *cenotes* and the many carved stele. Fernando was less interested in my quest to bring Eb Zotz to life. He wanted to travel on to Chichén Itzá via Vallodolid, check out this ancient *conquistador*-settled city established in 1543. Records say the settlement was situated on a lagoon, but early settlers complained about the mosquitoes and they moved the town to its present location in 1545. I completely empathized. One night on a pond, and I was over insects!

However, in typical European style, they re-built the

town on top of a Mayan town, dismantling the buildings to use the stones to build the city. The Mayans revolted, but were suppressed. Two more Mayan uprisings occurred, one in 1705, which caused the cathedral to be torn down and rebuilt. The new cathedral is unique as it faces north, not east as Spanish cathedrals traditionally did. Fernando navigated us through the narrow *centro* to look at the lovely Moorish influenced Spanish architecture. Even though it was Friday, we found a parking space and entered the cathedral.

Fernando was feeling guilty he hadn't been to confession in a while. I enjoyed the serenity of the churches we visited while he took communion and confessed his sins. It was an on-going conversation while we drove.

"Fernando, what do you have to confess?"

"I'm living with you, and we aren't married."

"So you confess, receive absolution, and go right back to the same behavior, and that's okay."

"Exactly."

"Isn't the idea to stop sinning?"

"Sure, but Catholics get a pass if they confess."

"So I'm going to Hell but you get to say a few Hail Marys and go to heaven?"

He would laugh and shake his head. There was no way he could explain the system—no way that would allow him to continue his free ride. But it wasn't Mary or Jesus he would want to forgive him. At this point in the conversation, he would start talking too fast for me to comprehend. By Valladolid, I was catching on. Fernando was confessing smaller sins to hide the big ones.

We admired the main square and the colorful area surrounding the market where we ate lunch and plotted our route out of Valladolid on the road leading to Chichén Itzá, another short hop. We enjoyed the scenery as we motored farther from the coast into the jungle on a typically narrow, paved two-lane highway. In 1992, most of the roads were narrow blacktop. I enjoyed cruising at about forty mph, able to take in all the sights. Farms, roadside stands of fruits, vegetables, dream-catchers and, of course, tacos. On our way, we passed through several tiny villages, mostly assemblages of small thatch-roofed huts and corrals. Ebtun, Kaua, X-Calakoop. Not even blips on my map, but recognized by the school bus discharging children in front of a tiny church.

Soon we came to the Hacienda Chichén Itzá Resort at the entrance to the ruins. We were close to San Felipe Nuevo, the name someone mentioned as the location of the camping site. How to find it? We drove on and eventually saw some hippie-looking types walking along the road near an intersection. Fernando pulled over.

"*Hola, amigos. ¿Saben dónde está el camping?*" Fernando asked, leaning across me.

"*Claro, mano. Está ahi a la izquierda varios kilómetros. No lejos,*" the young bearded man said, pointing to the right.

I smiled. "*Muchas gracias, nos vemos.*"

We were almost there. It would be on the left. We turned the corner and continued for several minutes until we reached a turnout into a grassy area surrounded by trees—full of vehicles, tents, cooking fires, and rock and roll music. People milled around in colorful clothing or barely any clothing—I inwardly groaned, *not again*. I saw lots of long hair and dreads, and plenty of joints burning. Fernando looked like he'd died and gone to heaven. He pulled in.

One of the campers was the self-styled director. He motioned us along a narrow aisle to a spot about a half-block on the road side of the field. Fer maneuvered the bus around so our sliding door faced the party and we climbed out. Parsley was delighted to be outside without a leash in a place with a million smells and plenty of food. She and Fernando set off to satisfy their cravings. I stowed my money in the hidey-hole, locked up the bus, put the keys in my pocket, then set out to find the bathroom.

I found the communal fire pit, learning there would be a bonfire that night. On the other side of the field, I bumped into Xochitl and her crowd, and discovered there wasn't a bathroom. "Use the bushes," she said.

Great, so I was going to carry a poop bag for my dog *and* myself. Inconvenient, but I was no stranger to roughing it. I could always set a bucket in the shower.

Fernando waltzed up while I chatted with the Tepoztlán hippies. They offered us beer. I declined and accepted a tamarindo. After lapping up a bowl of water, Parsley sprawled out in a patch of shade. We lounged around talking about Tepoztlán, their jobs; they all had straight jobs, and how cool it was we got to come for this amazing, magical event. Or I guess that's what we talked about. The air was thick with *mota* and I had a definite contact high.

About the time the mosquitoes appeared, we returned to the *combi* to set up for the evening. Of course people stopped by to check out our decidedly fabulous rolling home. Fernando proudly showed off the accessories, like the swing-out gas cans, the extra-long tube from the propane to the stove, and how the table rolled up.

As night fell, and we were fed and doused in DEET, he said, "Let's lock it up tight, Anita. Put everything inside and make sure the propane is strapped down."

"Why? We'll be right over there." I nodded at the campfire, now starting to blaze.

"There's going to be a lot of *borrachos,* drunks. People will steal. Leave Parsley inside."

"Parsley, you want to go to a bonfire or be a guard dog," I asked my girl.

She didn't bother to reply, too busy snapping at mosquitoes. I took that as my answer. She stayed inside.

The party was fun with music cranked up with plenty of dancing and talking. I ignored the drunks and passed the joints on. People were excited about the next day. The party wound down earlier than the bonfire on the beach at Tulum. But not before jars were passed to collect payment to the farmer who'd loaned us the field. Fernando dropped the change from our last food stop into the kitty. We returned to the bus via the bushes then went to bed. We were not bothered during the night.

The campers got going early. I awoke on March 21st, the spring equinox, to the smells of wood fires, coffee, tortillas, eggs cooking, and meat roasting. I rolled out. After a trip to the bushes with Parsley, I made coffee and started on breakfast. By the time we'd eaten, cleaned up and packed, half the campers were gone. A lot of their trash remained. I made sure we left a clean spot then we hit the road back to the ruins.

Again we found a shady parking lot. The day was warm, humid, and as the morning wore on, cloudy. I worried that if the sun didn't shine, we wouldn't see Kukulkan come down the great pyramid. We headed off to the ball court, where I took a picture of Fernando shirtless in his turquoise and red shorts draped around the half of the stone ball hoop, which had fallen to the ground. I paced around the court, checking out the carvings along the length and width of the ball court. I needed to know everything.

"Ana, all the glyphs around the sides are sponsor advertising. You know: *Paco's Tacos, El Banco de Puuc, Balanario Cenote Itzá,* " he said, grinning.

I laughed. He was probably right. "So Eb Zotz was carving advertisements?" I replied.

"A *publicista? Claro!*"

Eb Zotz—an ad man.

We trudged down to the cenote where I listened to a tour guide tell the English speaking tourists all about tossing virgins in to drown as sacrifices to the gods. The cenote itself was beautiful. The deep green water filled the circular pit about forty or fifty-feet down. The walls of the hole were stratified white limestone giving the illusion of giant steps. Because it is a jungle, plants and trees rooted in anywhere they could, giving the cenote a wooded look.

On the path, we met three Mayan women wearing traditional *huipiles,* stunning square necked white tunics intricately embroidered around the neck, shoulders and hems in vibrant red, yellow, orange, blue and green flowers. Even their toddlers were decked out in similar clothes. The two babes in arms had been draped in embroidered cloth; the school-aged boy wore a tee-shirt with a Mickey Mouse-type character carrying a baseball bat. Go figure. In the photo, I stand head taller than the tallest woman.

We visited the Chacmool statue and the skull rack to take pictures, but as it grew more overcast and muggy, Fernando and I disconnected. I felt anxious. I always felt anxious when he turned his attention away. I wouldn't stay in Mexico, yet I wanted, craved, his love. When he turned his eyes on me, I floated above the ground. I became imbued with confidence and danced through my life. In short, I was the happiest I'd only ever experienced once before. I wanted this euphoria all the time. I was addicted. Wasn't that love?

We went back to the parking lot to walk Parsley. She had continued to decline. She now had trouble getting up, tottered as she walked, and had to be lifted in and out of the *combi*. She was a good sport, but on top of my anxiety over Fernando and the pregnancy, I added guilt for dragging a geriatric dog away from home. Parsley had been my loyal companion for thirteen years. I'd adopted her from a box of puppies outside the Lagunitas store in 1979. Didn't she deserve a comfortable dotage? I carried a heavy heart knowing the loss the near future held. Fernando may not have adored me every moment, but he loved Parsley as much as I did. We discussed what was coming; he supported the humane solution. Watching her shuffling through the weeds along the parking lot, he turned his warmth back to me. "Anita, I'll be there for you."

I checked my watch—2:45. The full shadow coming down the pyramid, also known as Kukulcán's Castle, would be starting soon. I wanted to watch the marvel of the descending, *bajada*, as the angle of the sun cast shadows and the plumed serpent slithered down. The shadow snake would peak at four-thirty, but the *bajada* started earlier.

"We have to go to the pyramid. It's time," I said.

We slowly walked Parsley back to the bus and gave her some cold water from the cooler. She lapped up a few sips and grinned, ready to take a nap.

The esplanade in front of Kukulkán's Castle was full of people milling under the leaden sky. We pushed into the crowd, positioning ourselves slightly around to the right of the main face of the structure so we'd see the shadow. *If* we'd see the shadow. We discovered we weren't far from the Tepoztlán hippie group. That cheered Fernando up, and he swam through the mass to get in on the joints being passed.

He returned; the minutes ticked by. Three o'clock. Three-fifteen. Three-thirty. By this time, the shadow would have begun to descend but the light on the castle was as flat as can be. Our acquaintances started drumming and dancing. The crowd parted around them. Fer and I edged closer. Just after four, women started chanting, "*Sol. Sol. Sol.*"

I heard people pooh-poohing the chanting, but we joined in. People around us joined in. Soon the esplanade, ten or twelve thousand people, were chanting. *"Sol. Sol. Sol."* It was deafening and joyful. *"¡Sol. Sol. Sol!* I thought the entire area would lift off and soar.

At exactly four-thirty, a rent opened in the cloud cover; a thick ray of brilliant sun angled down. Kukulcán appeared on the pyramid! It was a miracle. The multitude cheered as he slithered the rest of the way over his carved head at the base of the pyramid's stairway. Then, the clouds closed up and the plumed serpent returned to his heavenly den. But he left us, all of us, awed. What engineers and astronomers the ancients were!

What message did he come down to give? How remarkable that thousands of people gathered to witness this mystery, and unified to create the miracle of the serpent's appearance. The ancients claimed he came every year to deliver the message mankind needed. I wasn't sure what the message was—humans needing to live in peace and cooperation and harmony with nature before we destroyed ourselves and our planet? I don't know what his 1992 address was about, but Fernando and I enjoyed a detente for the remainder of the journey.

Chapter 25

The Beginning of the End

March 22-24, 1992

The Archaeological zone closed soon after the *bajada*. We hurried to the bus to beat as much traffic as we could. The plan was to find a trailer park in Mérida, about two hours northeast on Highway 180. We hoped to make it before dark.

Traffic was slow on the narrow highway and we arrived close to sunset. My guidebook didn't say anything about trailer parks in the city, but we found one near the Gulf coast toward Progresso at the top of the Yucatecan peninsula, Rainbow Trailer Park. It had a hot shower, although it was right by a big *henequén* factory producing sisal rope. Not that anything was going on over the weekend. We paid for our slip and searched out an inexpensive restaurant near a university. Sandwich and soda for less than a dollar.

The next day, Sunday, Fernando insisted we go to *misa*, mass, at Catedral de Mérida San Ildefonso. We hustled into our clothes after a quick cup of coffee and a walk around the property with Parsley, making it to the fortress-like church in time for the service. It is the oldest cathedral in the Americas, built between 1561 and 1598. I was taken with the soaring columns of white limestone and vaulted ceiling. While Fernando again paid his *get-out-of-purgatory* dues, I soaked in the grandeur of scale and lovely simplicity of this ancient house of God. That time, I prayed Fernando and I could come to an agreement, but I pled that the Goddess grant my doggie recovery. She was too busy listening to Fer skirt the real sin to worry about Parsley.

Mérida is another ancient city built by the Spanish. I found it pretty enough, but neither of us liked the vibe. We ate a delicious lunch after mass then strolled the main plaza with the dog. Then we drove around for a bit, landing in the crowded downtown, where we were stopped by the police for having a loud tailpipe. The *escape* again. The officer made it clear citizens didn't want "our kind" in their city. Hippies. If he only had known I'd given up my hippie lifestyle to become an accountant almost two decades before, but it wasn't worth explaining. I overpaid a fine on the spot. It probably fed the cop's family for the week. All we wanted to do was get out of town.

Mérida to Villahermosa took about nine hours on the route running along the dull grey-green of the Gulf of Mexico dotted with oil derricks and a few tanker ships. We took the toll road from Campeche City to Champotón but got back on the free road for the rest of the way, as the new toll-way was still under construction. The scenery looked dull and flat just like the Gulf. After the coruscating blue and silver of the Caribbean, and the dense greens of jungle, this was boring. We had a heart-to-heart talk to pass the time.

"Fernando, I can't keep this baby. We have no way to take care of it."

"I need to get my *negocio,* business, started. You have to let me. I can't continue to drop everything to run around with you. I'll move out when Blanca leaves, and we'll get a place. You can run the office."

"Fer! You already have a child you can't take care of and never see. Why would you want another?"

That always stopped him. He focused on the road. We motored in silence for a while. I thought back to our first long drive over the mountains from Huatulco to Oaxaca city. He'd told me about his daughter, a youthful mistake. Then, my Spanish hadn't supported learning more than Karina existed. Fernando confided his late teen romance with her mother. Fer had been twenty when his daughter was born. Now Karina was about twelve and lived with her mother somewhere in the State of Veracruz. Fernando had never seen her and, if I understood him correctly, she didn't know he was her father. Fernando's father took responsibility for the baby, sending money monthly until his death. Blanca had apparently taken over the support payments. Fernando felt guilty knowing he needed to step up and make sure his daughter was taken care of. One of the reasons he went to Germany?

"Why don't we go see your daughter while we're in Veracruz?"

"*Tienes razón*, but I'm not ready."

"When will you be ready?" I knew his ex-girlfriend needed money and Blanca, Fer's mother, wouldn't pay any more. Earlier in our relationship, I hadn't been sure Blanca knew her husband had supported the girl. I hadn't understood Fernando's admissions. Either that, or he'd been purposefully vague. But over the long, open roads of Mexico, we chipped away at the situation little by little. I could tell he was getting close to agreeing to visit. "We should give them some money."

"As soon as I start earning."

"You need to meet your daughter now."

He hung his head. The air settled heavy and humid between us, mimicking the sullen day outside our windows.

"How could I manage your office, Fer?

His head jerked toward me, "Answering the telephone. Talking to my clients. Scheduling. The regular stuff."

"But I can barely speak Spanish."

"You'd learn fast. It would help us build the service up."

"Pattie wants me to open Morelos to International Relocation. She's been so good to me, how can I refuse? I'll make money. She's already started training me. I'll be able to stay in Mexico."

"You could stay if we got married," he said.

"Are you asking me?"

"As soon as I get my *negocio* running."

"I'll stick with the relocation training." And get an abortion. Hadn't I had a similar conversation with Sam in October? If only I would do a man's bidding! I was developing a pattern: I could get married IF some situation changed. The embryo rolled over on a wave of nausea. I needed a nap.

Villahermosa. Another night at Costa del Sol, and breakfast. A blip on the map, nothing more. We were back on the road early, going north, retracing our steps from the month before. I had a better view toward the coast, but it was still the kelp green and grey expanse of boring scenery and endless discussion of our future.

"You didn't tell anyone you're pregnant?" he quizzed for the umpteenth time.

"No. I'd be pressured to go home. That would be a ..." I paused to look up the words: deal breaker. *"Factor dicisivo."*

"So is living in Tepoztlán. It's too far away."

"Why? We just made a bunch of new friends from there. You could come on the weekends and we wouldn't have to pay for lodging."

"They aren't friends."

I eyed him sideways, concealing my sneer. "But you need a connection."

"You need to run my office."

"You don't even have one."

"I will soon."

I closed my eyes. Napping cut off the endless circles we danced around.

I awoke to Fernando calling, *"Reina, Reina, ¡mira,!"* He pointed to a large lake in front of us.

We'd climbed into the coastal hills while I dozed and, although still overcast, the terrain had changed to a densely forested, mountainous region.

"Where are we?"

"Catemaco, the town where the *brujos* hold their annual convention."

"I thought it was earlier in the month."

"We missed it. *Además*, this isn't a place friendly to strangers camping in a *combi*." Fernando set the emergency brake and shut off the motor. I jumped out to open the door for Parsley. Fernando joined me in the majestic silence.

"But look at this huge lake. There must be a campground." We pulled along the shore of Laguna Catemaco gazing across the coruscating water and up into the cloud-ringed peaks of the Sierra de los Tuxtlas. Parsley stretched her legs and peed. Patches of deep cerulean blue opened between the clouds.

"We still have a ways to go if we want to make it by dark. We can't stay. Let's drive into town and get some lunch."

"Maybe get some tacos and have our future read?" I laughed. Fernando didn't believe in all that witchy stuff —but wasn't he the one tapping out the cross and kissing his fingers every time something unexplained occurred or he wished for something? I listed secret hand signs as *brujaría*, even if it came through the Catholic Church.

Catemaco sprawled down the western slope to the lake. It was a town like most: neatly ordered streets of stuccoed cinderblock and re-bar buildings, houses in some stage of being built up or torn down, fading colors one would never see chipping off homes in the U.S., lots of ironwork, a tiny *tienda* in every block, and brilliant bougainvillea exuberantly embracing anything it could climb upon. I noticed many businesses advertising card readings, cures, and charms.

We found a restaurant through Fernando's magical process—fitting right into a witch town—and ate a delicious lunch. I truly respected his food intuition. He knew how to pick 'em. I was into *mole* and loved scrambled eggs topped with *mole*. The little dives Fernando found came with delicious homemade *mole*, and good conversations with the *dueñas* and other patrons. We learned a bit about the Catemaco and the success of the recent convention. I logged Catemaco's witch convention onto my mental bucket list.

Back in the bus, we circled through town again looking for the road out. I saw more signs, icons and magical symbols I associated with the New Age community. Walls used as billboards advertised medical cures. Storefronts displayed herbs and candles. Lots of God's Eyes.

"The *brujos* live here," I announced, thinking I could live comfortably in this town.

"Many do. They're a secretive lot. That's why they don't like *extranjeros*."

"How do you spell that?"

The State of Veracruz was large. We had another three-to-four hours of driving. The sky cleared, and the glimpses of Gulf looked prettier the farther north we drove, but it dawned on me we were racing the sun. As far as I knew, Fernando had never arranged to visit with his friend Francisco, the sugarcane grower he'd gone to university with. I'd liked Francisco when I met him in November and knew we'd be welcome to camp on his property, but as the afternoon wore on, that possibility dried up. We'd never find Francisco's in the dark. We would have to stay in the city of Veracruz again.

"What do you want to do about a place to stay? Toto's?" I asked as the sun set over the highway. I was pretty low on funds and his brother's place was free.

"*¡De ninguna manera!* No way."

"*Pues, ¿adónde?*"

The question, *then where?* hung between us as we drove down into the harbor. I'd always liked Veracruz. A major shipping port, it had a huge harbor and an interesting palm-lined quay dotted with statuary. I loved to look at the giant ships docked far into the harbor, cargo ships piled stories high coming or going, the Imperial Walkers lining the piers. Always there was a cruise ship in port and myriad sailing vessels, tugboats, skiffs. Even at night the view was fascinating with port and starboard lights of red and green, flood lamps over the cargo loading and unloading, street lamps, lit portholes all twinkling and bobbing with the tide. It smelled like home on Richardson's Bay. We walked around in the harbor area, finding our usual hole-in-the-wall restaurant and sharing Huachinango a la Veracruzana, Snapper Veracruz **style**, a baked whole fish covered in a tomato-based sauce flavored with mostly European ingredients such as olives, garlic, and capers.

Hotel San Martin solved our housing problem. Breakfast at the Golden Pig got us going in the morning. We headed out to San Isidro and Francisco's with a bag of *pan dulces*. We stopped in San Isidro for some *comida* ingredients then barbequed with him before he sent us to our spot on Rio Frio. Parsley was dying. There could be no more denial. I was heavy hearted, even as we made plans to return for Francisco's birthday in three weeks over *Semana Santa*.

Chapter 26

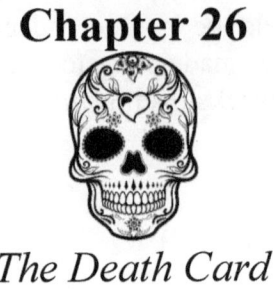

The Death Card

March 25-26, 1992

I may not have had my future read in Catemaco, but the cards were on the table. Parsley couldn't stand up on the banks of Rio Frio. On March 25th, we packed up our vacation and drove back to Mexico City. I spent the trip weeping and beating myself up for tearing my doggie away from her routine, her kitty, and her home in Sausalito. She was thirteen but I knew she would have had more good years if I hadn't been so selfish. If I hadn't wanted to break away from my dysfunctional family. If I hadn't thought I could write a book. What did I have to show for it? Nine pages of entries on three column accounting paper detailing what Fernando owed me. Eight million pesos I'd never recoup, and a baby on the way. Hardly a best seller.

"Fernando, she's dying."

"I know, *amor*. I'll make arrangements as soon as

SAINTS AND SKELETONS

we get back to Blanca's." He looked across the cab at me with tears in his eyes. Fernando loved Parsley nearly as much as I did. And she loved him.

I hung my head. "I can't have a baby, Fer. We've got to terminate."

He turned the radio up and crooned along. *'Perdóname mi amor por todo el tiempo te hice daño. Te sigo amando.*[9]*'*

I studied him from under my hair—his adorable curls and innocent visage, those beautiful blue eyes, the warm smile, even the shaggy mustache and beard, results of a month of roughing it. I was losing him. He felt the same. I knew it; he knew it. In the city he needed me more than I needed him. Everything was falling apart. Twisting up. How would I live without my doggie? How would I live without Fernando's heat? The love I had for each had twisted into a mass of barbed-wire squeezing my heart. Already I regretted my decision. Already I couldn't breathe.

'Estoy augando sin tu amore...'[10]

We pulled into Viveros de la Loma in the late afternoon. Fernando went directly to the telephone to call his vet friend. Then he phoned Uncle Beto, Blanca's youngest sibling, a hip man about my age, for help. Beto knew everyone; he could arrange anything. He suggested we come over for drinks and pizza the next evening. We had a lot to talk about. I looked forward to visiting Pilar and little Chareni again; they would cheer me up.

We stayed in Blanca's house in Fernando's

---

9 © 1980 Juan Gabriel *"Te Sigo Amando"*
10 © 1992 Maná Donde Jugaron los Niños "Vivire Sin Aire"

childhood room. I hadn't enjoyed staying there, but las Blancas were still in Veracruz. Still, the vibe was oppressive. We barely spoke. I slept on the floor wrapped around Parsley.

After breakfast, Fernando finalized the arrangements to get a lethal dose of whatever vets used to put dogs to sleep in Mexico, and the appointment at the *horno* at UNAM. The oven. All Mexico City pets were cremated at the University facility, Fernando said. I carried Parsley to the postage-stamp lawn in front and held her up to pee. She hadn't eaten much of anything in a couple of days. What she did eat, I hand fed her. She tried so hard to please me, even up to the final moments of her life.

Although I'd met Fer's vet friend on several occasions, I can't remember his name or picture his face. I remember he came to the combi, was gentle examining Parsley, and kind to me, taking time from his busy schedule to explain what we needed to do and what would happen. Fernando assured us he knew how to inject her. The vet gifted me the injection and some supplies for cleaning up. We thanked him before getting underway. The drive to the university could take two hours if traffic was bad. We had a cremation at four.

Everything about March 26th, 1992 is hazy. I can see the bus parked along a curb shaded by tall trees. A deep lawn ran between the sidewalk and a red brick building housing the crematorium. This is most likely my mind filling in. The lawn was probably a strip and the building cinderblock, but it doesn't matter. On the way to the south of the city, Parsley was so weak she couldn't stay on the seat. I crawled back with her. When we arrived, I slid open the door. Fernando climbed in with me, and as I held my old girl, whispering to her so she'd stay calm, Fernando injected her.

I watched her eyes close and felt her body relax into sleep. But her breathing continued, regular, deep. She was at peace. In my arms. Breathing. I thought she would live. I couldn't let go.

Fernando went to the crematorium and finagled a second injection for 20,000 pesos. The attendant came out with him. Although he wasn't pleased with the arrangement, he passed the syringe to Fernando and Parsley died in my arms on her seat in our bus. Fernando carried her to the *horno.* I cried. I was devastated, ripped out of myself by grief and guilt. Fernando tried his best to comfort me. I sobbed all the way back to Blanca's house in the north of the city.

I sobbed for my old dog, and I sobbed for the nameless baby growing inside me. Neither would be with me much longer. How could I possibly even think of keeping a child at my age and lifestyle? I swam in an ocean of guilt and grief.

The instructions were for the cremains to be returned to me, but Fer's friend stressed I leave her collar on her to recognize the ashes. While it wasn't unusual for the crematorium to give the cremains back, they were known to give people the wrong pets. We made the trek to UNAM four days later on the 30th. After another pizza for lunch, from another crematorium attendant, I received a plastic bag of ash and bones with her Marin County tags still on the metal collar ring.

Everyone was kind to me in the days after Parsley died. Beto and Pilar especially, since we had confessed our baby predicament over drinks and dinner. Beto, Fernando, and I disappeared into another room to have a private talk while Pilar put Chareni to bed. Beto said he knew a doctor who would take care of everything. A Doctor Ávila. He'd make arrangements. Fernando held me all night as I mourned my dog.

I drove back to Privada de Roseleda the next day. I needed to empty the bus, clean everything, repack the camping gear into the *bodega,* do laundry. I remember nothing. Maybe Patti and Rick were down in Tepoztlán. Fernando and I probably spent much of the day and night on the phone. I wanted information of Dr. Ávila and his clinic before I agreed to anything. In 1968, I'd gotten pregnant. Of course my parents had a fit. Abortion was illegal in California. But I've always remembered what my father said when I said I'd go to Tijuana. "I wouldn't send my dog to a Mexican clinic."

The week before I started my freshman year at University of Denver, I was sent to Tokyo, where it was legal. Twenty-four years later, I was hoping things had changed. We couldn't find any information about him. Most Mexican doctors trained in the U. S. I clung to that.

I fretted all day Sunday. We were summoned to Beto's office on Monday the 30th. The same day I was to pick up my dead dog.

Beto took us to the *consultorio.* It was all arranged and would cost 15,000 pesos or about $1200 dollars.

Expensive, but the good doctor was breaking the law. I had a preliminary exam and received instructions. Dr. Ávila had studied in the U.S. He spoke English about as well as I spoke Spanish. I was to return on April 1st—was he joking? —with an empty stomach and cash. This was beginning to feel like that back alley affair Dad had warned about. I looked around. The office was in a seedy, run-down area, but many parts of el D.F. looked disreputable. It was clean, the equipment sterile and in good repair. Beto vouched for him, admitting he'd used his services a time or two, totally shocking Fernando. I said I'd see the doctor on the first, and Fernando agreed. The die was cast; the future looked bleak. We both knew what this meant.

Beto dropped us off. Fernando got a haircut before we scarfed a few street tacos and he put me on the bus to the metro. I had to go back to Pattie's for the American Society Annual meeting the next day. I was keeping up appearances.

Chapter 27

April Fool's

April 1- 20, 1992

My diary entry for the 1st reads, *Last night I dreamed about the baby. It said, "You can't get rid of me." It wouldn't go away. I could see it, a redhead.*

I was freaked. There was no other way to describe it, but the die was cast. I would terminate the day. I couldn't talk to anyone about what was going on. Everyone knew Parsley died, and attributed my downcast manner to be that. I was alone in this weird nightmare. And scared. Abortion was illegal in Mexico.

I picked up Fernando. He drove us to Dr. Ávila's consultorio in Colonia Gustavo A Madera, near the airport. He called it a *Sanitario* and he might have been the doctor who delivered Chareni. I wasn't nervous until I realized Ávila wasn't there. I read. Fernando slept. We snapped at each other.

Finally, about five hours later he appeared, ushered me in to the large room, leaving me me to undress and settle onto the examination table positioned in the middle of the room. Fernando paced in the waiting room.

The doctor returned. He tried to get me to agree to total anesthesia. No way was I letting this guy put me to sleep.

"It will hurt," he said, pulling a speculum and some long torture instruments from his table.

He wouldn't be using a vacuum. It was the old "you rape 'em, we scrape 'em" method. "I've done this before," I said, refusing the anesthesia once again. But I was anxious. What if he punctured my uterus or...or... The specter of the back alley operation in TJ hovered over my head.

Dr. Ávila lectured and reprimanded me in English and Spanish throughout the procedure. I was a terrible person for having relations outside of wedlock, and a she-devil for terminating the pregnancy. Worst, I was an American. I was going to hell. Throughout the ranting, he roughly scraped away Fernando's and my love child. I feared I'd bleed to death on the table. Nobody but Fernando and Beto knew I was here. I'd be at the UNAM crematorium next. I gripped the table, trying to defend myself from his verbal attack. He didn't want to hear anything I said. He wanted me to feel the pain and cry. Plead. Repent. I gripped the table harder keeping my mouth closed, jaws clenched. Nothing about this abortion was clean. The methods this doctor used humiliated me.

As soon as he was done, I slid off the table and looked him in the eye. "I may have had sex out of wedlock, but *you* are the murder of the fetus, Doctor," I said as I shuffled to the recovery room. The joke was on me. I found Fernando lying on one of the cots, crying. I was the one who had endured the hateful speech and the painful scraping of my uterus! I snapped right out of the grief.

"God! What a baby, Fer. Why are *you* crying?" This was not what I expected. I needed him now and apparently he needed me more. What a letdown! I had to hold him, stroke him, whisper comfort, while my guts felt ripped to shreds.

I burned. I had the exhaustion, the sickness and the pain. And the humiliation. He wanted a mommy while I hemorrhaged.

We practiced avoidance for the rest of the afternoon until it got late. He interpreted my anger for grief and thought he was kind when he drove me to MacDonald's for a hamburger. He took me back to Pattie's. We watched the movie *Grand Canyon* on TV then ate candy and ice cream. He wanted to go home. I forced him to stay. Punishment.

The next day we set out to see a movie in Zona Rosa. Instead we drove to Tlalnepantla and parked in front of his house in Viveros de la Loma where I tried to get him to divulge his feelings, to no avail. I cried on his chest, but all I got was a terse, "If I want to leave you, I will say so." He said he still wanted me to move in with him and he'd get me a puppy. The irony: his speech was devoid of warmth. I wrote, *I'm depressed.*

After the abortion, I had dreams of Parsley, not the baby. Almost every night. I was a mess, bleeding heavily for the next week, and forced to keep my happy face in the house. When I dreamed of Parsley I felt close to her, could stroke her silky ears, hug her furry body. I missed her desperately. Too keep busy, I cooked: stuffed chayote for dinner, and food for ten guests at Pattie's friend Liz's birthday party, an amusing diversion while it lasted, except for the worsening intestinal distress I had begun to suffer. I shopped in Zona Rosa trying to get tickets the B.B. King concert in Chapultepec. Sold out. It dawned on me I felt depressed only when I was alone. I called Marty and was invited to go to Valle de Bravo for the weekend.

On Friday, I got up at six but we didn't make it to Valle until much later. Between the bleeding and the intestinal problem, I felt like total crap. I didn't want to do anything except eat, which caused pain, and shop, which also caused pain. I was practically broke. The trip was nice, how could beautiful Valle de Bravo be otherwise, but I missed Fernando and Parsley. When I confessed my gastrointestinal upset to Marty at our favorite barbacoa stand on the highway leading out of Toluca, she told me I had amoebas.

"Did you drink water somewhere?"

"From the pumps on the highway in Belize."

"How long ago?"

I counted back to March fifth.

"When did you start having symptoms?"

"A week or ten days ago."

"It's amoebas. We'll stop at the pharmacy for Flagyl when we get to Valle."

I was surprised. No doctor, just some pills. In no time, my gut was happy again.

In Valle I rode horses with Marty's second born, Christy, through beautiful forested country, catching glimpses of the lake, a reservoir that supplies water for Mexico City, between the trees. The damp forest smelled of pungent pine and herbs. I worried riding might make my bleeding worse, which it did. I also suffered from small, sharp pains. I went to bed early.

Every day it got harder to get up. I watched too many movies, but started a diet. Fernando and I talked on the phone. We met at VIPs magazine rack in Zona Rosa. A favorite stop for me, VIPs had books and magazines in English; their stores were located all over the city. For once Fer wasn't late. We had coffee and talked about what I needed in our relationship. Fernando didn't express any needs, but as a good will effort, he walked over to the Benjamin Franklin American Library with me and waited while I applied for a card, the first of many little steps toward residency.

My diary says we dined at a Denny's with terrible service; nowhere had B.B. King tickets; we bought a watch at La Rosa; our friends weren't home when we dropped by; and I was still bleeding. His friend's wife was pregnant. It made me sad for Fer, *He rationalized that it was for the best.* But I wondered what he was really thinking.

He said, "*Todo esterá mejor pronto.*" Everything will be better soon.

My response—we'll see, *vamos a ver.*

We spent most of the week getting ready to go to San

Isidro for *semana santa*, Easter week. We'd promised Francisco we'd celebrate his birthday with him. The *combi* needed some work Fernando could perform, and we ran around buying parts. Keeping busy distracted both of us from what I was now thinking of as "death week". On the 8th, I had my post-op check-up with Dr. Ávila and was pronounced, "doing well". I have an entry listing a visit to Shoe Street, a place that probably lifted my spirits. I cooked gumbo *file* for everyone and watched several dark movies, including *Cabo de Miedo,* Cape Fear. The movies matched my mood. It had been a terrible three weeks. I was ready to travel, but I had the feeling it would be our last trip.

We began it with coffee at Beto and Pilar's when we picked up Fer's laundry. I wondered what he promised her for the service. I found out: babysitting four year-old Chareni. I went to Charlie's salon for my wax, pedi, and hair trim. Another awful experience. She botched the wax, burning me in the process. Fer and Chareni ran errands, then picked me up to grocery shop and get money at Banamex in Satélite before we took her to MacDonald's and returned her home.

Finally packed, we swung by Fernando's, grabbed his bag, and hit the highway. We always forgot something, this time the huge water bottle. Eventually we stopped for excellent tacos al pastor in a dive in Lecheria. The establishment displayed posters of scenic places. I was drawn to one of Lake Tahoe. I realized I was homesick.

So much for our "early" start. Fernando was exhausted. We pulled off the highway to sleep. In the morning, we continued on to San Isidro. Francisco, or

Pancho to his friends, was already at work on his farm. We wiled away the time exploring the small town. Over coffee, I read in my guidebook about a pyramid nearby in a place called Zempoala, and added it to my list of touring for another day. At the time, we wanted to get to Francisco's and find our camping spot.

Francisco was delighted to see us, offering me many condolences over Parsley. He surprised us with his new girlfriend, a vivacious curly-haired beauty. We immediately hit it off and concocted the idea of everyone coming to our camping spot for a cookout. The men gathered up a couple of chairs, several cassette tapes, some fresh pork from a neighboring farm, and we caravanned to a copse of trees at the edge of one of his cane fields along the river we called Río Frío, although it was probably Río Actopán. We set up camp quickly to get the dinner started before the bugs came out.

April 15th was Francisco's thirty-first birthday. We spent it at Playa Chachihuecan, a six-mile long curve of pristine sand ringed by low trees at the mouth of Río la Antigua. The day was almost clear; the dull Gulf looked blue gray instead of kelp green. Sets of low waves broke in tiers across the gently sloping sand. My records say I bought ice and water for the beach trip. Did we barbeque on the beach? I only remember Fernando and I were happy, possibly the influence of Francisco's new love.

The 16th was the big day. I'd finally convinced Fernando to meet his daughter. Karina and her mother, stepfather, and siblings lived in an area called Chachalacas close to San Isidro. Possibly they lived in the town of Úsulo Galván. I picture the town with many

SAINTS AND SKELETONS

tall trees and much green. The family's house was one-story. It did not have a high wall around it. In fact it was very comfortable and light with windows all along the back looking into a verdant garden. Fernando and Karina were nervous as expected, but the mother, Fernando's ex-girlfriend, was a gracious hostess. In no time we were chatting and getting along well. The girl was sweet and lively. I'd brought some gifts for Fernando to give her, possibly the watch from La Rosa, among more interesting things, for a thirteen-year-old. I did not keep notes on what money they were given, but I know I arranged something. We went out for ice cream. Karina showed us around. She was a happy kid. I hoped Fernando would stay in her life.

We slept in a motel that night, because my bath and hair washing in the river had been a bust. We may have been on Francisco's property, but the river ford was right in my bathtub. First a *campesino* on a donkey splashed through, profusely apologizing for disturbing me. Then some women came to do their washing. Even Fernando harassed me with the camera! Finally I'd had enough. I needed a shower.

The next night, after exploring what is a now a glitzy ten-mile swath of coast called Costa Esmeralda, we dined in an inexpensive restaurant. The beaches were lovely and the sun shone. We decided to go south the next day to Papantla, the home of vanilla, to the ruin of El Tajin, known for its unique architecture.

The next morning, I found my fabled *mole* at Bonanza Café. It was a little hole-in-the-wall with bright tablecloths and a cheerful *dueña* then. I ate scrambled eggs with *mole* Veracruzano, an exquisite mixture of chiles, nuts, Mexican chocolate, plantains, plums, and raisins. *¡Qué Rico!* Hot and sweet, exactly like Fernando when we met. No wonder I loved it.

The Tajin archeological zone cost 26,000 pesos to get in, but was worth every cent. The city was inhabited from about 900-1300 C.E. after the decline of Teotihuacan in central Mexico. Its architecture, which is unique in Mesoamerica, displays elaborate carved reliefs on the columns and frieze. The "Pyramid of the Niches", is masterpiece revealing the astronomical and symbolic significance of the buildings. We did not climb this pyramid. It probably wasn't allowed. The black color comes from a fungus eating away at the stone. To enhance the day, Fernando and I were happy together.

From the ruin we passed through Papantla, also the home of la Danza de los Voladores. I bought several bottles of pure vanilla extract in a tourist market. Since it was Saturday, the town was full of visitors. As we walked around, we happened on a troupe of Voladores performing in the plaza. It was magical. The dancers, as they are called, climb up a tall pole and "fly" down, circling the pole as musicians atop the pole play drums and flutes. Round and round the dancers go, slowly being lowered to the ground. I flew right along with the voladores—on the magic of our happiness. Things were going to work out.

Before dark, we raced back to the *caña* field to bed down. The magic flew along with us that night.

On Sunday the 19th, we drove to Zempoala to find the archeological site I'd read about, with the pyramid located in town. We would be driving back to Mexico

SAINTS AND SKELETONS

City the next day. Two young men—English speakers—sat at the top observing the town and forest stretching to the Gulf. Zempoala was the Totonac capital city when Hernan Cortez set foot on the shores of Veracruz and is estimated to be over 1500 years in occupation. The name, Zempoala, means abundance of water, or twenty waters. In 1992, the site was free, and open to explore. We were the only tourists. We shared a couple of joints, basking in the light winds and antiquity of the area, talking about this and other ruins we had visited.

Eventually, we scrambled down the Temple of the Sun and parted ways. Hotel Royalty, Veracruz our destination. We wanted one last night to stroll the wharf in the clean tropical air. And one last turn through the ancient city. On our morning stroll, we found several marimba players set up on the wide sidewalk outside bustling restaurants playing for pesos. One played a tune Fernando liked just because he claimed to see our love. He thought we were newlyweds. More magic!

We got underway, making it to Xalapa, the capitol of the State of Veracruz, for lunch. Near our restaurant, we found a festival of flowers going on. I couldn't pass it up; Fernando was a good sport. The displays of orchids sent me to the moon and back.

The trip was a success. We were happy again. On the long drive to Mexico City, we negotiated a future. Deep down, I knew the trip and the talk were just more opportunities for us to avoid reality.

Chapter 28

Detox

April 20-May 5, 1992

Fernando went home to Viveros de la Loma. I went "home" to Privada de Roseleda. If I were to stay in Mexico, I had to put my nose to the grind and start acting like a professional housing specialist. Fernando insisted his uncle knew a guy, who knew a guy, who could push through legalizing the *combi* to stay in Mexico. We parted company, promising to continue our negotiation about living together in Tlalnepantla. We'd had an exciting trip and grown closer for it. I didn't want to lose him, but I couldn't move to the far north of the city, onto the local economy. I was close to the end of my money. Opening the Cuernavaca region to the expats pouring into Mexico with their companies since NAFTA ratified was a safer and more lucrative bet. And Pattie wanted a commitment.

I barely had time to take a proper shower and unload the bus before we sat down to have a chat about

B & Bs—something she was interested in doing with Hacienda Clementito. I could live in the room off the workshop and laundry, at the time roofless, but on a private patio across from the main house. She wanted me to do the advertising, bookings, run the cleaning and maintenance crew, and cater. When we were empty, I could find houses and contract with owners for International Relocation Services, Pattie's company, to rent to the American, Canadian, and English personnel of the companies flooding into the area. My work would include showing properties to prospective renters, helping families settle in, talking to their cooks and drivers, finding schools for the kids, teaching the wives how to grocery shop through basic Spanish lessons, and getting them into the Cuernavaca Newcomers Club, which I joined around that time.

She promised if I'd take the "job", Pattie would have the roof finished and the attached bathroom plumbed. She argued: "It will be a great way to improve your Spanish." "You'll meet so many interesting people." "Liz is a realtor. She will help you." "You love to run around and get to know Mexico and its people." "And you've said you'd like to live in Tepoz."

The list went on. I couldn't refute any of her points. I'd probably be great at the job. I already did some accounting for IRS, as Pattie called the company. In fact, the prospect excited me and gave me stomach cramps. I saw the distance between Fernando and me widening, not just in miles and hours—it was about seventy miles and might take three hours depending on the time of day and day of the week—but in lifestyle, social circle, communities. He was going to the dogs, literally, and I'd be going to the English-speaking expat community. You might say, I was going to the Americans, somewhere Fernando tolerated but didn't want to become a part of. This decision made me anxious and clingy. How could we solve the conundrum and stay together?

Two days after arriving back in el D.F. I drove to Valle to join Marty and Christy, to "think about it". The drive took a couple of hours, passing over the towering mountains to the east of Mexico City and down through the capitol of the State of Mexico. From Toluca, the route turned north into a mountainous region, passing Nevado de Toluca, Mexico's fourth highest mountain. The trip from Toluca on the typical two-lane highway was beautiful through pine and deciduous forests. At the turn-off to Valle is one of the world's monarch breeding grounds, a quarter mile of an orange and black monarch blizzard, one of the wonders of the world. But not on April 22nd. The traffic mirrored my mood. I growled at the selfish truckers crawling well below the speed limit, with twenty cars following instead of moving over. I gripped the wheel and tensed when idiot daredevil drivers pulled out to pass the train of cars on the curvy highway. I was so uptight, I missed my turn off to Avandaro and got lost near the golf course, finally finding the house in time for a short rest and lunch at four o'clock, then a trip into the city of Valle de Bravo to shop at my favorite *mercado de artesenal*. I bought a tortilla warmer. At the grocery, I learned about *nata,* the cream that thickens and congeals from boiling raw milk. We bought melon and prosciutto, and ate too much fresh bread slathered in *nata* at supper, and later, pie, ice cream and candy. I went to bed feeling bilious and adrift without Fer.

I stayed in Valle for the next couple of days on a whirlwind of luncheons with Marty. She, very kindly, counseled me to get away from Fernando and start doing something useful. I'd had my exciting travel, now get busy. She was right—if only I would recognize it.

On Saturday, I drove over the shoulder of Nevado De Toluca to Cuernavaca through a district of lakes—stunning green mountains with fresh rivers and many bodies of water. This area was known for its *trucha*, trout, which was popular as street food across the region. Whenever I went down, I patronized a Saturday vendor at the market in Tepoztlán, then happily passed through the zocalo, stopping for a snack before the *trucha* was gone.

Pattie's circle of friends was vast. That day was someone's birthday. We gathered for the weekend to celebrate. I enjoyed Pattie's crowd, but Fernando didn't fit in, so I had passed on many opportunities to make connections. Now, if I were going to work in relocation, I needed to know people. The inner circle loved to party. Everyone cooked, talked, played Trivial Pursuit and card games, told stories, swam, played tennis, and drank. Everyone could hold their liquor but me. I don't remember birthday-boy Edgar or his birthday. I was probably blitzed the whole time. As a teetotaler, Fernando was both a deterrent to drinking, and a caretaker after the third beer. All the drinking depressed me more. I went back to Roseleda, spent some time in the kitchen, and the Ben Franklin Library.

When I went out, I still rarely drove the bus. Parking was difficult; the traffic heavy at any time of day. I learned the main routes to the places I needed to go, and got to know the Zona Rosa, where I'd taken classes when I arrived, pretty well. But I often got lost on the one-ways and dead ends of the city. It was easier to use public transportation, which I did, coming to know the metro service well. To get to the library, I took a *pesera* from the intersection of Rosaleda and Observatorio, down the mountain to the Tacubaya metro stop on the pink line #1—the location of the best tacos *suaderos* in the city. Zona Rosa was three or four stops, depending on which end I wanted to go to. Sevilla stop for the Mercado Londres, my favorite place to shop for silver jewelry, and where I finally broke down and spent a hundred dollars on an embroidered tablecloth I'd lusted over since arriving in the city. The library was near the Insurgentes stop, as was a good pharmacy I frequented.

On the way back from the library during rush hour, laden with groceries, shopping bags and books, as I stood in the crowded line waiting for my *pesera* back up the mountain, a thief slashed my brand new handmade black suede purse that went with the pumps I had made, pinching a little zipper pouch. It was a cosmetic bag with a lipstick, of which I had another in the same color. Bastard! Ruined my lovely new handbag. I had it repaired at the cobbler's but it wasn't the same. I learned the hard way the city was full of dangers. I pined for Fernando, who had kept me safe for so long. After watching *Hook* on TV with Pattie and Rick, I spent an hour on the phone with Fernando. We planned to meet at Zona Rosa Sanborns the next day.

It was the 30th of April. I spent 8700 pesos on us—another seven bucks. If Fernando was getting his act together, it didn't come with money. I was tired of buying him. I needed to invest in myself. I'd decided I'd make a life in Mexico on my own, then spent May, 1992 doing things without him. As long as I was occupied, I was not exactly happy, but I was able to deny my depression. It was a sort of limbo. I joined the Cuernavaca Newcomer's Club, and the American Society, and started to get involved. I participated in a women's group, signed up for yoga in colonia Roma, which I absolutely loved. It probably saved me. I worked on my collection of recipes for a cookbook, even taking some cooking classes. I attended all the IRS meetings to learn about the relocation business, learned to use PageMaker on Pattie's Apple to start doing promotions by writing titles and blurbs for the photo album of my travels. My May calendar was packed with appointments, dates, parties. We celebrated Marty's birthday on the 15th. I went out with some of the women I'd met. Mom and my brother planned a visit. I made several trips down to Tepoztlán. And still found time to go to the library.

Life was pretty exciting and full. If I hadn't been so lovesick over my waning relationship, I would have had the time of my life! I'd probably live in Mexico City now. The city had a magic that excited me through to my bones. I felt good in The Capital, energetic and alive. Regardless of the awful pollution, my skin looked clear. The altitude and culture of taking the main meal in the afternoon made me thin. Getting out of my vehicle and walking made me fit.

I really needed to let go. Rip off the band-aid—cold turkey. Keeping busy helped. But we talked on the phone regularly, a difficult activity due to my imperfect Spanish. We couldn't agree on anything. It was around this time that the verb *discutir* began to crop up in our talks.

Fernando: *No discutas conmigo.*
Me: *¿Discutas?*
Fernando: *Búscalo. Discutir.*
Me: *Sí discutir, we need to talk about it.*

At this point he usually said he had to go. I failed to look up *discutir* because I was certain it meant "to discuss." Why wouldn't he want to discuss a path forward? The irony is, I didn't learn the meaning of the word—argue—until I started writing this book.

On Cinco de Mayo, a day not celebrated in Mexico, I woke up tired and depressed at Fernando's house after our fun outing to Xochimilco the day before. I had to pretend to be happy. I should have been happy—we'd eaten my favorite, *barbacoa*, and I bought carved saints for us. Pilar was visiting the house that morning. We took her and Blanca out to buy *pan*. Later Fernando and I went to Superama for chicken and cereal. I read an old copy of the English paper, The News, in the sun while Fernando tinkered with UYOLKAN's engine until it was timed. Then I drove back to Roselada to pot primroses with Jennifer, one of the relocation agents, and Susan's daughter.

Fernando stood me up, again, for the chicken dinner. I wrote, *But who cares? We've probably come to the end of our time. He's dear, but I find myself* *wanting someone who speaks English and has $ and standing. At least I'm not pregnant* (I'd gotten my period that day), *now there's only the issue of money between us.* I spent the evening reading lime recipes from one of Pattie's excellent collection of cookbooks.

Chapter 29

I Should Have Stayed in California

May through July first, 1992

During mid-May, we spent several days together in Tepoztlán. I tallied the pesos spent: tacos, 16,000; gas 20,000; food from the market 27,800; more food 48,000; cash for Fernando's metro. My money dwindled. I couldn't afford any more trips. If I wanted to move down to Hacienda Clemente Jacques and start putting ex-pats in homes, I needed cash. Running back and forth between *Privada de Roseleda*, Tlalnepantla, and Tepoztlán strained my budget. Just the tolls alone cost around twelve dollars.

Nothing had changed between Fernando and me. We fought over the phone. I wanted to try my hand at relocation real estate, see him on weekends and whenever I could get away for a trip. Fernando wanted me to move in with him to run the business side of his dog training service, the subtext: I'd fund his non-existant enterprise.

SAINTS AND SKELETONS

"Te amo, Anita. No puedo vivir sin ti. Ayúdame en mi negocio. Tan pronto como se ponga en marcha nos casaremos." Help me. As soon as this gets going, we can get married.

"I need to do this for Pattie. We can see each other every weekend. I love you."

"If you loved me, you'd help me. You're going to leave."

"I'm running out of money, mi amor. I have to work too."

Round and round and round. It was exhausting. I should have gone home. I couldn't leave him. I threw good money and emotion after bad. I was addicted—always looking for my next fix of his attention. We needed a trip to plan. A big one. That would fix everything. I called Dad.

After eleven months, I missed my family and friends. I wanted to scatter Parsley's ashes into the bay off Sausalito, the home she'd loved most. I needed to negotiate a loan. Fernando had never been to California. It was a no-brainer. Dad missed me and bought us round-trip tickets.

We flew out on the 15th of June and returned on the 21st. I was eight grand richer and had an agreement with Dad to pay my credit card bills for a year. If I weren't earning money in one year, I'd come home. I didn't share this information with Fernando.

I'd slimmed down after the abortion. The pair of us together looked great, especially after I took us clothes shopping. At forty-one, I looked Fernando's age. I saw the envious glances from my single friends. Fer had learned a bit of English and tried it out. Even my mother liked him. He had the capacity to be charming and polite. It was pretty cute watching him help her in the kitchen, neither understanding what the other said. Fer did not charm my sister. Dallis had gotten chummy with my ex, Sam, and disapproved of what I'd done.

For a week, we enjoyed barbeques with all my friends in Sausalito's houseboat community while we bunked with my former next-door neighbor, delighting Fernando. He'd never been on a houseboat. We sailed around Angel Island catching glimpses of the Golden Gate Bridge, and San Francisco, toured the Marin Headlands, Muir Woods, Bolinas Beach, and finally, my dear friend Ebbie took everyone who knew Parsley out on Richardson Bay on his sternwheeler, for a ceremony. Half of Parsley's ashes rained on the breeze into the water as the sun dipped behind Mill Valley and the coastal hills. The other half of Parsley now resides with Lab Chocolatte and cat Alison on my pet altar.

Like our time in Belize, I was the caretaker, manager, and tour guide. I liked it. I felt like I was in charge of my life again. I was the envy of the crowd with my running translation to Spanish of everything going on for my cute, charming arm-candy. One of my close friends commented he was my pet. A replacement for Parsley. I was probably offended, but she was right. I confessed what had been going on to my closest friends, who all pegged him as a freeloader, a gigolo. I'd heard that from Pattie, Marty, and his mother, but I wasn't able to accept it at the time. When I told my friend Judy we were talking about getting married she laughed.

"He's already married."

"No, he says he's divorced."

"You're in denial if you believe that."

I flashed back to the living room at Toto's in Veracruz. The talk of responsibility, doing the right thing, getting his wife straightened out. I hadn't understood all the words, but something had stuck. Outside of the environment of our relationship, it made sense. I'd convinced myself the family was angry because he wasn't paying his alimony. Clear, even to me, Fernando's family disapproved of our affair, although I knew they liked me personally. Hadn't his mother warned me not once, but several times? Blanca said he wasn't trustworthy. I refused to believe any of them, especially Blanca. She tried to warn me: Fernando wasn't available.

I was supporting him when we were together, and in Mexico saw him only when he needed something. His family and my friends were right. I knew it. But in California, we were riding high, connected, and in love, the effect I sought. We promised each other we'd figure out how to make it work. Like we'd done on every trip we'd taken. What was the matter with me? I was barreling toward a cliff and was about to pass the last exit. I could have stayed in California, flown down to pick up my bus and souvenirs later. I could have done lots of things, but I got on that plane to fly to Mexico City with Fernando Leon.

Afterword

On July first, 1992, I moved to into my newly roofed shack at Hacienda Clemente Jacques to start my job as a relocation agent. Fernando moved out of Blanca's house into his duplex cum *oficina*, in Tlalnepantla. The vultures circled; the funeral bells tolled. I want to say I veered away from the cliff, let go and moved on, but I sailed right over that precipice into a black withdrawal.

Everyone was right about Fernando. I couldn't deny it any longer. I was addicted to love, and the drug was gone. The withdrawal was long and painful. No, I didn't go home for another nineteen and a half months. Much of that time I suffered greatly on the emotional rollercoaster of grief and anger, extreme isolation, loneliness, and depression. But that part isn't the story I tell here. This is the story of Mexico and the Mexican who filled my heart, then broke it, as we adventured like gypsies through his homeland, loving, fighting, lying, and denying the truth as we sampled the riches and dangers of his world.

Mole Veracruz Style

Adapted from Diana Kennedy's "Mole de Xico" in *My Mexico—A Culinary Odyssey with More than 300 Recipes,* Clarkson Potter Publishers, New York, 1998

Over the twenty-nine years since I returned to California from Mexico, I've continued to search out superior *moles*. My husband and I frequent Mexican restaurants where I sample their *mole* atop enchiladas, in tamales, with meats or fish, and if they offer it, over my favorite—scrambled eggs. If I like the *mole*, and the restaurant is owner-operated, I ask what region they and the *mole* are from. Too often I can taste the *mole* is from a commercial paste, but sometimes it's the real deal— homemade from authentic *mole* ingredients. We're lucky, our local *Mi Pueblo* serves homemade red mole from the Mexico City region. I've never enjoyed Veracruz style mole in the U.S. except when I've given up a day to the kitchen, and made my version of *Mole de Xico*.

The original recipe was featured in an out-of-print, limited edition, collection of recipes sponsored by a former governor of the State of Veracruz, *La Cocina Veracruzana.*

This recipe will serve twelve. Leftover *mole* will keep for a month in the refrigerator; longer in the freezer.

Ingredients:
12 oz. *mulato* chilies dry
9 oz. *pasilla* chilies dry
pork lard (best) or flavor neutral cooking oil
1 small-medium pungent white onion sliced

9 small cloves of garlic or 5 large peeled
about 4 quarts of rich chicken broth
½ c. almonds (I use blanched and skinned almonds)
2/3 c. skinned peanuts (for a richer-flavored sauce, exchange 1/3 c. each pine nuts and hazelnuts)
¼ c. pecans (you can use almonds and pecans if you don't want peanuts)
4 T. sesame seeds
1/3 c. raisins
2/3 small plantain sliced
10 pitted prunes
3 small slices of stale French bread
2 dry corn tortillas, tiny street taco sized
2 medium sized tomatoes broiled, see directions
6 peppercorns toasted and crushed
6 cloves toasted and crushed
2/3 inch cinnamon stick crushed
1/3 c. *piloncilo* grated or soft brown sugar
1 ¼ oz. Mexican drinking chocolate such as Tazo
12 generous servings of chicken (or turkey) pieces
salt to taste

Equipment:
a saucepan large enough to hold the chilies
a frying pan
a blender
a deep heavy Dutch oven (I use Le Cruset)
a large deep skillet to cook the chicken

Steps:
01. Remove the seeds and veins from the chilies, place in the saucepan and just cover them with water, simmer for five minutes. Set aside to soak for up to ten minutes and drain completely.
02. Place the tomatoes on an ungreased pan or

comal over medium heat, turning often to evenly brown and blister. Or broil two inches under the oven's broiler on a foil-lined baking sheet until browned, blistered and soft inside.

03. Heat $2\ 1/2$ tablespoons of lard or oil in the frying pan. Add the onion and garlic and fry without browning until the onion is translucent. Drain the oil. Add mixture with 2/3 cup of broth to the blender. Blend until smooth. Add a cup or so of broth and blend a few of the chilies to a grainy puree in two or more batches, adding enough broth to keep the blades turning.

04. Add 1/3 c. lard or oil to the heavy Dutch oven. Add the pureed chilies and fry very gently, scraping the bottom of the pan often to prevent scorching. Fry for about ten minutes. Set aside.

05. Put some lard in the skillet and fry each of the remaining ingredients through the corn tortillas separately and draining each in a strainer to remove the fat. Between ingredients add only enough fat to cover the bottom of the pan. Crush the fried nuts, bread and the tortillas after draining to blend more easily.

06. Add about 2 c. of broth to the blender and blend the fried ingredients in small batches, adding broth as needed. Pour the fried ingredients into the chile puree.

07. Blend the tomato and spices together. Add to the mixtur the pot with the sugar and chocolate. Cook over low heat for about ten minutes. Add about a quart of broth and continue cooking for about a half hour. Stir often to keep the mole from sticking to the bottom of your pot. The *mole* should be thick and the flavors well blended. Pools of oil will form on the surface.

08. Heat 1/3 c. of lard in the frying pan to brown the

pieces of meat. Drain the excess fat and add the meat to the pot. Cook over low heat for about 40 minutes until the chicken is fully cooked. Dilute with more broth as needed and adjust the salt before serving.

Mole is delicious served over fluffy long grain white rice or with plenty of warm tortillas of your choice to sop up extra sauce.

¡Buen Provecho!

About Ana Manwaring

Ana Manwaring is the award winning author of the JadeAnne Stone Mexico Adventures and three volumes of poetry, as well as many essays, short stories and flash memoirs.

Ana teaches creative writing and autobiographical writing in California's wine country. She is the founder of JAM Manuscript Consulting where she coaches writers, assists in developing projects and copy edits.

When Ana isn't helping other writers, she posts book reviews and tips on writing craft and the business of writing at https://buildingabeterstory.com/. She produces the North Bay Poetics, a monthly poetry event.

She's branded cattle in Hollister, lived on houseboats, consulted brujos, visited every California mission, worked for a PI, swum with dolphins, and outrun gun totin' maniacs on lonely Mexican highways —the inspiration for The JadeAnne Stone Mexico Adventures. Read about her transformative experiences living in Mexico at www.saintsandskeletons.com.

With a B.A. in English and Education, and an M.A. in Linguistics, Ana is finally able to answer her mother's question, "What are you planning to do with that expensive education?" Be a paperback writer (e-book and audiobook, too!)

If you enjoyed Saints and Skeletons, please consider going to your favorite online bookseller and leaving a review. Reviews help authors continue to write their books for your enjoyment.

To find out about new books and upcoming events, please take a moment to sign up for my mailing list at www.anamanwaring.com.

A JadeAnne Stone Mexico Adventure Book 5

Backlash

Venom and Vengeance from 'Nam

Chapter 1

The Past is Always With You

September 30, 2007

Jackman Quint hovered outside the TSA checkpoint at the Denver airport, despondency a blue funk like Tule fog swirling around him. JadeAnne was leaving—going home. He felt his heart cracking open. After he'd finally found his child, lost to him before her birth, JadeAnne was flying away. He hadn't expected to feel like this.

Obscured behind the snaking line of travelers inching through the TSA checkpoint, he watched his daughter slip back into her shoes, scoop up her small carry-on and take her man's hand. They headed into the wide hall toward the train to Concourse C. Quint watched as they disappeared into the crowds, eyes stinging from pinpricks of hot moisture. Would she come back? He shuddered, gulping to stifle his sorrow, and swiped away the visible signs of emotion from his face. *Get a grip, soldier.*

Irritated at acting like a broken-hearted teenager, he exhaled and strode toward the drop-off area in front of Jeppesen Terminal East. Horacio would be navigating back around the airport loop to pick him up. He couldn't keep his partner waiting, or risk a ticket and police interest. It would be gamble enough driving back to El Paso in the shot-up SUV, one of the cartel attackers still in the wind.

Anyway, public displays of emotion weren't his thing. The first time he'd lost her—the last time he'd cried—it was either buck up or bitch up. And he wouldn't be anybody's bitch. At least JadeAnne and Dylan were safe. He blew his nose on his Starbucks napkin. No, he wasn't going to start blubbering now. He dropped the empty coffee cup and soiled napkin into a receptacle then pushed through the revolving door onto the wide sidewalk, crammed with travelers and luggage scurrying to check-in to their flights.

But the question, *would she return to their home and business in Mexico City?* pecked at his thoughts. Would she? A series of honks startled him back to the airport. A man, scooting out of a black SUV, the side riddled with bullet holes, gesturing.

"Queent. ¡*Queent!*¡*Aqui yo!*"

Quint waved his arm, and broke into a jog, shoving his sadness into a dark crevasse of his heart to inspect later. The sooner they got out of Denver the better. And the sooner they dumped the SUV back with his contact on the border, the sooner they could get back to Colonia Roma and the op.

Horacio held the shotgun door open. A sudden sharp crack rang through the departure area, sending Quint diving into the SUV, ducking below the window. Horacio slammed the door behind Quint and stumped around to the driver's side, sliding his ogre bulk behind the wheel.

"Thanks, H. They're off. Let's get out of here. Dump this SUV. You okay to drive?" he asked, straightening up, nodding toward the bulky dressing under his partner's shirt.

"Only hurts when I laugh, *jefe*," He grinned, slamming his door shut as the ping of metal on metal rang out. Then another.

"What the hell—"

"Get down, *jefe*," Horacio shouted. He floored the gas pedal, cutting off arriving travelers to honks and shrieking brakes.

The vehicle shot into the left through-lane into the curve as the rear window spider webbed, but held. H laid on the horn as they blasted away from Denver International to loop onto Peña Blvd. headed toward I-70 West.

Quint craned around in his seat. "Can't see a damned thing out the rear. Anything chasing us?" He peered through the side mirror. The white peaked roofline of DIA, like a giant circus complex, receded into the endless blue sky spread over the prairie.

"Nothing going as fast as we are," Horacio said, "The sniper wasn't in a vehicle. Not a moving vehicle."

"Parking garage?"

"*Sí.*" His answer slipped into the sibilance of air breeching the cracked glass.

"Get off the road at the next opportunity."

"On it, *jefe.*"

The SUV's body might look like hell, but the engine hummed. Quint wouldn't have considered anything less of his El Paso contact. They'd worked together several times. Quint knew from experience Gonzo ran a tight ship, regardless of his outward appearance as a gangbanger. And he would be pissed. Quint resigned himself to buying Gonzo a new vehicle. But only if he agreed to help catch the bastards who shot up the car. The Mexican cartel bastards operating the human trafficking ring. A joint taskforce—as it were.

Quint stiffened. "*Oye* H. If they followed us here, do you think they followed us to the Medina's?" After everything…what if Nader had snatched the rescued teen and sold her back to the cartel?

"We weren't followed, Quint. Nader knew the plan. They were watching the airport." He tapped the gas and spun around a slow-moving truck carrying bottled water. "He's acting alone. I shot the fourth man. The other two are dead—"

Quint dropped his head into his hands. Muttered, "I was a fool."

"*No te castigues por eso*, don't beat yourself up. What's his angle, do you suppose?"

"I haven't a clue. I thought we were something like friends. He was my CO back in 'Nam." Quint paused, looked out the window at the interstate businesses rushing past. "Take that next exit in a quarter mile—Tower Road—" he pointed north— "Sign says there's a Walmart Superstore. Pick up supplies. Hide in the parking lot until we're sure no one is following us. We have ten hours to the border if it goes right." He paused, peered through the side mirror again. "You sure you're good to drive?"

Horacio grunted. Quint nodded. "Okay then."

"We need gas," Horacio said, inching the vehicle toward the right-hand lane through the thickening morning traffic.

"We'll probably find a station nearby. We should eat before we hit I-25 South."

"Any decent Mexican food?"

Besides the usual gastrointestinal distress cluster of Burger King, MacDonald's, and Taco Bell squatting on Walmart's coat tails, Horacio sniffed out two Mexican restaurants on a cross street in the neighborhood. He pulled into the parking lot behind the second restaurant, a ramshackle-looking affair tucked into the edge of an equally downtrodden housing district, and wedged the SUV between two jacked-up pickup trucks. He nodded his head toward the back door as a pair of mestizo-looking men in cowboy hats and boots sauntered out. One carried a cup to go. Quint heard a snippet of Spanish as they passed by.

Horacio squeezed through the narrow door opening only after shedding his jacket. A tight fit, but no one looking for it would see the SUV.

"H, if you eat two orders of *huevos rancheros*, you aren't going to fit back into the vehicle."

Horacio bellowed his infectious laugh. "True dat."

Quint snorted. "True dat? You been taking English lessons from Chucho? Speaking of Chuch, I should call. See if everything is okay at the office."

"Mrs. P will keep him in line, *jefe*."

"True dat," Quint retorted, grinning as Horacio pulled open the back door to the enticing steam of hot tortillas and roasting chilis. Quint almost felt at home. *Damn. I'm getting too comfortable in Mexico.* There was no telling where his op would take him. So why was he obsessing over Jade's return?

Three orders of *huevos rancheros* later, a thermos full of black coffee, and a packet of a dozen each chorizo tacos and mushroom quesadillas to-go, the men eased out into the weedy parking lot. Quint felt better.

Maybe his emotional weakness was brought on by hunger. One of the trucks was gone, but the other remained, protecting the bullet-ridden side of the SUV. Probably belonged to the two guys in the corner flirting with the middle-aged proprietress. Regulars. If he was staying in Colonia Roma and finishing his work for Senator Aguirre, he needed to find a local breakfast dive with good food and a cheerful staff.

Reading Quint's mind, Horacio said, "You know there's a place two blocks from the office even better than this one for breakfast. A lot cheaper, *támbien.*"

"Well, this is the U.S. Everything costs more."

They pulled up to pump 6 at the EXXON Mobil on Tower Rd. "Grabbing a six-pack, H," Quint said. "I'll pay inside. Keep your eyes open."

When he'd finished filling the tank, Horacio pulled over to the Tower Liquor and Quint clambered in with a bag of beer and chips. He held up the bag of hot chili Cheetos and a Coors. "Ever try the Rockies' best? Made from pure Rocky Mountain spring water."

"Ay, that piss water? *No gracias.*"

"Good thing I got a six-pack of Dos Equis." Quint grinned. "But let's get out of Denver first. By the way, I called Medina and warned him to be careful."

Horacio slowed for a red light. "I thought you might. What did he say?"

A low rider pulled up in the left lane and stopped next to them. Four gangbangers stared at the side of the SUV. The kid riding shotgun cocked an air AR15 and made like he was blasting them. Quint heard the laughter over the booming bass. The light turned green; the kids roared ahead, fingers cocked.

Horacio finger blasted back. "We're drawing attention. *¿Qué piensas?* The *entrada* to I-70 is coming up."

"I dunno. Which is worse? Explaining what

happened to the police when we're pulled over in town, or risking an attack by Nader? The thing is, Nader knows where we're going and where we'll end up. He'd be insane to attack us here. Too much traffic. Too many witnesses. There's a lot of empty country before the border. But we have to get on the interstate."

Horacio nodded and pulled over then veered onto I-70 West.

Quint pushed down his seatback and closed his eyes. "Wake me up when you want to switch drivers."

"Where are we?" Quint yawned, rubbed his eyes, and sat up. "It looks like a desert out there."

"We're almost in Santa Fe. Just passed the halfway mark. You've been sleeping for five hours."

"Didn't get much sleep last night. Want to trade now?"

"No, I'm fine. I'll take us into Santa Fe so we can get out. Stretch. I'll swap then. I could eat."

Quint fished around behind his seat and grabbed the bag of snacks. "Cheetos and beer?"

"I was thinking about some of that famous *carne adovada* with hatch chilis."

"How do you know about New Mexico food?"

"My wife and her sisters took a trip to Santa Fe. She's still raving about a restaurant called Cafe Pasqual's in the old town. Here's the map." He handed Quint a new road map with city maps of Santa Fe and Albuquerque. Quint flipped to Santa Fe.

"Where'd you get this?"

"Stopped at a visitor center when we crossed into New Mexico, *jefe*.

"Damn. I must have been tired. Sounds good, *amigo*. Let's find those hatch chiles."

The SUV garnered a ration of stares and glares.

Quint wanted to pin his credentials to his shirt or shout, *We're the good guys here,* but kept his head in the map, trying to ignore the tourists. Horacio looked nonplussed. Maybe he didn't realize they were being taken for narcos. But inside the quaint adobe restaurant, the food was worthy of remembering, the other diners at the long communal table congenial. A Russian woman, her American daughter, two gay men from California, one a muckety-muck in high tech, a couple from Toronto celebrating their thirty-fifth anniversary, and a young German running a humanitarian aid organization for immigrants displaced by wars and poverty, traveling with his vivacious Italian girlfriend. Quint relaxed enjoying the lively talk, the exchange of ideas observations, and, of course, the food. Horacio proved to be a warm, entertaining social addition to the group. For a moment, Quint's sadness lifted.

After a bison burger and two servings of toasted piñon ice cream with fleur de sel caramel sauce, Quint was ready for another nap. Horacio wanted another dessert. Where that man put all the food, Quint couldn't say, but he'd managed to wheedle the cook into making his adovado, not on the luncheon menu, and put away a plate of *mole* enchiladas as well. "Amigo, let's take a stroll and do some sightseeing? Whaddya say? I've got to walk off some of this food."

"All for it, *jefe.* I need to pick up some trinkets for *mi marida y hija.*"

"Let's go. I saw plenty of shops on the plaza."

An hour later, Quint had a stunning silver necklace of green turquoise and Mexican jade for Jade's birthday. Horacio bought a silver ring inlaid with turquoise and coral for his girl, and a handmade silver and turquoise bracelet set with several tiny sapphires, her birthstone, for his wife. Everything had been made locally.

When Quint and Horacio returned, two local officers were inspecting the SUV, their patrol car double-parked, hemming in the vehicle.

"Can I help you, officers?" Quint asked, his tone mild.

The younger officer's hand hovered over his gun. The older man asked, "This your vehicle?"

Quint replied, "No, sir. Borrowed." He patted his pockets. The younger cop rested his hand on the butt of his revolver. "License," he said.

The older cop nodded. Quint pulled out his wallet, handing over his driver's license, carry permit, and a second ID. Quint noted his nametag: Quintero.

"You're attached to the State Department? You carrying?" the cop asked, handing the IDs over to his partner.

"Not on me. Glove box. I'm on loan to the Mexican government, actually."

The cop eyed Quint skeptically. "This is *New* Mexico. What happened to the vehicle?"

"Registration's in the glove box. H, give the man the keys." Quint replied, ignoring the question. The younger patrol's hand tightened around the gun. Quint swung his chin toward Horacio. "My assigned minder. Horacio, *dale al oficial las llaves.*"

Horacio fished the keys out of his pocket and tossed them to the younger cop who let go of the sidearm to catch them. *Good thinking, H.* A tourist family with three school-aged kids flowed around them, the kids gawking open-mouthed.

"Your man don't speak English?"

"Nah, but my *español* is improving."

"Ask him for his papers," Quintara demanded, waving Quint toward the side of the SUV. "Hand them to Herdez."

"Horacio, muestrale al hombre tus papeles." Again, he gestured with his chin.

"Claro, jefe," Horacio replied as he handed over his passport to the junior patrol.

Herdez nodded to his partner and unlocked the door, reaching into the glove box. He retreated to the patrol car with the registration and Quint's gun, checking the license plate on the way.

"What happened to the vehicle?" Quintara demanded a second time.

"We're guessing they were gangbangers. Shot it up while we ate breakfast in a dive in Denver. Maybe thought we were someone else."

"Make a police report?"

"No. I can't talk about the mission. You'll have to call and verify. Partner's got the number." Quint tossed his chin this time toward the kid in the patrol car.

The older cop motioned to Horacio to stand next to Quint. "Is he carrying?"

"No sir," Quint snapped back. "Not authorized in the U.S." He prayed they wouldn't search the SUV. The cache of weapons would boggle the bored tourist cops' minds. And probably land them in jail.

"So what're ya doing in Santa Fe?" the man asked, obviously making small talk until the plate was run.

Quint chuckled. What did anyone do in Santa Fe? "Lunch at Cafe Pasqual's. Shopping for the girls." He held up his gift bag from Malouf's. Quintara raised his eyebrows and gave a quick nod.

Herdez returned and leaned toward his partner. In a low but audible voice he said, "All clear, Quintara. Vehicle checks out. It's a Fed permit to carry and matches the ID. Only problem I can see is the SUV could be connected to the shootout in Hernandez— black, shot up. Whadda we do?"

Car tires squealed around the corner and it's motor revved as it peeled away from the plaza. A second car in hot pursuit.

"Let's go!" Quintara sprinted to the patrol car. Herdez thrust the papers and gun into Quint's hand and ran.

Quint settled behind the wheel and shifted into gear. "Someone is watching over us, H. Let's blow this town. Five more hours if the gods continue to clear our path."

"Police are the same everywhere. It's why I quit. What did they want—money?"

"Not so common in the U.S. You didn't hear the young guy. He made the SUV for the one in Hernandez. Someone saw what went down. Or Nader made a report."

"He would have had the *placa*."

Quint shrugged and turned left toward I-25. Traffic was light pre-rush hour. "I dunno, H. Nader was never the most observant character. If he'd reported it we'd be in the back of that squad car, cuffed." *But now they have the license plate.*

The men sank into silence as Quint maneuvered them onto I-25 and set the cruise control to 75 mph, the posted limit. He punched on the radio, dialed in a jazz station to some peppy driving music. Lots of clarinet. The station identifier cut in. "103.7 The Oasis. We'll take care of your thirsty ears. Your best stop along Route 66."

Horacio dropped his seatback and stretched out as far as he could. "Wake me up when we get there, *jefe*."

Fifty minutes later, the SUV snarled into Albuquerque afternoon traffic. Quint kept an eye on the signs for the throughway to Las Cruses, the termination of I-25 at the Texas border. He'd pull off there and contact Gonzo to expect him. Maybe have a coffee. They could eat in El Paso at the airport. If all went well, they'd be in Mexico City before morning.

Outside the windshield, the urban landscape morphed into a dun-colored drone of emptiness bordered by dark crags and monotone peaks. Along the highway he could see evidence of irrigation, but this late into the year, most of the cultivation would be done. What did they grow in New Mexico, anyway, besides chilies and corn? Goats probably. After all, he was essentially in Mexico. Listen to the ads: Valencia sopapillas. Even the city names: Santa Fe, Las Lunas, Belen, Las Cruces. No question who immigrated here first. Were there missions like in California?

Further south, the scenery began to resemble a moonscape. Dry. Bare. Rocky—driving him into the blue funk again, but now the mists morphed to dusty haze. He could always fly to California and beg her to come home. *But Sausalito is her home.* Quint had a hankering to pull over, dial JadeAnne's number, ask about the dog. Dylan. Their trip. But he had another two hours and forty-seven minutes of this mind-numbing scenery to go before Las Cruces. He hoped to arrive before dark. Easier to see attackers during daylight. *Would Nader be so stupid?*

Convinced Nader hunted him, he pondered why. *Why would Nader hate me?* What nagged at Quint was, he'd done time for Nader's operation and never given him away. Quint never revealed the kingpin—and Nader walked scot-free while, for five years, he languished in Lompoc. Lost his commission. Dishonorable discharge. Everything expunged if he signed on with NSA. Everything he hated—dirty dealing—spying on citizens—assassinations—you name it. Only, you didn't name it. Top secret. Few with clearance. Not even Nixon was privy to what those fuckers were up to in Vietnam, Laos, and Cambodia. Or, maybe the politicians just didn't want to know. Or now, for that matter. Not that Quint was NSA anymore. He'd completed his indentured servitude. Got out. *But did I really get out?*

The radio program changed, with a new DJ coming on shift. An evening program. Mellow. Easy. So unlike Quint's life. He'd paid his dues. Why was Nader after him now? "Hold on! Because I know the truth. I know everything!" he bellowed.

Horacio stirred, snuffled and shifted his weight toward the door, but didn't wake up. "Sorry, man," Quint whispered and punched the door lock. Didn't want to lose his partner, but he did want to lose Nader. They'd never really been friends. Nader played him back then just as he was doing in Mexico City.

How long had the man been looking for him? *Congratulations, asshole. Took twenty-seven years to find me*—now that Quint had something to lose. Nader knew Jade was flying back to California. No coincidence he was shooting at him, or had he been waiting to kill JadeAnne? Maybe he planned to hop a flight to San Francisco. Quint banged the steering wheel. The vehicle shimmied and swerved into the right-hand lane, cutting off a farm truck piled with hay bales. He stepped on the gas. Horacio snored. The sky streaked pink, orange, and purple between the peaks as the western mountains shadowed to black. Quint needed a telephone. But there wasn't any cell service in this God forsaken desert.

Horacio woke up chipper and hungry at the Shell Station just off I-10 East outside Las Cruces.

"*Good morning, amigo.*"

"*¿Qué hora es, Queent? ¿Dónde estamos?*"

"Las Cruces. I figured it out. Nader is going after Jade. I have to call her. Need a pit stop? It's another fifty minutes to El Paso."

"*¿Pit estop?*"

Quint pulled up to the pump. "*Baño.*" He opened his door and dropped to the ground. Horacio called across the seats, "I'll be back. Want anything? How much on the gas?"

"Forty. Thanks. I'll park over there." He pointed to the front of the convenience store and extracted his cell phone from his jacket pocket. Three bars. He dialed.

"It's Quint. Heads up, I'm in Las Cruces. One hour. You ain't gonna be happy, Gonz." He hung up. The pump was ready and he filled the tank. At least Gonzo would get the SUV back with a full tank.

The pump clicked off. Quint hung up the nozzle and capped the tank. Horacio hadn't returned, so he moved the vehicle to the parking space then wandered into the convenience store. H appeared with the bathroom key. *Might as well hit the john.* "Grab something to go with the tacos. We'll eat dinner at the airport in a couple hours."

In the bathroom, Quint dialed JadeAnne. No answer. They had to have arrived. Maybe out grocery shopping. Or...he let the thought hang unfinished. He couldn't go there. She and Dylan would be doing something. Visiting her friends or her parents. Her parents. He should have raised her. He should have rescued Thuy, his gentle woman. He didn't even know she was pregnant. Because of Nader and his "mission" he was pulled out of Saigon, sent to Laos to move heroin into Vietnam. White-hot hate boiled through him, scalding his veins. Charley promised to protect Thuy, had tried to find her as the NVA swept toward

Saigon, but it was too late. She was dead.

Quint slammed his fist into the metal bathroom door, splitting open his knuckles. The pain soothed him. It was real. And he was a free agent. He could do something about the tragedy of his life. Not like 1975—addicted, incarcerated, and disconsolate, Quint had been helpless. He signed over the papers for Charley Stone to adopt his baby. He hadn't even read the documents to find out the child's gender. But now he'd found her. His flesh and blood, and he'd be damned if anyone was going to take her away from him.

Pounding on the door. "Queent? You okay in there?"

Quint washed his bloodied hand, looked for towels, then wiped his palms across his jeans, and opened the door. "The big question, H. Why'd Nader turn up right when I found JadeAnne?"

www.ingramcontent.com/pod-product-compliance
Lightning Source LLC
Chambersburg PA
CBHW060350080526
44583CB00012B/244

* 9 7 8 1 6 4 4 5 6 6 1 6 9 *